The Great SOUTHWEST NATURE FACTBOOK

A Guide to the
Region's Remarkable
Animals, Plants, and
Natural Features

Susan J. Tweit

Alaska Northwest Books ™
Anchorage • Seattle • Portland

Ten percent of the royalties from the sale of this book will be donated to organizations dedicated to habitat conservation and education in the Southwest.

Third printing 1995

Library of Congress Cataloging-in-Publication Data
Tweit, Susan J.
        The great Southwest nature factbook : a guide to the region's remarkable animals, plants, and natural features / by Susan J. Tweit.
             p.   cm.
        Includes bibliographical references and index.
        ISBN 0-88240-434-2
        1. Natural history—Southwestern States.   I. Title.
QH104.5.S6T84   1992
508.79—dc20

                                                92-21599
                                                     CIP

Edited by Carolyn Smith and Joan Gregory
Cover and book design by Cameron Mason
Cover illustration and text illustrations by Robert Williamson

Alaska Northwest Books™
An imprint of Graphics Arts Center Publishing Company
Editorial office: 2208 NW Market Street, Suite 300, Seattle, WA 98107
Catalog and order dept: P.O. Box 10306, Portland, OR 97210
    800-452-3032

Printed on acid-free paper in the United States of America

To my maternal great-grandfather, William Austin Cannon,
who began studying the Southwest's deserts in 1903.

And to my parents, Robert and Joan Cannon Tweit,
who taught me how to know the desert
and to not sit on fishhook cacti.

ACKNOWLEDGMENTS

Thanks to Marlene Blessing for recruiting me, and to Carolyn Smith and Joan Gregory for their clear editorial vision. My husband, Richard Cabe, generously shared my enthusiasm as I dug up facts and anecdotes; my step-daughter, Molly Cabe, inspired me to tell interesting stories and was patient when I worked long hours, even on weekends. My parents, Joan and Robert Tweit, loaned references and carefully checked my facts. Thanks also to friends and colleagues who answered my odd and sundry queries. Any errors or omissions are, of course, my own responsibility.

CONTENTS

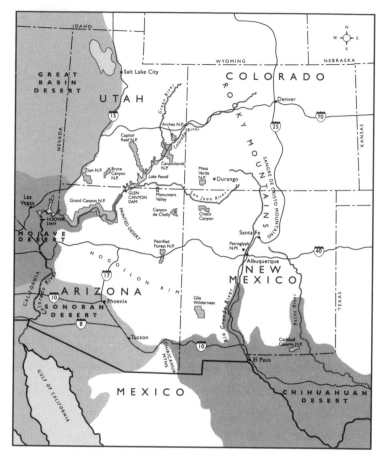

THE SOUTHWEST

THE SOUTHWEST

I love the Southwest, with its searing heat, its miles of spare landscape that seem empty but are not, its secrets and its silences. Although I am a new resident—my husband, stepdaughter, and I moved to southern New Mexico just two years ago—I have visited these landscapes since childhood. My family's roots in this arid country go back some ninety years, beginning with my great-grandfather, a botanist who moved to Tucson in 1903.

The Southwest is a powerful region. Its sere and spacious landforms may not fit some definitions of beauty, but those who explore here come away changed, awestruck. From the high mountains, some snow-spotted, others dry and bare as weathered bones, to the fiery-orange slickrock mesas slit by narrow canyons and desert basins shimmering with fantastic heat mirages, the landscape dominates. Here are some of the nation's great natural treasures: Grand Canyon, Canyonlands, Mesa Verde. A rich variety of cultures—Hispanic, Anglo, Native American—flourish here. And here are found myriad animals and plants unified by their ability to adapt, in an astounding variety of ways, to the region's aridity.

The Great Southwest Nature Factbook is neither a field guide nor an all-inclusive encyclopedia. It is a browser's collection, a guide to help you begin your exploration of the Southwest. By showing you the beauty and the intricate interrelationships of life here, I hope to kindle your sense of wonder and inspire you to discover your own love for this magical combination of desert, mesa, slickrock, canyon, and mountain. With that in mind, I have selected examples of the region's inhabitants and features that I thought characteristic and unique, ones that gave the "feel" of the region.

For the convenience of the reader, entries in this book are divided into three sections: animals, plants, and natural features. Introductions to each section show the big picture; entries within each section, arranged alphabetically, detail the region's inhabitants and features. You can look up specific entries, like DESERT VARNISH or NIGHT-BLOOMING CEREUS, or you can read through from ANTLIONS to ZION CANYON. Words in SMALL CAPITAL LETTERS are titles of other entries. If you don't see what you are looking for, try the index. A short annotated list of recommended reading at the back of the book guides you to other sources.

THE REGION

There are probably as many definitions of "the Southwest" as there are inhabitants and visitors. Choosing boundaries is difficult, because clear lines rarely exist. For this book, I have picked a common definition that considers the Southwest to comprise Arizona and New Mexico, west Texas, extreme southern Colorado, and Utah south of Interstate 70. All four of North America's deserts occur here—the Sonoran, the Chihuahuan, the Mojave, and the Great Basin—as do mountains rising higher than 13,000 feet above sea level. Since animals, plants, and natural features do not abide by our boundaries, many of the entries refer to areas adjacent to the region as defined.

The one physical characteristic that knits together this diverse region is lack of water. Ironically, the region has not always been arid. Long ago, shallow oceans covered much of the Southwest, depositing many of the thick rock formations that today are visible as cliffs, MESAS, HOODOOS, buttes, domes, arches, mountainsides, canyon walls. During the wetter glacial ages some 15,000 years ago, water eroded thousands of cubic miles of material from the landscape, drowning the basins in layers of rocky debris. Today, water runs through the region, often in muddy torrents, but rarely stays, except in the highest mountains and behind the dams of reservoirs.

THE CLIMATE

Part of the Southwest is considered true desert, where annual precipitation is far eclipsed by evaporation from the abundant sunshine and relentless winds. The remainder of the region is simply classified as arid, except for the scattered mountain ranges. Annual rain and snowfall average from 7 to 18 inches across the region except, again, in the relatively wet mountains. But "average" means little. The lower the average, the more it varies from year to year, and from place to place. For instance, at my home in the Chihuahuan Desert of southern New Mexico, the "average" is 10 inches, but 3.5 inches of rain is just as normal in a year as 15 inches. Temperatures also oscillate widely. Summer midday temperatures soar into the hundreds at the lower elevations, but even there nights are cool since the dry air cannot retain heat—the mercury can plummet 50 degrees after sunset.

Summer is the Southwest's "MONSOON season." Sudden, intense

thunderstorms between July and September bring the region's most reliable precipitation—occasionally as much as 4 inches in an hour. The mountains catch the most rain; the low-elevation deserts the least. When late fall and early winter bring cyclic storms off the distant Pacific Ocean, snow falls in the mountains and the north, and day-long "mizzles" bring fog and rain to the south and the lower elevations.

WHEN YOU ARE THERE

Be prepared for extremes of weather—the summer temperatures that can be over a hundred degrees in the shade at midday, but downright cold at night. Always carry plenty of water and protection from the intense sun.

Never enter a dry ARROYO or a canyon in a thunderstorm, or if a storm is visible up the drainage. Never try to drive through a flash flood—a trickle can, in moments, become a torrent capable of carrying away a large motor home. Ironically, drowning is a common cause of death in the desert.

RATTLESNAKES live in much of the Southwest, except in the highest parts of the mountains. Be alert—never put your hands or feet in places that you can't see. If you encounter a rattler, back off and treat it respectfully; rattlers won't bother you if you don't bother them. If you are bitten, stay calm, drink plenty of water, and get yourself to a medical facility as quickly as possible. Rattlesnake bites are rarely fatal—people die more commonly from exposure or dehydration—but they are very painful.

Travel carefully in this magnificent region. Treat these landscapes as sacred spaces, home to many other lives. Our thoughtless activities— whether overdrawing groundwater that once recharged rivers, abandoning piles of radioactive mining waste, or uprooting a tiny cactus that took fifty years to grow—have caused enduring damage. If we can live lightly on them, these awesome landscapes will nurture generations to come.

ONE

ANIMALS

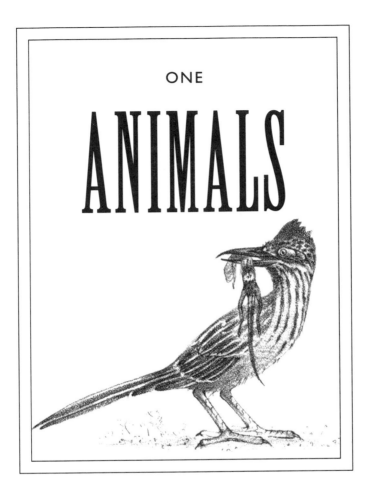

THE SOUTHWEST'S widely varying landscapes, from low deserts to high mountains, provide homes for thousands of kinds of animals. From the tiniest—microscopic cyanobacteria living in MICROBIOTIC CRUSTS on desert soil surfaces—to the largest, BEARS, the region's diversity of animals is astounding.

Deserts, often thought of as barren or lifeless, are neither. Animals abound in these arid regions, including TARANTULAS, SCORPIONS, RATTLE-SNAKES, DOVES, QUAIL, pocket mice, JACKRABBITS, BATS, HAWKS, and COYOTES. Many desert insects and reptiles are unique to the Southwest and adjacent northern Mexico.

Grasslands and shrublands, which occur at elevations higher than the deserts, provide homes for animals adapted to open country, such as GRASSHOPPERS, HORNED LIZARDS, PRAIRIE DOGS, MAGPIES, meadowlarks, burrowing OWLS, red-tailed HAWKS, coyotes, and pronghorn antelope. Moving farther up in elevation to the foothills, MESAS, and dry mountain slopes, PIÑON-JUNIPER and OAK woodlands shelter animals such as western bluebirds, PIÑON JAYS, WOODRATS, badgers, mule deer, and MOUNTAIN LIONS, which depend on the short, scattered evergreen trees for food and shelter.

Densely forested SKY ISLANDS—high mountain ranges rising above the deserts and plateaus—provide cool, relatively wet oases for animals that cannot tolerate the desert heat and/or aridity. Sky islands also provide "highways" for subtropical mountain species to move north. Tiger swallow-tail BUTTERFLIES, SALAMANDERS, kingsnakes, Mexican spotted owls, RAVENS, blue grouse, TASSEL-EARED SQUIRRELS, beavers, black bear, and elk inhabit these high-elevation oases. Sky islands harbor subtropical species more common in Mexico and Central America, such as COATIS and blue-throated HUMMINGBIRDS.

Alpine habitats exist on only the highest mountains in the northern Southwest. Common residents in these cold, harsh places are mosquitoes, fritillary and checkerspot butterflies, ptarmigan, water pipits, voles, PIKAS, and marmots.

Rarest in this parched region are the oases, or rivers, lakes, streams, ponds, and springs. The myriad animal residents include dragonflies, water striders, treefrogs, tiger salamanders, TROUT, herons, kingfishers, ducks, dippers, ORIOLES, great-horned owls, and raccoons.

Most of the Southwest's denizens must cope with aridity and have evolved elegant ways to live with the scarcity of water. Some avoid drought by becoming dormant or by leaving the area altogether in the hottest and driest times; others prevent dehydration by coating themselves with water-tight layers or storing water in internal "canteens"; all thrive within the boundaries imposed by harsh conditions.

The most extreme drought-avoiders grow and reproduce only during the brief MONSOON season, passing the intervening months or years of drought as desiccation-resistant seeds or eggs. FRESHWATER SHRIMP, racing from egg to adult to egg in as few as two weeks, exemplify this strategy. Other animals vacate the deserts. PHAINOPEPLAS, for example, fly to the mountains for the summer. Some drought-avoiders retire to sheltered burrows or crannies and essentially go dormant until more clement times. Amphibians such as tiger salamanders and SPADEFOOT TOADS spend most of their adult lives dug into the soil, emerging only after summer rains. Drought avoidance can also mean spending the hottest, driest parts of the day in the shade or in a den. Nocturnal creatures such as scorpions and CORAL SNAKES forego daytime altogether, taking advantage of night's coolness and higher humidity.

Protection from dehydration takes many forms. Some arid-country animals, such as white-winged doves, weigh more than similar-sized counterparts not adapted to arid conditions—their higher mass-to-surface-area ratio makes their bodies more resistant to fluctuating temperatures and dehydration. Arid-country inhabitants also conserve water metabolically. Some, like pocket mice and KANGAROO RATS, need never drink water—they derive all of their moisture from their food. Lizards, many other reptiles, and some birds and mammals also save water by concentrating their urine into uric acid crystals rather than watery urea.

During the summer, most arid-country residents are active (and therefore easier to see) in the cooler, moister hours after the scorching sun sets, from late evening until early morning. In winter, animal watching is most rewarding during the relatively mild middays. Whatever time of year, the Southwest's diverse landscapes are home to a surprising variety of lives.

ANT More than one hundred species of ants (family Formicidae) live in the Southwest. Some ant species eat seeds and plant leaves; many sip nectar, honeydew produced by aphids, and plant juices; others are carnivorous and eat other insects; one species farms, cultivating its own edible fungus. Whatever their diet, the total population of ants makes these tiny and often overlooked animals major consumers in their respective ecosystems.

Ants are social insects related to wasps and bees. Most ant colonies, whether a few dozen or a million members in size, consist of a large fertile female—the queen—and numerous smaller, sterile, wingless females, divided into worker and soldier castes. The queen's function is to reproduce—she lays eggs, which hatch into larvae, pupate, and mature into adults. Workers tend the eggs and larvae, and gather food for the colony. New colonies begin when the queen lays a special brood of eggs that hatch winged females and males. This generation leaves the colony, swarms, and mates. The males die after mating, but the fertilized females—new queens—build a nest or nests, lay eggs, and raise the first generation of the new colony themselves, feeding the larvae from their fatty deposits.

> **Ants are long-lived insects. Individual workers live as long as six years, queens up to fifteen years. More than one hundred species of ants live in the Southwest.**

Ants are long-lived insects. Individual workers live as long as six years, queens up to fifteen years. Like many insects and reptiles, ants are poikilothermic (cold-blooded), their body temperature depending on the temperature of their surroundings. They avoid both extreme cold and heat by remaining below ground in their extensive nests.

Harvester ants (*Pogonomyrmex* species), seed-eating ants with powerful jaws and a potent sting, are the most conspicuous ants in the desert Southwest. Harvester ants have elaborate defenses. Only old, nearly inedible workers are allowed out of the nest, and when a harvester ant is killed, it spews an alarm scent that draws other ants to attack. All harvester ants pack a painful sting, injecting a venom highly toxic to vertebrate animals that contains a red blood cell–destroying compound. When tested on mice, the ant venom was more toxic by volume than that of vipers, cobras, and RATTLESNAKES. In humans, a harvester ant sting is not fatal but does induce excruciating pain lasting twenty-four hours. Many desert animals eat ants, but most avoid the venomous harvester ants. Only HORNED

LIZARDS, with an antitoxin in their blood specific to harvester ant venom, prey on these poisonous ants.

Workers from a single colony of harvester ants can collect as many as 7,000 seeds a day—more than 2 million seeds a year. Each worker can lift up to 50 times her own weight. Some plants rely on harvester ants' predilection for seed gathering to scatter their seeds. For example, DATURA (*Datura* species), a mounding vine with fragrant, night-blooming flowers, produces seeds with tiny carrying handles designed to attract harvester ants. The ants carry away the seeds before rodents can find and eat them, but then abandon the seeds uneaten, discouraged by the thick seed coat.

Harvester ants dump their trash—seed husks and excavated soil— around the entrance to their nests, accumulating cone-shaped mounds up to 2 feet in diameter. Nest tunnels extend up to 10 feet underground. Such tunneling, and the organic matter that harvester ants transport underground, enrich and aerate dry, hard desert soils.

Arid lands honey ants (*Myrmecocystus* species), found in Southwestern deserts, shrublands, and grasslands, tide themselves over periodic droughts by storing food in the swollen abdomens of special workers called repletes. These currant-sized living jars hang from the nest ceilings and regurgitate food droplets for the colony.

Texas carpenter ants (*Camponotus festinatus*) live throughout the Southwest wherever trees are abundant, from urban areas to mountain forests. These large, big-jawed ants speed the decay and recycling of nutrients in wood by chewing out nest cavities in partly decayed wood. Unlike TERMITES, carpenter ants do not eat the wood; they feed on other insects and sugary juices.

Leafcutter ants (*Atta* species) cultivate and dine on their own species of edible fungus. Workers harvest leaf bits from above ground to feed the fungus. When a queen starts a new colony, she takes a piece of fungus in her mouth to begin a new crop. Only one species of this group reaches north into the Southwest, in the Sonoran Desert of southern Arizona. Most leafcutter ants live in Mexico and Central and South America.

Some species of ants act as bodyguards for BUTTERFLY caterpillars in the metalmark (Riodinidae) and blue (Lycaenidae) families. Their soldiers protect the caterpillars from predacious wasps by spraying the wasps with poison. Caterpillars attract the ants by rhythmic drumming that mimics ant communication, enticing them to stay by feeding them sugary secretions.

See also HORNED LIZARD, TERMITE.

ANTLION Antlions are named for their carnivorous larvae that trap and eat ANTS. Other predators, such as HORNED LIZARDS, flickers, and Gila woodpeckers, also prey on ants. But the tiny, eyeless larvae of the antlion (family Myrmeleontidae: *myrme* for "ant," *leo* for "lion") have evolved a unique ant-hunting strategy. They dig small, conical pits in the soil surface, and simply wait for randomly foraging ants to stumble into the trap. Antlion traps dot dry soil throughout the Southwest, from the deserts to the PONDEROSA PINE forests in the mountains. Antlion larvae are also called "doodlebugs" because their clumsy, backward locomotion leaves "doodling" tracks in the soil. Barely half an inch long, their bodies are soft, flattened, and grublike. But attached to each larva's head is a marvelous, all-purpose tool—a huge pair of sickle-shaped jaws that the larva uses to dig its traps and capture its prey.

A larva begins digging its ant trap immediately after hatching. Walking backward in an ever-tightening spiral, it shovels dirt with its jaws. When it reaches the center of the spiral, it has dug itself into the bottom of a steep-walled, conical pit, about an inch deep and 2 inches across. There the larva opens its fearsome jaws and waits for its prey. The tiniest footfall of a wandering ant on the steep sides of the pit starts a landslide, sweeping the ant into the antlion's jaws. The antlion grabs its often larger victim, injects it with venom to quell its struggling, and eats it.

Antlion larvae eat and grow until their hormones dictate a change, whereupon they spin a cocoon and metamorphose. In late summer and early fall, an entirely dissimilar creature, the delicate, winged, and dragon-flylike adult, emerges. Its mission: reproduction. Adults do not eat, and

Antlion

they die soon after mating. Mated females lay single eggs directly on the soil surface; from these eggs hatch the carnivorous larvae.

BAT   From April to October, when night-flying insects are active, bats inhabit every Southwest ecosystem except the alpine. Among the Southwest's twenty-eight bat species are North America's smallest and largest bats. The smallest, western pipistrelles (*Pipistrellus hesperus*), have walnut-sized bodies and weigh a mere one-fifth of an ounce. Western mastiff bats (*Eumops perotis*), the largest, have a 15-inch wingspan, big, floppy ears, and weigh 2.25 ounces—about as much as a large chocolate bar.

When food is not available, bats migrate south and/or hibernate, subsisting on stored fat. Some bat species hibernate in large groups in caves, abandoned mines, under bridges, or on other human-made structures. Other bats hibernate singly in cracks in rocks, on tree trunks, or, like western pipistrelles, under flat stones on the ground. During hibernation, bats' temperatures may drop nearly to freezing, but they revive regularly to warm themselves. Solitary bats that hibernate in trees (*Lasiurus* species) can drop their body temperatures as low as 26°F without harm. Disturbing a hibernating bat can be deadly to it. Each time a bat rouses, it uses from ten to thirty days of stored fat reserves and may starve before food is available again.

Contrary to popular belief, bats are not blind. They can see everything but color and many have excellent vision. However, in order to navigate and communicate in the dark, bats use echolocation, producing high-frequency sounds (most above the range of human hearing) that bounce back to their antennalike ears, allowing them to "see" so accurately that they can detect a single human hair in total darkness.

Bats are the major predators of night-flying insects, including mosquitoes and numerous crop-eating insects. Tiny mouse-eared bats (*Myotis* species), the most widely distributed North American bat species, are effective organic mosquito control, able to consume 600 mosquitoes in an hour. Mastiff bats wing hundreds of miles over the desert during their nightly insect hunts. A large colony of bats, such as the colony of several hundred thousand inhabiting CARLSBAD CAVERNS, New Mexico, consumes several tons of moths, pests on agricultural crops mostly, in a single night.

Not all southwestern bats eat insects. Pallid bats (*Antrozous pallidus*) hunt lizards, SCORPIONS, small rodents, and GRASSHOPPERS and beetles in deserts and dry grasslands. Eating such juicy prey, pallid bats can live for over a month without drinking water. Long-nosed bats (family Phyllostomatidae), named for their elongated snout, feed on nectar as they pollinate the flowers of two desert giants, SAGUARO cactus of the Sonoran Desert and AGAVES or century plants of the Chihuahuan Desert. The bats migrate north just in time to feed from night-blooming saguaro and agave flowers. Hovering in place like hummingbirds, the bats insert their entire head into the flower to slurp the high-protein nectar with their retractable tongue. When they emerge, they carry a mantle of pollen on their fur, their gift to the next flower.

Hordes of Brazilian free-tailed bats (family Molossidae) roost in summer and autumn at Carlsbad Caverns and other large caves in the Southwest, their nursery roosts containing up to 20 million baby bats. A mother bat returning to the roost after a night of feeding can fly directly to her own baby, somehow recognizing its voice in the squealing din. Carlsbad's free-tailed bats cloud the evening sky as they exit the cave: five to ten thousand bats a minute rush out, spiraling in a counterclockwise column that can rise as high as 10,000 feet in the air and is visible from miles away. Tail winds at these high altitudes push free-tailed bats as fast as 60 miles an hour, helping them fly 50 or more miles to their nightly foraging grounds.

Many Southwest bat populations are plummeting. In the last two decades, Brazilian free-tailed bat populations in Carlsbad Caverns have decreased from some 5 million to only several hundred thousand bats. Human harassment is one factor: for example, one summer evening in 1990, two men shot and killed more than 500 free-tailed bats and their young at a nursery roost under a bridge near Phoenix, Arizona. Pesticide poisoning is another cause. Pesticides like DDT are still used on crops in Mexico and Central America, where many bats winter. Bats ingest the pesticides along with the insects that they eat; the poisons accumulate in their fatty tissues and eventually kill the bats when they use their fat reserves.

See also AGAVE, CARLSBAD CAVERNS, SAGUARO.

BEAR Before 1850, grizzly bears (*Ursus arctos*) lived throughout the Southwest, roaming the plains grasslands, PIÑON-JUNIPER woodlands, and PONDEROSA PINE forests around the larger mountain ranges, feeding on plant roots and bulbs, and berries; animals from insects to elk calves; and carrion. It was said that these big, southern plain grizzlies grew even larger than the still-surviving grizzlies of the northern Rockies, which can weigh up to 900 pounds and measure as much as 7 feet from nose to rear haunches. But when millions of domestic livestock were trailed into the Southwest after the Civil War, grizzlies were hunted down. *El oso plateado* (Spanish for "the silvery bear," because of its silver-tipped fur) was considered extinct in the Southwest after the 1930s. A female killed in the San Juan Mountains of southern Colorado in 1979 raised hopes that isolated grizzlies might remain, but no more have been sighted.

Black bears (*Ursus americanus*), the smallest of the North American bears, are common in the forested parts of the Southwest. These omnivores have adapted readily to human habitat and often forage at the edges of towns and cities. *El oso negro* ("negro" means black in Spanish) is smaller than the grizzly, standing 2 to 3 feet high at the shoulders, stretching 5 to 6 feet and weighing as much as 450 pounds, with black or cinnamon-brown fur. Black bears usually move with a deceptively clumsy, shambling gait, but can accelerate suddenly to 30 miles per hour.

Black bears' preference for verdant mountain forests makes them an "island species" in much of the Southwest, confined to the small, high mountain ranges that rise above the desert and SLICKROCK mesas. These SKY ISLANDS provide homes for many species that were once more widespread in cooler, wetter climates and that are now isolated—sometimes by hundreds of miles—from others of their kind by the surrounding arid country. If isolated for long enough, these pocket populations may eventually evolve into distinct species adapted to local conditions.

See also PETROGLYPHS AND PICTOGRAPHS.

BEE   Several thousand species of bees occur in the Southwest, from deserts to alpine regions, living wherever nectar-producing flowers grow. Most species are not social, and nest in the ground or in natural cavities; only bumblebees and nonnative honeybees live in organized colonies. Bees are the most important of pollinating insects. Thousands of wild and cultivated plant species, including fruits, many vegetables, and other crops such as COTTON (a major crop in the Southwest) depend on bees to cross-pollinate their flowers.

Common Southwest bees range in size from the tiny, 1/8-inch-long *Perdita larrea*, which forages on CREOSOTE BUSH blossoms in the deserts and low-elevation shrublands, to the inch-long, robust, golden northern bumblebee (*Bombus fervidus*), found feeding on summer wildflowers in clearings in forests and mountain meadows.

European honeybees (*Apis mellifera*), introduced to North America in the 1600s by Spanish priests in the Southwest and California, are the basis of the commercial honey and crop-pollinating industry. Some two million colonies are trucked south to north each year to pollinate crops from orange groves to cranberry bogs. Feral honeybee hives are common in the Southwest in the fat, hollow trunks of COTTONWOOD trees. In fact, Utah's state emblem is an old-fashioned conical bee skep or hive. But three recent immigrants threaten North America's only honeybee: two parasitic mites, which are wiping out cultivated honeybee colonies in the northern United States, and the honeybee's relative, the African honeybee.

The African honeybee is an aggressive race of *A. mellifera* that reached the United States–Mexican border in 1991. It will likely displace European honeybees in much of the Southwest and the South. Nicknamed "killer bees" because they defend their hives more vigorously than do European honeybees, African honeybees sting aggressively and may pursue intruders for a mile. Although humans have died from African honeybee stings, their killer image may be overstated. More people die each year from wasp stings.

First introduced in Brazil in 1956, because European honeybees did not survive in the tropical climate, African honeybees are now the domestic honeybees of Central and South America. Feral swarms have been moving north at a rate of about 300 miles per year. Honeybee researchers hope that interbreeding with mild-mannered European bees will cool the African bees' fire, without lowering their resistance to the parasitic mites.

See also DIGGER BEE.

BIGHORN SHEEP Frequently depicted in Southwest PETROGLYPHS AND PICTOGRAPHS, bighorn sheep (*Ovis canadensis*) were prized by native peoples for their meat, hides, and horns. The first European to see these native sheep may have been Francisco Vasquez de Coronado, who, traveling through New Mexico in 1540 in search of the legendary cities of gold, wrote of these big-horned, sturdy animals. Excessive hunting after European settlement, plus introduced diseases and competition with domestic and introduced sheep and goats, decimated bighorn populations. By the 1920s, few remained. Bighorns are now being reintroduced in their former habitats—rocky terrain throughout the Southwest, from cliffs in the low deserts to precipitous slopes in the high mountains.

Two kinds of bighorn sheep live in the Southwest. Desert bighorns, the smaller, paler-colored of the two, inhabit the arid southern mountains and lower elevations. The larger mountain bighorn sheep are found up to the alpine in the northern high mountains and mesas.

Although both sexes have horns, the massive, curled horns of the males give bighorns their name. A full curl, which can measure 30 inches from base to tip, takes seven or eight years to grow. When the horns grow around and block their peripheral vision, older sheep deliberately "broom" their horns, breaking off or filing the tips on rocks.

In rutting season, pairs of bighorn rams engage in dramatic butting contests over the right to mate with small bands of females. Horn size determines status, and contests occur only between rams with similar-sized horns. After snorting and pacing, the rams rear up on their hind legs, drop down with heads lowered, and lunge at each other at speeds of more than 20 miles an hour. Their foreheads collide with a loud *crack* that can be heard for more than a mile. Bighorns are truly "hard-headed"; thickened skulls and horns enable them to withstand repeated collisions unharmed. Butting contests continue for hours, until one ram grows exhausted and wanders off.

Like cows, domestic sheep, and goats, bighorns are ruminants: their multichambered stomachs harbor microorganisms that can turn cellulose (woody fibers) into food, allowing them to squeeze the maximum amount of nutrients and water from the grasses and shrubs they eat. In wet seasons, bighorns obtain all of their water from their food. When grasses and shrubs are dry, they must drink water. Bighorns can tolerate extreme dehydration—losing up to 20 percent of their body weight without ill effects. (In contrast, people die after losing just 12 percent of their body weight to dehydration.) The ability to drink and rehydrate quickly allows bighorns to spend very little time at waterholes, minimizing their exposure to predators.

See also CANYONLANDS, ZION CANYON.

BLACK-THROATED SPARROW
Black-throated sparrows (*Amphispiza bilineata*) are known as "desert sparrows" for their ability to thrive in arid conditions. Named for their large, black chin bibs, these small sparrows drink less water than any other seed-eating bird. Like KANGAROO RATS, black-throated sparrows obtain most of their water from their food, eating seeds or insects—whatever food contains the most moisture. After the winter rains, they eat new green vegetation and plump new seeds; in dry spring and early summer, juicy insects; after the summer rains, they search out moist seeds again.

Black-throated sparrows also conserve water by using very little water to process and eliminate their droppings and by resting in cool underground rodent burrows on extremely hot days. In addition, they can drink saltier water than many other birds. Their ability to conserve water allows them to live year-round in the extremely dry CREOSOTE BUSH stands of the Chihuahuan Desert. (Other birds winter there, but few can withstand the hot, dry summers.) Black-throated sparrows are characteristic of shrub deserts and dry shrublands in the Southwest, from the Chihuahuan Desert to the SAGEBRUSH communities of the Great Basin Desert.

> **Black-throated sparrows drink less water than any other seed-eating bird and are known for their ability to thrive in extremely hot, arid conditions.**

BLACK WIDOW SPIDER
Black widow spiders (*Latrodectus mactans*) are named for the female's habit of eating any small intruder that disturbs her web, including her mate. Males literally live only to mate. A male seeks out a female's web, courts her, mates, and before he can philander further, she bites and eats him.

Female black widows manufacture one of the world's most potent venoms. Desert Native Americans once used crushed black widow bodies to poison their arrows. Fortunately, black widows are not aggressive—they retreat into their web and bite only if cornered—so the chance of dying from a black widow's bite is slim, much less than the chance of being struck by lightning. The coal-black, inch-long females, easily identified by bright scarlet markings on the underside of their abdomen, and the smaller, light brown, venomless males, are common throughout the Southwest, except in the mountains.

Able to store sperm to fertilize future generations, female black widows need mate only once. After laying 300 to 500 eggs, they wrap the eggs in a protective cocoon of silk and hang them near the web. After thirty days, the young emerge and forage for themselves. The silk produced by black widows has the tensile strength of steel and replaced silkworm silk in making gun sights during World War II.

Female black widows build their irregular webs in dark, sheltered places where insects are plentiful, such as in garages, under porches, or at the entrance to rodent burrows. When insects become trapped in their webs, black widows fling silk strands around them from a distance, subduing them with silken straitjackets before approaching to bite and inject venom to paralyze and partly digest the insect. A female black widow may eat 2,000 insects, from flies to DARKLING BEETLES, in her one-year lifespan.

The succulent spiders are appealing prey to larger animals, especially lizards, some of which appear to be immune to black widow venom. Several tiny fly and wasp species lay their eggs on black widow egg masses. When the fly or wasp larvae hatch, they eat the spider eggs.

See also DARKLING BEETLE.

BLISTER BEETLE Blister beetles (family Meloidae) are common in Southwest desert ecosystems. They defend themselves by excreting a toxic liquid containing cantharidin, or "Spanish fly," which can blister human

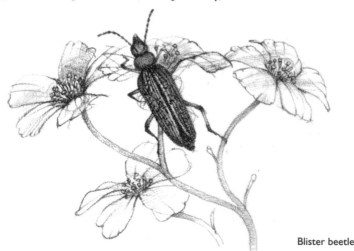

Blister beetle

skin and damage the digestive systems of humans, other mammals, and some birds. Once thought to be an aphrodisiac, cantharidin is still extracted from crushed beetles for external medicine.

Adult blister beetles are conspicuous for their size (1 to 3 inches long) and their bright coloring. Leathery wing covers of bright orange or red and blue-black serve as a warning to insect-eating birds and lizards. After once sampling a cantharidin-laden beetle, a predator avoids similarly bright-colored insects. Adult blister beetles feed on plants; larvae feed on grasshopper or bee eggs. Groups of feeding and mating adults of one Chihuahuan Desert blister beetle (*Megetra cancellata*) are sometimes so common along the highways between El Paso, Texas, and Carlsbad, New Mexico, that travelers stop to gawk at them.

One blister beetle has a close relationship with CREOSOTE BUSH, the olive-green shrub of the Chihuahuan Desert. The adult beetle eats the flowers, and the larva—wingless, sightless, and deaf—parasitizes BEES that pollinate creosote bush. After hatching, the larva climbs to the top of the nearest flowering plant and stations itself on a blossom where it can detect approaching bees by vibration and odor. When a bee hovers within reach, the larva attaches itself to the bee, hitches a ride to the bee's nest, and eats the bee's eggs. After molting through a series of grublike stages into the adult beetle, the insect heads for creosote bush again.

See also CREOSOTE BUSH.

BURRO   Native to Africa, burros (*Equus asinus*) were originally brought to the Southwest by Spanish explorers in the 1500s, along with horses, cattle, and domestic goats. Overgrazing by all four has had a profound effect on Southwest ecosystems: once-fertile grasslands have degenerated into shrub deserts, and accelerated rainwater runoff has carved deep ARROYOS where streams once flowed. Further, the domestic livestock have displaced many native grazers such as elk and BIGHORN SHEEP.

Of the domestic livestock, burros have thrived most readily in the wild because of their adaptation to arid environments. Like bighorn sheep, burros can tolerate high water losses and rehydrate quickly when drinking water is available. Their long life (up to twenty-five years), fecundity, and the lack of predators also have helped swell their numbers. Burros compete directly with bighorns and are blamed for the decline of these animals in some areas, including GRAND CANYON National Park.

BUTTERFLY Shimmering butterflies—cobalt blue, sulfur yellow, iridescent black—flutter through every ecosystem in the Southwest, from the Mojave Desert at nearly sea level to alpine tundra above 13,000 feet. Dependent on plants for their existence, butterflies lay their eggs on specific host plants, which then become food for the hatched caterpillars. The voracious caterpillars munch on their hosts as they grow, swell, and grow more. Once mature, they spin a cocoon, usually on the host plant. Weeks or months later, the familiar, gracefully winged adults split the cocoon, emerging to mate, sip flower nectar, lay eggs, and die. Although butterfly caterpillars are often considered pests because of their insatiable appetites, the adults are important pollinators, often of the very species consumed by their hungry progeny.

Among the hundreds of species of butterflies living in the Southwest are two of North America's three largest: giant swallowtails (*Heraclides cresphontes*) and tiger swallowtails (*Pterourus glaucus*). Both of these dark-colored swallowtails, named for the "tail" protruding from each hind wing, have wingspans up to 5.5 inches. Giant swallowtails, a tropical species found only in the extreme southern Southwest, feed on trees of the citrus family. The short-lived adults are capable of flying hundreds of miles; strays roam as far as the Midwest and northern states.

Tiger swallowtails, found throughout North America, are usually yellow with black tiger stripes and black wing margins. Some Southwest females are all black with a bluish iridescence. These females mimic the coloration of a foul-tasting species found in similar habitats, the pipevine swallowtail (*Battus philenor*), in order to fool potential predators.

Eight other swallowtail species live in Southwest ecosystems, usually near permanent water sources. One, the western tiger swallowtail (*Pterourus rutulus*), is a striking lemon-yellow butterfly with black tiger stripes across its wings. Its pale-green caterpillar has a swollen front end with prominent "eye spots," which it may use to frighten predators. The western tiger swallowtail is the most conspicuous butterfly in the woodlands and wet canyons of southwestern mountains and the COLORADO PLATEAU.

The great purple hairstreak (*Atlides halesus*), a small butterfly of the Sonoran Desert in Arizona and Mexico, is not purple; it has cobalt-blue wings, with black margins dotted red and white. Great purples, like other hairstreaks, fool avian predators into attacking a false head on their hind wings. They rub their hind wings up and down, causing a lobe with long,

narrow "hairs" protruding from the hind wing to resemble a
head with moving antennae. The bird bites
this false head, and the butterfly escapes
with only a beak-shaped notch missing
from its hind wing.

Adult male great purple hairstreaks engage in a
common insect
ritual called
"hill-topping,"
selecting and
d e f e n d i n g
perches with a com-
manding view of the surrounding landscape in
order to spot and perhaps mate with passing females.
Fast and agile fliers, great purples hold high-speed flying
contests to defend their perches in lookout trees. When
another male approaches, the first male begins a zooming
chase around the perch tree. If the newcomer doesn't retreat,

Purple
hairstreak

the defender chases the intruder straight upward several hundred feet
into the air, the two spiraling so tightly that their wings brush. Next they
plummet earthward in a suicidal dive; at the last moment, the victor
pulls out and returns to its sentry post to scan for potential mates. The
loser flies away.

The painted lady (*Vanessa cardui*), rosy-brown with black and white
spots, may be the world's most well-traveled butterfly. Each year in late
winter, North America's population of painted ladies emigrates east, west,
and northward from the Sonoran Desert. Laying eggs as they go, successive
generations of these fragile insects fly as far as Canada and the Atlantic and
Pacific coasts, winging over mountains at altitudes up to 12,000 feet. But
these farflung populations do not survive winter—new migrants repopulate
the following spring from the Southwest. In especially wet years, when their
food supply is abundant, the population explodes and consumes all available food. Spectacular emigrations occur when millions of adults take flight
in search for new food sources. In 1879, one such flight of European
painted ladies was so dense that the butterflies darkened the sky.

The Chiricahua pine white (*Neophasia terlootii*), one of two white
butterflies common to Southwest pine forests, displays dramatic sexual

dimorphism (having two distinct "morphs," or kinds). The adult male is white, with heavy black markings; in contrast, the female is brick-red with black wing margins. Chiricahua pine whites live in the CHIRICAHUA MOUNTAINS and other mountains of southern Arizona and northern Mexico. Pine white caterpillars eat the needles of long-needled pines such as PONDEROSA, Chihuahua, and Apache pines.

North America's most recently discovered butterfly species was found in 1978 in the harsh alpine environment high in southwestern Colorado's San Juan Mountains. The Uncompahgre fritillary (*Clossiana acrocnema*) descended from arctic fritillary (*Clossiana improba*) populations that became isolated in the San Juans as climates grew warmer and drier after Pleistocene glaciation. Eventually, with no way to continue mating with their parent population, the small, dusky-colored butterflies evolved into an "island species," a separate, isolated species adapted only to its unique environment.

See also SKY ISLANDS, SPHINX MOTH, YUCCA MOTH.

CENTIPEDE AND MILLIPEDE

Although neither centipedes nor millipedes possess as many legs as their names imply, both are many-legged. Centipedes possess one pair of legs for each of their flattened body segments, and millipedes' numerous cylindrical body segments grow two pairs of legs each. Centipedes are predators and can inflict a painful, but not fatal, venomous bite with the sickle-shaped pincers at the end of their first pair of legs; millipedes are herbivores and repel predators by emitting a smelly vapor from their "repugnatorial gland."

Centipedes have poor sight, relying on smell and touch to locate and identify prey, which they then subdue with their venomous pincers. Smaller centipedes make good housemates, eating insects and spiders, including cockroaches, clothes moths, and houseflies. The 9-inch-long giant desert centipede (*Scolopendra heros*), North America's largest, lives in the Sonoran and Chihuahuan deserts and dines on side-blotched lizards, GECKOS, and even small toads and rodents.

Desert centipedes, lacking the impermeable wax "shell" possessed by most other arthropods (critters with hard outer skeletons and jointed feet), avoid desiccation by hunting at night and spending the day under rocks or wood, or, in the hottest parts of the year, burrowed into the soil. Their large size and high mass-to-surface ratio helps minimize water loss. Female giant desert centipedes wrap themselves around their egg clutch until the eggs hatch, licking them constantly to keep them from drying out (they die if the relative humidity drops to 3 percent, not unusual in the desert), and to cleanse them of a potentially fatal FUNGUS.

Millipedes feed on dead leaves, the bark of shrubs, and other plant material, making them important recyclers of organic material, especially in arid environments. Desert millipedes avoid dehydration by spending three-fourths of the year deep underground, often taking up residence in abandoned burrows or nests of other animals, or sharing them, including nests of harvester ANTS, and emerging only after rains. They also eat moist soil and can take up water anally to rehydrate their bodies.

Predators generally avoid millipedes, repelled by their smelly vapor. One exception is the larvae of one species of glowworm beetle. Sightless and unable to smell, the larvae are apparently undeterred by the stink.

COATI Coatis (*Nasua nasua*), 40 to 50 inches long, resemble large, dark brown raccoons, except for their long, anteaterlike snout used to root in the soil for food. The most social of all raccoon family members, female and young coatis live in troops, extended family bands of from four to twenty-five individuals. They run on all fours, holding their 2-foot-long tail erect, and climb trees and vines readily, wrapping their prehensile tail around stems for balance and using it as a brake when they descend headfirst.

Coatis

A tropical species of mountain woodlands and forests as far south as South America, coatis are a recent immigrant to North America. First noted along the United States–Mexican border in the 1870s, they were probably attracted by the carcasses of thousands of cattle killed by range overstocking and drought. Between 1881 and 1883, at least 360,000 cattle died in south-central Arizona alone.

Coatis, also called *chulos* ("bandits"), forage for carrion and eat fruit and small animals. They've become common campground raiders in the mountains of extreme southwestern New Mexico and in Arizona as far north as the MOGOLLON RIM.

See also CHIRICAHUA MOUNTAINS.

COCHINEAL INSECT These tiny scale insects are common in the arid parts of the Southwest wherever cactus grows. Cochineal insects (*Dactylopius confusus*) conceal their bright red body under a dense mat of white, waxy strands (hence *confusus*, or "deceptive"). They feed on cactus juices, especially PRICKLY PEAR, in colonies that form white, mold-like blotches, or "scales," on the plants' skin. Their crushed bodies yield a brilliant crimson dye.

Like mealybugs, which are also scale insects, female cochineals lose their legs and antennae after the first molt, becoming immobile. Their larvae hatch in place and crawl out from underneath the dead parent.

CORAL SNAKE Western coral snakes (*Micruroides euryxanthus*), brightly colored, small snakes related to mambas and cobras, live in the rocky upland parts of the Sonoran and Chihuahuan deserts, from Mexico north into southern Arizona and extreme southwestern New Mexico. Coral snakes' pencil-thin, glossy body is marked with a distinctive, gaudy pattern of black and red rings, each separated by a yellow or white band.

Although western coral snakes' venom is about twice as poisonous as that of most RATTLESNAKES, their bites have caused no known human deaths. Their nocturnal, burrowing habits make encounters with people rare, and the snake's small head and fangs, while effective for killing lizards and small snakes, keep it from injecting much venom. Coral snakes spend much of their lives underground, avoiding desiccation and extreme temperatures by emerging to hunt only at night or on overcast days, usually during or after rains.

Numerous small, nonpoisonous snakes, including red-banded kingsnakes, shovel-nosed, ground, and banded sand snakes, echo coral snakes' body pattern and colors. Biologists once assumed that they imitated poisonous coral snakes to fool predators. However, mimicking coral snakes' bright color holds no advantage for these nocturnal snakes—their predators are generally color-blind. Probably both color and banding pattern act as camouflage, echoing nighttime dark and light shadows and serving to diffuse the snakes' outlines on the ground.

These nonpoisonous snakes also share a unique behavior with western coral snakes. Both coral snakes and the nonpoisonous imitators coil when cornered, hiding their head and elevating and waving their tail—colored like their head—at the aggressor. They may even feint a "strike" with the false head, and exert their cloacal lining with a sudden popping sound, effectively frightening away predators.

COYOTE Coyotes flourish from Southwest deserts to mountain meadows. Once common only in the West's open spaces, these pale-colored wild dogs began spreading across the country after wolves were nearly exterminated in the late 1800s, and are now moving into urban areas as well.

Coyotes are intelligent animals, able to adapt their behavior and diet to most situations. Where they hunt primarily large game, such as deer or young BIGHORN SHEEP, coyotes travel in small packs; in cities and suburbs, where they thrive on urban rodents, dumpsters, and dog food, they hunt singly or in pairs. A "typical" desert coyote's diet includes up to 40 percent plant material; the remainder is mainly JACKRABBITS, carrion, and insects, although coyotes will eat any easily obtained food. (Ironically, although thousands of coyotes are killed each year in the Southwest to protect livestock, they may benefit livestock by consuming large numbers of jackrabbits, the major competitor to livestock for range forage.) Southwestern coyotes sometimes raid farms and gardens, eating grapes, melons, raspberries, and even CHILES. According to local lore, the wily canids eat only the succulent chile flesh, spitting out the fiery seeds.

Coyotes have adapted physiologically to survive in the Southwest's deserts. Desert coyotes weigh about half as much (20 pounds versus 40 to 45) as other coyotes, with shorter, thinner fur, and so are more able to dissipate excess heat. Also, they are paler-colored, and so absorb less heat and blend into light-colored desert landscapes.

The speedsters of the canid world, coyotes lope as fast as 25 to 30 miles per hour, sprint up to 40 mph, and can travel several hundred miles in a night.

Social animals, coyotes mate for life and maintain family territories. Pups often stay with the family for more than a year, sometimes helping provide food for the next year's litter before traveling as many as several hundred miles to find a territory of their own.

Called "song dog" in some Native American languages, the coyote's scientific name is *Canis latrans*, or "barking dog." Coyotes' sophisticated vocabulary involves a wide variety of growls, whines, yips, barks, howls, and combinations thereof. They also speak with body language and behaviors such as tail wagging, lip curling, play-fighting, and marking scent posts. Communication helps coyotes maintain their social structure and facilitates group activities from play to hunting. The most distinctive of coyotes' songs—a series of barks and yelps followed by a drawn-out howl and ending with short, sharp yaps—broadcasts the locations of group members and reunites the band before or after hunting. Eastern coyotes rarely howl this familiar nighttime chorus, but it is commonly heard in the West and Southwest.

Once common only in the West's open spaces, these wild and adaptable members of the dog family are now moving into urban areas.

"Old Man Coyote" is an important figure in most Southwest Native American traditions. Stories about Coyote, a wily trickster whose blend of naiveté, charm, intelligence, and greed constantly involves him in scrapes, are told to entertain, to pass on societal mores, and to remind listeners of the many facets of their humanity.

See also JACKRABBIT.

CRANE Flocks of North America's two crane species—sandhills (*Grus canadensis*) and the larger, very rare whooping cranes (*G. americana*)—winter in the southern Southwest. Cranes, tall, stately birds with long necks and long legs, summer and nest in marshy areas and wet grasslands from the northern Great Plains and valleys in the Rockies to the tundra as far north as the Arctic Circle. The Southwest's largest flock of sandhill cranes winters at BOSQUE DEL APACHE National Wildlife Refuge on the RIO

GRANDE in central New Mexico. And among the thousands of slate-gray sandhills are thirteen taller, striking white whooping cranes, the offspring of an experimental fostering program.

Each spring, eggs from captive whooping cranes are placed in the nests of sandhill crane pairs at Grays Lake National Wildlife Refuge in southeastern Idaho. The foster parents incubate the 4-inch-long, nearly half-pound eggs and teach the whooper chicks to grub for insects, arthropods, and plant bulbs and tubers. Once fledged, the big whoopers migrate to the Southwest with their family flock, returning north the following spring. Unfortunately, despite biologists' best efforts, the thirteen foster children have never paired or mated.

Whooping cranes, the tallest North American bird, stand 4.5 feet tall, with a 7.5-foot wingspread. They are named for their loud, French horn–like calls, which, issuing from their 5-foot-long windpipe, can be heard up to 2 miles away. One of North America's rarest birds, whoopers have been the subject of captive breeding and habitat conservation programs since 1941, when only sixteen remained. The wild population has grown slowly, and now numbers around 155 birds.

Both cranes perform graceful, balletlike dances in pairs during courtship and throughout the year. The movements are spontaneous and varied. A crane will suddenly leap 8 feet in the air with its wings stretched wide, then bow. Or perhaps a pair will cross their long bills, then leap together with wings partly folded, trumpeting, stretching their necks straight toward the sky.

Strong fliers, cranes ascend as high as 13,000 feet in order to ride favorable winds, and migrate long distances—from a thousand to 2,500 miles—between their wintering grounds and nesting areas. Flocks take wing in the evening and migrate at night in the less turbulent air. Dozens of the huge birds fly in a shallow V or a straight line with long necks extended, legs dragging and big wings flapping slowly. Their sonorous calls, which help keep the flock together, echo as they pass overhead.

DARKLING BEETLE Among the most conspicuous insects in the Southwest, from the deserts to the PIÑON-JUNIPER woodlands, are inch-long, jet-black darkling beetles (family Tenebrionidae). Over a hundred different kinds of these common beetles, which walk with their rear end raised as if their struts were jacked up, live in the Southwest. Darkling beetles feed on wind-blown organic matter and fungi, making them vital to nutrient recycling in arid ecosystems where physical decay is incredibly slow.

Darkling beetles' behavior has earned them additional names. They are known as stinkbugs because they repel predators by spraying a noxious, black liquid smelling like kerosene from the tip of their abdomen. Another name, *piñacate* beetle (slang for "presumptuous" in Spanish), refers to the beetles' stance when threatened: they stand on their head and shove their abdomen toward the predator. In the Navajo language, darkling beetles are called *k'ineedlishii*; the same name in Navajo is also given to a common small car, the Volkswagen "beetle"!

Darkling beetles are elegantly suited to arid country life. Their ungainly, up-tilted posture raises them from the hot ground and allows them to collect nighttime dew, channeling droplets formed on their back into their mouth. An insulating air space under their fused wing covers helps buffer them from both cold and hot air. To avoid baking on hot summer days, they burrow or seek shade. Their black color allows them to collect solar heat (in full sun, a black object absorbs 25 percent more heat than a white one) and be active in winter when their food is plentiful and their predators less so. Black pigment also screens their tissues from ultraviolet radiation and strengthens their shell against abrasive desert soils. Further, black is conspicuous, advertising their noxious spray to predators.

Not all predators are deterred by the darkling beetle's repellent. When a beetle wanders into a BLACK WIDOW SPIDER's web, the spider simply flings a line around it to tie it down, stays out of range until the beetle exhausts its spray, then eats it. Grasshopper mice grab darkling beetles and swiftly stuff their abdomen into the soil, disarming the sprayer, then consume the juicy beetle at leisure.

DESERT COTTONTAIL

Desert cottontails (*Sylvilagus audubonii*), found throughout the arid West, are the most abundant and commonly seen of the Southwest's three species of cottontails, inhabiting shrubby areas in all of the Southwest's desert ecosystems. They also live in dry GRASSLANDS and PIÑON-JUNIPER woodlands.

Desert cottontails avoid heat, spending hot days resting in trees, bushes, or the burrows of other mammals. These voracious browsers are active at dawn, dusk, or night, nibbling on plants, including cactus. They rarely drink, obtaining most of their water from their food. Their light-colored fur—buffy above, white below—reflects solar heat; their relatively large ears (smaller than those of JACKRABBITS) radiate metabolic heat.

Unlike precocious young jackrabbits, cottontail young are born blind, furless, and helpless. Both rabbit types, however, are speedy and prolific breeders. Cottontail females can produce twenty to thirty young in four or more litters a year. They breed as young as 80 days old, mate immediately after giving birth, and wean the young in two weeks. However, because they are the staple food of many predators, such as RATTLESNAKES, OWLS, COYOTES, bobcats, and humans (archaeological sites in the Southwest contain thousands of rabbit bones), their average lifespan is only two years. Without predation, populations of these rabbits would explode; they can consume all of the plant food available, thus eating themselves out of house and home. The rabbits then starve and their populations plummet, rebuilding as the vegetation grows back.

Cottontails are host to two bacterial diseases that are potentially fatal to humans: tularemia and relapsing fever, both transferred when a tick or other insect bites a person handling a sick or recently killed rabbit.

See also JACKRABBIT.

DESERT TORTOISE The scientific name for desert tortoises is *Xerobates agassizii*, with *xero* meaning "dry" and *bates* meaning "walks"; thus, "one who walks dry places." A fitting moniker: these long-lived denizens of the Sonoran and Mojave deserts excel at water and energy conservation in the harshest of conditions.

Vegetarians, tortoises derive most of their water from their food. Storing their carbohydrate-rich food as fats, they metabolize these fats to yield water, storing up to a cup in an internal "canteen" (their bladder) for use during seasons when the plants they eat are dry. In spring, after a long, dry, winter hibernation, the tortoises rehydrate by eating juicy annual plants, consuming 3 to 4 percent of their weight each day. When water is available, usually after the summer rains, tortoises guzzle long and deep. After drinking at a puddle, one tortoise weighed 43 percent more than before drinking.

As do all reptiles, tortoises conserve water by excreting their waste as uric acid crystals rather than as liquid urine (human urine is 95 percent water); they can tolerate high salt and ion concentrations in their blood.

Desert tortoise

Their greatest water loss occurs from breathing. To control this and to escape summer's heat and winter's cold, they hibernate in humid burrow systems dug as far as 30 feet down into loose soil of wash or ARROYO banks.

Hard, dark-gray shells—high domes that look like a hardhat supported on four elephantine legs—protect these slow-moving reptiles from predators and insulate them against moisture loss and temperature change. On cool mornings, tortoises bask in the sun, absorbing solar radiation with their shells to raise their body temperature.

A long-lived species (captive tortoises have lived seventy years), tortoises do not breed until they are over 15 years old. Full-grown males weigh as much as 20 pounds and grow up to 15 inches long from nose to tail; females are slightly smaller. Males joust, snorting and banging shells, for the chance to mate with mature females. Females lay clutches of two to fourteen Ping-Pong ball–sized eggs in a hole dug near the burrow entrance, then urinate on the soil, perhaps to disguise the smell from predators such as GILA MONSTERS, KIT FOXES, and COYOTES. The tiny, 1.5-inch-long baby tortoises hatch about three months later and fend for themselves from birth. Their shells remain leathery for their first five years, leaving them vulnerable to predators.

Sadly, human activities endanger these gentle creatures. Thousands are crushed each year on highways or by off-road traffic. Their desert habitat is rapidly shrinking, decimated by off-road traffic and urban development. Even thoughtless handling can kill tortoises: as a last-ditch defense they squirt an attacker with the contents of their bladder, using up their precious water supply and leaving them vulnerable to death from dehydration.

DIGGER BEE   Digger bees (*Centris pallida*), small, nonsocial bees of the Sonoran Desert, spend eleven months of the year underground, timing their emergence to the blossoming of PALOVERDE trees.

Digger bee larvae live and grow in a buried brood cell that their mother constructed and stocked the previous year with paloverde nectar and pollen. Just before the first paloverde trees bloom, male digger bees metamorphose and chew their way up through about 6 inches of desert soil. Once free, they fly close to the ground in search of still-buried females, sniffing with their antennae. When they detect a buried female's odor, they land on the ground and begin digging her up, sweeping the soil with their antennae to hone in. After unearthing a female, they fight off any males attracted by her scent, mate for a few minutes, then resume searching. (Sometimes they mistakenly dig up late-emerging males!)

> **Digger bees spend eleven months of the year underground, timing their emergence to the blossoming of paloverde trees in the Sonoran Desert.**

Mated females work frenziedly to build and provision as many brood chambers as possible during the short blossoming period of paloverdes. The two species of paloverdes that depend on digger bees for cross-pollination have flowers which, to humans, look nearly identical. To help the bees forage more efficiently, the paloverdes have evolved ultraviolet pigments—visible to the bees but not to humans—to enable the bees to distinguish their flowers. Further, the top petal of an already pollinated flower, which has quit producing nectar and pollen, folds down over the flower, signaling the bees to avoid this blossom.

See also BEE.

DINOSAUR   An enormous skeleton currently being excavated near San Ysidro, New Mexico, may be the world's longest dinosaur, *Seismosaurus*. Stretching perhaps 120 to 160 feet from nose to tail, twice as long as the next largest-known dinosaur, the lumbering *Seismosaurus* grazed river valleys 150 million years ago in what is now the FOUR CORNERS region. Some 50 million years earlier a small dinosaur named *Coelophysis* hunted nearby.

Ponderous giants with long necks and tails, *Seismosaurus* resembled the familiar *Brontosaurus* (now called *Apatosaurus*), but probably weighed less. With its stubby legs and a low-protein diet of plants,

Seismosaurus (Greek for "Earth-shaker lizard") was not built for speed. Rather, these massive grazers crawled along, pivoting their head in an arc on their long neck and using their rakelike teeth to mow down and pull in all of the vegetation within reach.

Seismosaurus could not use their long neck to browse from the tops of trees—their heart simply would not have been able to pump blood up their 60-foot-long neck to their brain. Like modern birds that swallow gravel to help grind their food, *Seismosaurus* swallowed stones, called gastroliths, to help digest the half-ton of food they ate every day. But with their huge stomachs, a handful of gravel would not do: a couple of hundred gastroliths the size of large cobbles were found in the abdomen of the *Seismosaurus* now being excavated.

In contrast to the huge, slow-moving Earth-shaker, the lightly built *Coelophysis* was only between 6 and 10 feet long. *Coelophysis* moved upright, running swiftly on strong hind legs like some modern lizards. Its speed and formidable mouthful of sharp teeth allowed it to capture even the quickest of insects and smaller reptiles. The biggest-ever find of *Coelophysis*, New Mexico's state dinosaur, came in 1947 when paleontologists digging in a fossil-bearing layer of red sandstone and siltstone near Ghost Ranch, New Mexico, found 1,000 skeletons of the little speedster.

DOVE The soft cooing of doves or pigeons (family Columbidae) provides a gentle background sound for many Southwestern ecosystems. Six species live in the Southwest—more than in any other region in the United States—and include North America's largest pigeon, the band-tailed pigeons (*Columba fasciata*), 15 inches long and weighing in at a stout 0.75 pounds; and the smallest, the common ground dove (*Columbina passerina*). These last, diminutive birds measuring just 6 inches long including their tail, are a tropical dove whose range extends only as far north as southern Arizona's Sonoran Desert.

Band-tailed pigeons' owllike hooting is heard in summer in OAK woodlands and oak-pine forests of the foothills and lower mountains from Mexico north to southern Colorado and Utah. Before migrating south in the fall, these big pigeons gorge on fatty, protein-rich acorns. Although their dark-gray and dusky purple coloration helps them blend into forest shadows and avoid predators like Cooper's HAWKS, it offers no protection from being killed and eaten by exploding human populations on the doves'

White-winged dove

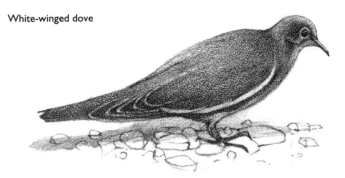

wintering grounds in Mexico and Central America.

Another Southwest species, the white-winged dove (*Zenaida asiatica*), named for its bright white wing patches, is the most desert-adapted of the family. A plump body gives white-wings a high mass-to-surface-area ratio, minimizing moisture loss and insulating them from both extreme heat and cold. White-wings' diet of dry seeds, supplemented by cactus fruit, leaves them dependent on drinking water. But they can go four or five days without drinking, and fly 10 or more miles to reach a water hole. (Because they fly directly to water, with no searching about, both animals and people often locate water holes by watching doves.) White-wings can survive losing 20 percent of their body weight by dehydration, are able to drink salt water, and can rehydrate quickly—they suck up water like mammals, rather than sipping and tilting their heads up to allow the water to trickle down their throat like most birds.

EEL Snakelike American eels (*Anguilla rostrata*) are the landlocked Southwest's only ocean fish. They spawn in the deep ocean waters north of the West Indies. The transparent, ribbonlike hatchlings feed on plankton in the ocean for their first year, then, as 2-inch-long eels, migrate toward the North American continent. (European eels spawn in the same area but head in the opposite direction.) At the coast, eels forsake the ocean for freshwater rivers and develop camouflaging pigment. Muddy, river-colored olive-brown upper parts hide them from predators above the water, such as osprey, herons, and humans, while their whitish belly and sides disguise them from aquatic predators swimming below.

American eels that inhabit Southwest rivers swim several thousand miles from their birthplace to the mouth of the RIO GRANDE at the Gulf of

Mexico. Males remain in the lower river, where they feed and grow to 2 feet long. Females push onward, journeying another thousand miles up the Rio Grande and the Pecos River into New Mexico and growing up to 4 feet long. (Until high DAMS blocked their passage up the Rio Grande, these amazing fish migrated into southern Colorado, probably bypassing low dams by traveling overland in marshy areas.) The female eels remain inland until they reach full size, usually six to eight years. Then they stop eating, swim downstream to the ocean, turn silver again, and journey back to their natal waters, where they breed, spawn, and die. Males also return to their natal waters and die after mating.

See also RIO GRANDE.

FRESHWATER SHRIMP Wherever water temporarily collects in the Southwest—small puddles, basin-filling PLAYA lakes, and alpine snowmelt ponds high in the mountains—fairy shrimp, crab shrimp, tadpole shrimp, and other freshwater shrimp appear miraculously. These tiny crustaceans, no bigger than a thumbnail, survive the months of drought either as desiccation-resistant eggs laid the last time their ephemeral habitat dried up or as adults in a dormancy-like state called diapause.

Freshwater shrimp resemble miniature horseshoe crabs with a shrimplike segmented tail and are more closely related to long-extinct Paleozoic trilobites than to edible saltwater shrimp. External gills attached to their abdomen provide oxygen; the paddlelike gills also help them swim and feed, stirring up the silty sediments of the pond bottom to reveal algae, protozoa, and bacteria. The shrimp, in turn, are food for fish, tadpoles, and insect larvae.

Freshwater shrimp are incredibly productive. Their whole life cycle, from egg to egg-laying adult, requires as little as fifteen days, a necessity in their short-lived world. To thrive in temporary waters, freshwater shrimp produce two kinds of eggs: nonfertilized eggs and thick-walled "resting eggs." The first kind, produced when water and food are abundant, hatch females only; in some species, males have never been found. But when their ephemeral ponds show signs of drying up (the water becomes crowded and saturated with excrement, and the mineral content rises along with the temperature), the shrimp produce eggs of both sexes. This generation's mating results in resting eggs, designed to survive freezing, broiling heat, and complete drying until the next flush of water revives their world, perhaps as much as a century later. (Resting eggs cannot hatch without drying out; otherwise, they might hatch as the pond that produced their parents was waning and not survive to produce a new generation.) Freshwater shrimp can also survive drought by going into diapause, an inactive state of arrested development and lowered metabolic activity. When conditions improve, the tiny arthropods "come alive" again.

See also CANYONLANDS, PLAYAS, WATERPOCKET FOLD.

GECKO Western and Texas banded geckos (*Coleonyx variegatus* and *C. brevis*), nocturnal lizards of a tropical and subtropical family, live in the southern parts of the Southwest, from the hot CREOSOTE BUSH deserts to PIÑON-JUNIPER woodlands in the foothills. These tiny, delicate lizards, measuring 4 to 6 inches long, have soft, yellowish-pink skin marked with brown bands on their back and whitish belly. When seen on back roads at night, they look like tiny ghosts in car headlight beams. Toe pads, like the bumps on the soles of footed pajamas, make geckos excellent climbers, able to grip vertical rock surfaces, as well as walls and ceilings.

> Banded geckos sacrifice their tail for their life. When a predator grasps a gecko's tail, the tail breaks off and the gecko escapes unharmed.

Unlike most lizards, which, active in the daytime, communicate visually with their colorful scales and their behavior, geckos, active at night, communicate and defend their territories by chirping and squeaking. In fact, "gecko" describes the sound made by an Asian species.

Vulnerable to ultraviolet radiation and desiccation because of their soft, translucent skin, banded geckos spend their days sheltered in burrows or cracks and crevices in rocks, protected from extreme heat and cold, and dryness. They emerge at night to hunt small arthropods such as spiders, young SCORPIONS, and CENTIPEDES. Adapted to nightlife, banded geckos have extra-large eyes and are active at body temperatures as low as 84°F, about 18 degrees cooler than day-active lizards. They exhibit curiously feline hunting behavior: they stalk their prey, swishing their tail continuously, and wash their face with their tongue after eating.

Banded geckos hibernate over the winter and during dry years when food is scarce. They can survive for up to nine months in their cool, moist hideout by slowing their metabolic rate and burning the fat stored in their tail. A gecko's tail contains more stored energy per unit of weight than its body or its eggs. Geckos even recycle their shed skin by eating it.

Like most lizards, banded geckos sacrifice their tail for their life. When pestered, geckos raise their tail and wave it laterally—the way a CORAL SNAKE does—attracting their attacker's attention. When the predator grasps the tail, the tail breaks off and the gecko escapes unharmed. Although other lizards have "break-away" tails, only geckos actively draw the attacker's attention to it. Geckos can grow complete new tails in just seven weeks, twice as fast as other lizards with break-away tails.

See also WHIPTAIL LIZARD.

GILA MONSTER Gila monsters (*Heloderma suspectum*) are aptly named. Two feet long, with a heavy body, massive head, stocky limbs with curved claws, and a swollen, sausagelike tail, gilas do indeed look monstrous. Their scientific name (*belo*, "warty"; *derma*, "skin") describes the beaded or warty look of their bright-colored skin—pink or orange with black banding. And gilas, along with the closely related Mexican beaded lizard, are the world's only known venomous lizards. Unique to the Southwest and northern Mexico, gila (HEE-lah) monsters are also the largest native lizards in the continental United States. Protected in Arizona since 1952, gila monsters are the only venomous animal protected by state law.

Despite their fearsome appearance, gilas are remarkably gentle. But when finally provoked, they live up to their image. After hissing in warning, they lunge and fasten a mouthful of sharp, grooved teeth on their attacker, holding tenaciously with a viselike grip. The tooth grooves channel venom into the wound from glands in the gila's jaw. The venom is rarely fatal to humans because it is diluted with saliva and not directly

Gila monster

injected. Still, the bites are severely painful; swelling is quickly followed by nausea and weakness. In smaller animals, the venom causes death by respiratory paralysis. Venom seems to serve these sluggish, fat-rich lizards primarily as a defense against predators, including OWL, KIT FOX, and RATTLESNAKE.

Gila monsters' eye-catching color and pattern actually provide good camouflage in the dim light and mottled shadows under shrubs and small desert trees where they usually hunt: on dark backgrounds, the black markings blend in, and the light markings look like sticks and rocks; on pale backgrounds, the effect is the opposite. Specialized carnivores, these lumbering lizards raid nests and eat ground-dwelling birds' eggs, DESERT TORTOISE eggs, and young mammals. Their high-protein, high-fat food is converted into fat and stored in their swollen tail, sustaining them through nine or more months of hibernation. Gilas hibernate in burrows dug in the damp soil of canyon bottoms or ARROYOS. When drought limits the production of baby desert animals—gilas' food supply—they can survive as long as several years on stored fat. Gila monsters live up to twenty years, patroling the same territory year after year.

GRASSHOPPER Hundreds of species of grasshoppers (order Orthoptera) feed voraciously on grasses, wildflowers, and shrubs in the Southwest from deserts to the alpine. With so many species, most have no common names. Those that do include some with quite curious names.

For example, Mormon crickets (*Anabrus simplex*), actually grasshoppers, not true crickets, are stout, large (1 to 2.5 inches long) dark brown or blue-black grasshoppers with reduced wings hidden under a shieldlike covering. Their common name commemorates a particularly dramatic example of grasshopper population explosions. In 1848, hordes of these big grasshoppers hatched in Utah and, migrating in search of food, began consuming crops planted by Mormon settlers, threatening the Mormons with starvation. The crops were saved by flocks of migrating gulls, which appeared and consumed the insects. (A statue of a gull still stands in Temple Square in Salt Lake City.) Mormon cricket populations periodically explode throughout their range in the Southwest and Great Basin SAGEBRUSH ecosystems. In the 1930s, Mormon crickets ate their way through 2 million acres in Nevada, one band advancing in a twelve-mile-wide front.

The female Mormon cricket has a swordlike ovipositor ("egg-layer") as long as her body, which curves upward from her rear end. Like all long-horned grasshoppers (named for their long, slender antennae), the males are songsters, producing a hoarse chirp to attract females by rubbing a "scraper" on the inside of one wing against a filelike ridge on the other. Mormon crickets provide important food for inland gulls, as well as small HAWKS such as KESTRELS, and other insect-eating predators.

Horse lubbers (*Taenipoda eques*, literally "banded-foot horse") received their curious common name for their physique and slow move-ments. These stout, large, and handsome grass-hoppers (from 1.5 to 2.5 inches long) are shiny black with orange or yellow markings and belong to the banded-wing grasshopper subfamily. Like all male banded-wing grasshoppers, horse lubbers make loud snapping noises by clacking their brightly colored wings together, when they can be persuaded to fly. Horse lubbers live in the deserts, GRASSLANDS, and PIÑON-JUNIPER and OAK woodlands in the foothills of the southern Southwest, wherever shrubby MESQUITE trees grow.

In 1848, hordes of grasshoppers began consuming crops planted by Mormon settlers. The crops were saved by flocks of migrating gulls.

Horse lubbers hiss when picked up, blowing air and fluid out the spiracles in their sides through which they breathe. Although the sound alone might startle a predator into dropping the juicy tidbit, the air and fluid also form a repellent foam.

Grasshoppers' abundance is correlated to the availability of their food plants. In years with plentiful spring or summer rains, adults appear from August to November; in dry years, not at all. Banded-wing grasshoppers are the primary food for many birds, including cactus WRENS and their young. Female wrens are able to judge the potential grasshopper supply and adjust the size of their clutches to match.

The creosote bush grasshopper (*Ligurotettix coquilletti*), a less-than-inch-long grasshopper found in the Mojave, Sonoran, and Chihuahuan deserts and adjacent shrublands, lives only on CREOSOTE BUSH. Females lay eggs in the soil beneath the fragrant shrubs; the eggs hatch after spring rains when nymphs can graze on soft, new creosote bush leaves. This is the only known grasshopper able to digest the toxic compounds that creosote manufactures as a defense against grazing. The adults camou-flage themselves by mimicking creosote bush: female grasshoppers resemble old stems; the males look like young leaf sprays.

See also CREOSOTE BUSH, WREN.

HAWK   Fifteen species of hawks (family Accipitridae), including accipiters, harriers, buteos, and kites, frequent the Southwest. *Hawk* comes from Old German and Old English verbs related to "have," and meaning "to grasp" or "seize." These birds of prey are most commonly seen soaring or perched in open landscapes, from low-elevation cactus deserts to PIÑON-JUNIPER woodlands of the high MESAS. In summer, hawks can be seen in the mountains above timberline.

Hawks are skilled fliers and often catch their prey by diving at great speeds from above, killing it instantly. They scan for prey while soaring in effortless circles on rising warm air currents, while perched, or when patroling a regular reconnaissance. Hawks can spot prey from great distances with their extraordinarily keen vision—up to eight times sharper than human sight. ("Hawkeye" aptly refers to keen eyesight.) Although different species of hawks may hunt the same area, they minimize competition by hunting different prey with different techniques.

Female hawks are as much as one-third larger than males, depending on the species. With the size difference, pairs can feed their young more efficiently by specializing in different-sized prey. The males can catch larger quantities of smaller, more abundant and easily caught prey, while the females catch fewer, but larger and less-abundant, prey.

Most hawks hunt in the uncluttered air spaces of open country. Only one group, accipiters (Latin for "hawk" or "bird of prey"), hunt in woodlands and forests, using short, wide wings and long tails to maneuver rapidly in the tight spaces between trees. Accipiters' plumage—solid gray or brown above, white with fine barring below—camouflages them in the dappled shade of forest canopies. All three North American accipiters are found in the Southwest: robin-sized sharp-shinned hawks (*Accipiter striatus*); crow-sized Cooper's hawks (*A. cooperii*), sometimes called "chicken hawks"; and raven-sized northern goshawks (*A. gentilis*), North America's largest accipiter.

Populations of northern goshawks are declining in part due to clear-cutting, which diminishes the large areas of continuous forest necessary for their prey. In the Southwest, goshawks live in the extensive PONDEROSA PINE and fir forests of the high Kaibab Plateau north of the GRAND CANYON, and in the higher mountains. More tolerant of disturbance, sharp-shinned and Cooper's hawks are frequently found in the urban "forests" of sprawling cities and suburbs, and are known even to snatch birds from residential feeders for a meal.

Harriers, long-winged, long-tailed hawks of open country, hunt small rodents and frogs in a unique way called "quartering." They fly close to the ground in a regular pattern, inspecting each square foot of ground; the dishlike arrangement of their facial feathers intensifies and directs the sounds of their prey. Pairs of harriers often quarter adjacent territory. North America's only harrier, the northern harrier (*Circus cyaneus*, formerly the marsh hawk) is common throughout the Southwest's GRASS-LANDS, from mountain meadows to low-elevation desert grasslands. The larger, brown female and the slender, pale-gray male both display prominent white rump patches.

Buteos are the soaring birds of the hawk family. Their broad, rounded wings and wide, fanned tails are marvelously adapted for riding rising air currents. From these mobile observation posts they spot their prey: mostly insects, reptiles, and small animals. Southwest buteos include North America's most common and widespread soaring hawk, the red-tailed hawk (*Buteo jamaicensis*), as well as rare subtropical species such as the gray hawk (*B. nitidus*). The red-tailed hawk is easily recognized by its bright rufous tail; the gray hawk, a fast-flying, small buteo, is found north of the Mexican border only in remnant riparian forests along desert and grassland watercourses in southern Arizona.

Two Southwest buteos soar with VULTURE flocks for "camouflage" when they hunt—prey animals are not wary of carrion-eating vultures. The common black-hawk (*Buteogallus anthracinus*) and the zone-tailed hawk (*B. albonatus*) each resemble a different vulture species, lacking only vultures' bare heads. Common black-hawks are coal-black with whitish patches at the base of their primaries and broad, rounded wings, and look just like soaring black vultures. Slate-black zone-tailed hawks, with pale barring on their flight feathers, mimic turkey vultures. Zone-tails even soar like their carrion-eating counterparts, holding their wings in a deep V and teetering on the air currents.

Swainson's hawks (*B. swainsoni*) and rough-legged hawks (*B. lagopus*) trade off on the Southwest's grasslands, hunting them in different seasons. Swainson's hawks summer in western North America, consuming grassland insects—especially GRASSHOPPERS and locusts—and some rodents. When Swainson's hawks migrate south to South America's grass-lands in the fall, rough-legged hawks (which, like Swainson's, are large, brown-backed, and white-chested) take their place, migrating from their arctic nesting grounds.

Mississippi kites (*Ictinia mississippiensis*) are the Southwest's least "hawklike" hawks. These small, gray hawks with 3-foot wingspreads use their buoyant, swallowlike flight to catch flying insects. They live on the western Great Plains, and can be seen in the Southwest on the LLANO ESTACADO of eastern New Mexico and west Texas, and in southeastern Colorado.

See also OWL, VULTURE.

HORNED LIZARDS
Horned lizards (*Phrynosoma* species), also called "horned toads" for the daggerlike spines crowning their head and for their flattened, toadlike body, are true lizards. Slow moving, with a body shaped like a hockey puck, and only 3 to 7 inches long, these reptiles are unique to the Americas. Most species are denizens of the deserts, GRASS-LANDS, shrublands, and dry woodlands throughout the Southwest. But one species, the short-horned lizard, is adapted to cold climates; it lives in forests up to 11,000 feet in altitude and bears live young, having no way to keep its eggs from freezing.

Most lizards rely on speed and adaptations such as "break-away" tails to avoid predators, but horned lizards, hampered by their awkward body and sluggish metabolism, cannot zip away. They rely instead on camouflage. When they are motionless, as they often are, their camouflaging color and form blend into the ground where they hunch. Their color varies from pale buff to yellow-brown to reddish to nearly black, matching the predominant soil color. Unevenly shaped dark blotches on their knobby back mimic shadows; fringelike scales edging their body break up their outline.

When a predator happens to discover a fat horned lizard, the lizard does not necessarily make a meal—its armor of sharp, spikelike scales makes it difficult to swallow. And the little lizards can inflate themselves by gulping air like a blowfish. One species can even splatter predators with a stream of blood, which, squirted distances of 6 feet from a pore in its eyelids, startles the predator sufficiently to allow the lizard to scramble away.

Horned lizards' tanklike form and slow metabolism result from the low nutrient value of their major food, ANTS—specifically the foraging workers of harvester ant colonies (*Pogonomyrmex* species). Harvester ants can sting with a highly toxic venom, and when one is killed, it spews an alarm scent that draws other ants to attack. Nonetheless, horned lizards prefer this difficult food and have evolved unique adaptations to make a meal of it. Horned lizards' enormous stomach, comprising 13 percent of their body weight (more than any other lizard), is designed to digest nutrient-poor ants. They hide by ants' foraging trails, munch a few workers, then move on before being detected and attacked. The lizards have even evolved an antitoxin specifically for harvester ant venom. Despite horned lizards' caution and defenses, many species of harvester ants discover and mob them, blowing their cover and exposing them to predators like ROAD-RUNNERS, shrikes, HAWKS, and COYOTES.

The horned lizard–harvester ant predator-prey relationship is apparently still evolving. At one location in southeastern Arizona, the ranges of three species of horned lizards overlap, producing unusual pressure on the local population of one harvester ant species. These ants' venom is four times as toxic as that of other populations of the same species—yet the lizards still eat them!

These small lizards are popular pets. Unfortunately, they usually starve to death in captivity since it is difficult to supply them with live harvester ants. In some parts of their range, especially south Texas, horned lizard populations are declining dramatically, perhaps because of the destruction of harvester ant colonies by nonnative fire ants.

See also ANT, GECKO, WHIPTAIL LIZARD.

HUMMINGBIRD Each year, bird-watchers trek to the mountains of southern Arizona, especially the CHIRICAHUA and Huachuca mountains, to see North America's widest variety of hummingbirds. Twelve of the fourteen North American species summer in the Southwest, including the two largest—the 5-inch-long blue-throated hummingbird (*Lampornis clemenciae*) and the magnificent hummingbird (*Eugenes fulgens*). Both are neotropical hummingbirds whose ranges reach the Southwest only in the southernmost mountains. North America's smallest are the 2.75-inch calliope hummingbirds (*Stellula calliope*), which nest throughout the Rockies and are found in the northern Southwest. Most Southwest hummingbirds frequent the foothills and higher elevations and are spring and summer residents only. These tiny birds migrate through the hot deserts, but do not stay to breed—partly because food supplies vary, and partly because their small size makes overheating a problem.

Creatures of the air, hummingbirds are most often seen hovering in one place to feed or zipping through the air at speeds up to 30 miles an hour. Flight muscles, making up a third of the bird's body weight, and mobile shoulder joints power long, narrow wings, which beat as fast as 80 times a second in the tiny calliope and 20 beats a second in the large magnificent hummingbird. (The name "hummingbird" refers to the audible whirr of their wings.) With these twin propellers, hummers can truly hover, remaining in place in still air, unlike HAWKS and falcons, which "wind hover" by flying into the wind at a speed equal to that of the moving air. And hummingbirds are the only birds able to fly backward. Their stiff, broad tails act as rudders, allowing the quick, precise flight and aerial acrobatics so characteristic of them.

Hummingbirds are voracious feeders. With the highest metabolic rate of any warm-blooded vertebrate (except perhaps shrews), these spectacular dynamos feed almost continuously in the daytime, gleaning insects and spiders from plants or out of the air, and pumping up nectar from flowers by capillary action with their long, extendable tongue and its brushlike tip. The only time they perch is to digest and make room for more food. To keep from starving when they cannot feed—at night and on cool days—hummingbirds lapse into torpor, lowering their body temperature as much as 50 degrees below their normal temperature of 104°F, cutting their metabolic rate to a third of normal.

Hummingbirds can fly at speeds up to 30 miles an hour and are the only birds able to fly backward. Voracious feeders, these birds perch only to digest their food.

The mating flights of male hummingbirds are perhaps their most dramatic shows. Often called "jewels of the air" by early naturalists, each species's characteristic choreography displays its brilliant colors and acrobatic control. For example, one flies back and forth in a tight horizontal arc just inches from the perched female. Another performs breathtaking, pendulumlike dives beginning high above her.

After wooing and winning a mate, the males resume a solitary existence defending their bit of territory, leaving the females to construct a tiny, cuplike nest. The females bind bits of lichen and other plant material with spider silk and line the inside with plant and feather down before laying two eggs inside. With only one parent to tend the eggs, the nest is designed for maximum insulating value, built under a sheltering branch or leaf clump, with sides curving inward at the top. When incubating, females cannot go into torpor at night—the eggs must be kept warm to develop—so they feed frenziedly late in the evening, storing enough food to sustain themselves. Broad-tailed hummingbirds (*Selasphorus platycercus*), the common mountain hummer in the Rockies and the Southwest's isolated mountain ranges, nest where temperatures often drop below freezing on summer nights. Temperatures at one broad-tail nest, measured before dawn, dropped precipitously from the toasty-warm eggs (92°F) to the chilly incubating female's back (54°F) to the air above her (38°F). Above the leafy canopy, the air was below freezing.

The Southwest's most widespread hummingbird is the black-chinned hummingbird (*Archilochus alexandri*), a small hummer with an iridescent-green back. It is named for the male's black chin, which is underlined by a violet-purple throat band. Black-chins nest throughout the West; in the Southwest they are found from the Chihuahuan and Sonoran deserts to alpine meadows, as well as in urban areas. They winter in Mexico, moving south in the fall when flowers and insects disappear.

Costa's (*Calypte costae*), a tiny hummingbird with a brilliant violet-purple crown and gorget in the males, nests in spring and winters throughout the Sonoran and Mojave deserts; during the hottest and driest months of summer, most Costa's head for cooler elevations. To avoid overheating on hot days, Costa's and other hummingbirds pant, evaporating comparatively large amounts of water. A female Costa's loses nearly half of her body weight on hot days. (A 150-pound person who lost water at that rate would have to drink more than ten gallons of water a day.) Costa's obtain the water they need from the nectar of desert flowers, or from hummingbird feeders.

Anna's hummingbirds (*Calypte anna*), medium-sized hummers with a rich rose-red crown and gorget in the males, have followed urban gardens and feeders eastward from the Pacific Coast, and now reside year-round in urban areas of southern Arizona.

JACKRABBIT   Five species of hares (genus *Lepus*) live in the Southwest. Four are nearly identical jackrabbits, denizens of arid country and easily recognized by their huge ears, slender bodies, long hind legs, and large feet. The fifth is radically different: snowshoe hares (*L. americanus*) have chunky bodies and small ears and are named for the broad web of

Jackrabbit

hairs on their feet that act like snowshoes to keep them from sinking in deep winter snow. Snowshoe hares live in the cold, moist forests of northern latitudes, and in the Southwest, in the highest mountains.

Jackrabbits save water by eating the juiciest vegetation they can find—succulent post-rainy-season annual plants, CACTI, the fleshy stems and leaves of shrubs and trees—and by excreting concentrated wastes. During the hot parts of the day, jacks often cool themselves by resting in the shade in a shallow depression scooped in the slightly cooler subsoil. They feed in the less-hot afternoon to nighttime hours. Their trademark ears, equal to one-fifth of their body length, are very sensitive antennae. But that is not all: with the veins dilated, jackrabbits can dissipate around a third of their body heat through their ears.

Jackrabbits rely on alertness and speed to escape their numerous predators. Their antennalike ears are aided by eyes located far back on their head providing near-full-circle vision. Powerful hind legs and feet propel them as fast as 40 miles an hour. Jackrabbits further confound pursuers by running an erratic course, making sudden zigzags, leaping as far as 17 feet, and bounding straight up in the air. COYOTES and Harris HAWKS, two common predators, have learned to use the big rabbits' lack of stamina: they pursue jacks in relays until the hares tire.

Jackrabbit young, like all hares, are practically born running. Fully furred, with their eyes open, they can hop after their mother soon after birth. Jacks breed prodigiously. In southern deserts, jackrabbits breed throughout the year, producing up to seven young per litter and three litters per year.

In the late 1800s and early 1900s, millions of jackrabbits' natural predators—coyotes, foxes, hawks, and OWLS—were slaughtered, leading to spectacular population explosions. In California in 1886, hunters shot 5,000 jacks in one day; a Kansas hunt during the dust-bowl years of the 1930s bagged 50,000. Biologists now blame the attempt to "control" (exterminate) wild predators and the subsequent explosion of jackrabbits and DESERT COTTONTAILS for some of the overgrazing which turned thousands of acres of the Southwest's GRASSLANDS into shrub desert.

See also COYOTE.

KANGAROO RAT Kangaroo rats (*Dipodomys* species) are named for their upright hopping gait, powered by huge hind legs and feet and balanced by a long furry tail with a tuft at the end. When pursued, a kangaroo rat leaps off in a wild, randomly zigzagging flight, like a ricocheting ball, changing course quickly by swinging its long, rudderlike tail and springing up to 10 feet at a leap. Like some lizards, kangaroo rats have "break-away" tails: when the tuft at the end of the tail is grabbed by a predator, it breaks off and can be regrown. These medium-sized, pale-colored rodents (8 to 14.5 inches long, including their tails) are widespread throughout the West's plains, basins, and intermountain valleys.

Astonishingly in this arid country, kangaroo rats can survive without ever drinking water. They manufacture what little metabolic water they need from carbohydrates in their food and have developed elaborate physiological and behavioral adaptations to conserve it. Elongated nasal passages cool their outgoing breath and recapture its moisture, and efficient kidneys concentrate salts and urea from ten to twenty times before eliminating them. Even kangaroo rats' feces are concentrated, containing 50 percent less water than human feces. They forage nocturnally, spending hot times underground in their extensive burrows and sealing the entrances to maintain relatively high humidity and cool temperatures. Food, stored in the moist burrows, rehydrates before they eat it.

Kangaroo rats feed on the prodigious numbers of seeds produced by annual plants. The big-eyed rodents hop across the ground on their big hind legs, keeping their front paws free to stuff food swiftly into fur-lined cheek pouches along their lower jaws. These commodious shopping bags hold a teaspoon each, or up to 900 seeds a load. Kangaroo rats do not eat out; rather, they return to their burrows to munch or stash the seeds, minimizing exposure to nighttime predators.

Kangaroo rats are well adapted for nocturnal life. Their big head (equal to one-third of their body) allows space for an inflated middle-ear echo chamber that magnifies sounds, especially in the low-frequency range of OWLS and RATTLESNAKES. Large eyes placed high on their head and keen night vision also help them to avoid predators, even in total darkness.

Adults live alone except during mating, when males tussle over females, rolling on the soil, growling, and sometimes leaping high off the ground like hares. A large mound, formed by excavation of 6-foot-deep tunnels and chambers, gives away the location of a kangaroo rat burrow. Burrowing breaks through caliche or alkaline layers in often-hard-packed arid-country soils, improving drainage and also aerating and fertilizing the soil. (In salty Great Basin desert soils, some plants grow only on kangaroo rat burrow systems.) Abandoned kangaroo rat burrows become homes for other Southwest animals, including SCORPIONS, burrowing owls, and KIT FOXES.

In the arid Southwest, kangaroo rats can survive without ever drinking water. They manufacture what little metabolic water they need from carbohydrates in their food.

Kangaroo rats' smaller, mouselike cousins, pocket mice (*Perognathus* and *Chaetodipus* species), named for their cheek pouches, share many physiological and behavioral adaptations with kangaroo rats, but lack their characteristic bipedal locomotion.

See also KIT FOX.

KESTREL American kestrels (*Falco sparverius*), North America's smallest and most common falcon, are often seen perched on utility wires or barbwire fences, or hovering over roadsides and other open areas throughout the Southwest, except in the high mountains. Other Southwest falcons include crow-sized, pale, prairie falcons (*F. mexicanus*), which hunt the deserts, MESAS, and GRASSLANDS, and the larger, dark, peregrine falcons (*F. peregrinus*).

Kestrels have extremely light, strong, and flexible skeletons, with pneumatic bones that hollow out and fill with air as the bird grows. Although their bodies are nearly a foot long and their wingspread 2 feet, these graceful birds tip the scale at less than a quarter of a pound. (Aircraft designers have yet to build a plane with the same ratio of weight to strength as a bird.)

Kestrels are speedy and agile fliers that hunt by scanning for prey from their perches or while hovering, beating their long wings quickly to hold themselves in place in the air. Falcons are aerial hunters, and kestrels often catch their prey by diving from above. They launch themselves with a few quick wingbeats, and then, partly folding their wings, plunge toward the prey, using the speed of their dive to stun or kill it.

Populations of kestrels' major prey—GRASSHOPPERS, crickets, and mice—periodically produce huge numbers of young. During these "boom years" kestrels and other predators hunt the exploding population almost exclusively. This benefits both the predators—who have an easy food supply—and the ecosystem, since the predators help keep the population from depleting its own food sources.

Unlike most falcons, kestrels nest in cavities—often abandoned woodpecker holes. Because they take well to nest boxes and regularly hunt freeway medians, some states in the Southwest mount kestrel nest boxes on the back of highway signs.

See also HAWK.

KIT FOX Kit foxes (*Vulpes macrotis*), one of North America's smallest canids, live throughout the Southwest's deserts, GRASSLANDS, and arid shrublands. The size of house cats, these nocturnal animals are pale-colored, with bushy, black-tipped tails and big ears.

Kit foxes are well adapted to every North American desert, from the cold sagebrush desert of the Great Basin to the hot Mojave, Sonoran, and Chihuahuan deserts of the southern Southwest and Mexico. They avoid extremes of temperature and drought by hunting at night, using extra-large eyes and ears to "see" in the dark, and spending hot days in a cool, humid underground burrow. Small body size gives them a large surface-area-to-mass ratio, enabling them to lose excess heat quickly. Their large ears—twice as large relative to their size as are gray foxes' ears—also help radiate heat from their bodies. Kit foxes rarely drink water, obtaining their dietary water from the meat they eat. Heavily furred paws give them good traction on loose, dry, desert soils and may insulate their pads from the hot ground.

By hunting at night, kit foxes can take advantage of one of the desert's most abundant food supplies: nocturnally active rodents. Their range closely coincides with that of their most important prey, KANGAROO RATS. Kit foxes also eat black-tailed JACKRABBITS (in Utah's Great Basin sagebrush desert, the big hares account for 94 percent of kit foxes' diet), and smaller animals, including lizards, SCORPIONS, and insects. Kit fox predation serves to check populations of plant-eating rodents, preventing them from over-grazing their habitat. Kit foxes are eaten in turn by larger predators such as bobcats and COYOTES.

MAGPIE Black-billed magpies (*Pica pica*) are striking black-and-white birds with streaming, foot-long tails and harsh voices. Denizens of open country, magpies frequent sagebrush shrublands, agricultural areas, and PIÑON-JUNIPER and riparian woodlands in the northern Southwest. Like most corvids, members of the crow family, magpies display high intelligence in their large repertoire of calls, skill at mimicry, fondness for keeping found objects—especially shiny ones—and ability to adapt to human habitat.

Although omnivorous, magpies are ground feeders that concentrate on insects. They pick up GRASSHOPPERS from rangelands or fields, dig maggots (fly larvae) and adult flies from carrion, and pluck ticks from the backs of elk, bison, or other mammals. They also clean up roadside carcasses and sometimes eat mice, snakes, grain, and fruit, as well as the eggs and young of small birds.

Magpies are monogamous and travel in family groups outside of breeding season. Nest building is part of magpies' courtship—the male brings nest material to the female to tempt her into mating with him. She alone crafts the 2- to 4-foot-high domed nest, cementing sticks together with mud. The commodious abandoned nests are sought after by birds as large as OWLS and HAWKS, and as small as bluebirds.

MOCKINGBIRD Northern mockingbirds (*Mimus polyglottos*), robin-sized, slender, gray-and-white birds with long tails that they often flick up and down, are vocal mimics extraordinaire. Male mockingbirds are the virtuosos, using their powerful voices and extensive vocal repertoires to delineate their territories, discourage competitors, and attract mates.

Mockingbirds' long bubbling songs imitate other birds' songs, mechanical noises like cars, sirens, and car alarms, and even human voices and household noises. The males broadcast their prowess from high perches—television antennae, roof peaks, or utility poles in urban habitat. During mating season mockingbirds' songs are common night noises in the Southwest's deserts and lower elevations. Unmated males sometimes sing all night long.

Once found only in scrubby woodlands across the southern United States and northern Mexico, mockingbirds have adapted so well to urban lawn and shade tree habitat that they have been moving steadily northward for the last twenty-five years. Unfortunately, urban areas can be deadly to these slender songsters. Lawn and garden pesticides often coat mockingbirds' food—insects in the warmer months; berries and fruits, including fiery chiltepines, native CHILE peppers, when insects are dormant—eventually killing the birds. While foraging in lawns and other open areas, mockingbirds often suddenly open and close their wings, flashing their conspicuous white wingbars to scare hidden insects into view and to distract predators, especially snakes.

MOUNTAIN LION
Mountain lions (*Felis concolor*) are the most widely distributed cat in the Americas, inhabiting wild areas from Canada to South America. Not limited to one ecosystem, they inhabit rain forests and deserts alike, following the distribution of their prey. The Southwest is home to an estimated 3,000 mountain lions—the healthiest concentration of mountain lions in the United States.

North America's second-largest cat (only the jaguar of Mexico and Central America is larger), adult mountain lions grow from 5 to 9 feet long, including the tail; stand 2.5 feet high at the shoulder; and weigh as much as a good-sized adult human—125 to 200 pounds. Despite their large size, mountain lions are agile, capable of jumping 20 to 30 feet, sprinting faster than a deer, and climbing trees with ease.

Even in the Southwest where these large wild cats are relatively common, mountain lions are rarely seen. Often the only sign of this secretive hunter's presence is a straight trail of 4-inch-long paw prints in damp soil, or the rare but unforgettable sound of its piercing scream. Curious mountain lions frequently follow people for miles without ever revealing their presence.

Except for mothers and kittens, who remain together until the kittens

Mountain lion

are about 2 years old, and during the brief mating period, mountain lions are solitary within their 10- to 20-square-mile territories. They frequently stalk their prey, sometimes covering 25 miles in one night, or they may wait silently in a tree over a game trail, their tawny color providing excellent camouflage. When a deer passes below, the lion leaps onto its back and breaks its neck. If deer are scarce, mountain lions hunt wild BURROS, BIGHORN SHEEP, livestock, and prey as small as rodents, reptiles, birds, and insects.

In the past decade, as cities and urban areas in the West have expanded into lion habitat, the big cats and people have begun to clash. Thousands of people and pets have moved into what once was mountain lion country in Colorado's Front Range above Denver and Colorado Springs; in 1990, a lion attacked and killed a jogger there. Still, attacks on people are rare: only a handful of attacks and two deaths have resulted from numerous people–mountain lion encounters in the past two decades. (In contrast, domestic dogs attack thousands of people each *year*.)

ORIOLE Three species of orioles (*Icterus* species), bright-colored songbirds of a mostly tropical group, dwell in the canopies of the Southwest's woodlands and in desert trees. They breed in the Southwest during the warm months and winter in Mexico and Central America. Orioles glean caterpillars and other larvae from foliage, sometimes catching adults in the air. They also eat a variety of fruit, including CACTUS fruit, and punch holes in flower nectaries with their sharp beak to sip the sugary nectar.

Orioles are the fiber artists of the bird world, weaving their sculptural cup- or bag-shaped nests from long grasses, plant fibers, aerial roots, and sometimes string or yarn, and lining them with soft material. One Southwestern species, the northern oriole (*I. galbula bullockii*), weaves a pendulous, 6-inch-deep bag that it suspends from the forked end of a branch high in a deciduous tree. In contrast, hooded (*I. cucullatus*) and Scott's (*I. parisorum*) orioles stitch their cup-shaped nests to the underside of YUCCA, palmetto or PALM leaves, or even to clumps of MISTLETOE.

Orioles are the fiber artists of the bird world, weaving their sculptural nests from long grasses, plant fibers, aerial roots, and string or yarn.

Cowbirds frequently lay their eggs in hooded orioles' nests. These blackbird-like cousins to both orioles and grackles never build their own nests; instead, they draft other birds as unwitting substitute parents. The aggressive young cowbirds hatch first, grow quickly, and out-compete the young orioles, which starve.

The strikingly colored male orioles are brilliant yellow or orange and black, with white in their wings. Females are colored drab yellow-green for camouflage in the leafy canopies where they nest. Male orioles' songs—loud, clear mixtures of whistles, warbles, and trills—are often all that reveal their presence. Their flashy plumage hides surprisingly well in tree canopies.

OWL Owls, nocturnal birds of prey, inhabit every ecosystem of the Southwest except the alpine. Among the Southwest's thirteen species of owls is the world's smallest owl, the 5.75-inch-long, fist-sized elf owl (*Micrathene whitneyi*).

Elegantly adapted to nighttime and twilight hunting, owls have large eyes with a high proportion of light-gathering rods (rather than cones) for excellent night vision. Asymmetrical openings in their large ears allow them to distinguish which ear is hearing a sound more strongly and thus to triangulate the location and distance of sounds. So acute is their hearing that common barn owls (*Tyto alba*) and some other species can precisely locate prey in complete darkness. The disklike arrangement of feathers around their eyes functions like a parabolic reflector, intensifying and directing sounds to their ears. Serrated leading edges on their flight feathers dampen air noise, allowing eerily silent flight.

Large heads, fluffy plumage, long, broad wings, and heavily feathered legs and feet give owls their characteristically stocky look. Somberly colored plumage, heavily patterned with streaks, fine barring, and spots, enables them to roost in trees during daylight hours, nearly invisible against shadow-dappled tree bark. Many species even have "horns"—tufts of feathers protruding from the front corners of their head, which make their silhouettes look like snags. The long-eared owl (*Asio otus*), a big owl of evergreen forests, looks exactly like a dead snag when it roosts close to a conifer trunk: its finely barred plumage echoes the bark pattern, and closely spaced ear tufts make its head look like a jagged broken branch.

Owls cannot chew their food; they swallow their prey whole or in large chunks, digest what they can, and later regurgitate bones, fur, and feathers in compact pellets. Two-foot-long great horned owls (*Bubo virginianus*), the Southwest's largest species, often seen in urban areas, hunt prey as large as skunks and domestic cats.

The range of the Mexican spotted owl (*Strix occidentalis*), is limited to the dense, moist forests of the southern Rockies and the Sierra Madres in Mexico. A big, quiet, decidedly nocturnal owl, the Mexican spotted owl needs daytime summer roosts with cool microclimates because its thick plumage and inability to dissipate heat make it intolerant of even moderately high temperatures. Never common in the Southwest's isolated mountain ranges, spotted owl populations are declining rapidly due to the clear-cutting of its forest habitat.

Moist mountain and riparian forests throughout the Southwest resound with the curious saw-on-sharpening-stone call of the sparrow-sized northern saw-whet owl (*Aegolius acadicus*). The northern pygmy-owl (*Glaucidium gnoma*), another sparrow-sized owl, prefers dry woodlands—dense OAK, PIÑON-JUNIPER, and PONDEROSA PINE—in the foothills and mountains. In spring, male pygmy-owls are visible and vocal, perching in the open, whistling, and flicking their unusually long tails up and down. Flocks of small birds often mob this gnomelike owl.

Tiny elf owls prefer open country, but only in a very restricted range, breeding in the Sonoran Desert and adjacent foothill canyons of Arizona and Mexico, and extreme south Texas. They winter in central Mexico. Elf owls nest and roost in the cavities drilled by woodpeckers in the trunks of the giant SAGUARO and cardón cacti, and sycamore and COTTONWOOD trees.

Their loud, yipping call wavers in the air at dusk and through the night as they search out large insects and other arthropods, including SCORPIONS.

Most owls nest in cavities, abandoned hawk nests, or buildings. But burrowing owls (*Athene cunicularia*) nest and roost in underground burrows to escape the heat and aridity of their treeless plains, basins, and desert homes. Often they enlarge abandoned ground squirrel, PRAIRIE DOG, or KANGAROO RAT burrows. They frequently share a nest with prairie dogs, roosting in prairie dog colonies, even acting like prairie dogs by standing at the entrance of their burrows in the daytime, bowing and chattering when disturbed. Pairs court atop their burrow. Like most owls, the male burrowing owl brings a tidbit of food to the female, and the pair quietly calls to each other, touching necks and bills, and stretching their wings.

Underground burrows, however, have significant drawbacks. First, the owls are vulnerable to predators such as badgers and RATTLESNAKES; burrowing owls must lay nearly twice as many eggs as other owls to compensate for increased predation. Fledgling burrowing owls attempt to fool some predators by giving a distress call that sounds like a rattlesnake's rattle. Second, adult owls often line their burrows with manure of other animals, perhaps also to confuse predators. However, the burrows eventually become infested with fleas and must then be abandoned. And because they inhabit ground squirrel and prairie dog burrows, burrowing owls have been killed by rodent-killing poisons placed in their burrows.

See also PRAIRIE DOG.

PHAINOPEPLA Phainopeplas (*Phainopepla nitens*), slender, dark birds with conspicuous crests, are often called silky flycatchers for their lustrous plumage and flycatcherlike "hawking" for insects. Like many winged dwellers of the desert or semidesert, phainopeplas leave in summer to escape the heat, aridity, and scarce food. Further, they raise a brood in both their summer and winter ranges. In the cool of early spring, they nest in the Sonoran and Chihuahuan desert scrub and adjacent agricultural areas of the southernmost West. The male phainopepla does the courting by setting up a territory and building a model nest. The female, attracted by the male's silky black plumage, inspects the nest. If it satisfies her, the two mate, and then the female lays and incubates the eggs. Pairs disband once the young are raised. After forsaking the desert for cooler summer weather in southern Nevada and Utah and along the Pacific Coast, phainopeplas nest again, in loosely communal groups.

Phainopeplas are the northernmost species of a group of birds that eat MISTLETOE berries. Their main winter food, the berries provide both nutrition and water. Phainopeplas and the parasitic plant are interdependent. The birds digest only the flesh of the salmon-colored berries, passing on the seeds—which may need to have their seed coats chemically softened in the birds' digestive system to germinate. The fertile droppings accumulate on mesquite branches beneath the birds' perching spots. There they eventually germinate, pushing their roots into the tree branches to feed. When mistletoe berries are not available, phainopeplas flycatch, snatching protein-rich insects from the air in graceful sallies.

See also MISTLETOE.

PIKA   Pikas (*Ochotona princeps*), guinea pig–sized members of the rabbit family, live in rock slides at the highest elevations of mountains throughout western North America. To remain active all year in the severe cold and aridity of their alpine habitat, pikas are completely covered—even the soles of their feet—in super-insulating three-layer fur; their ears, tail, and other extremities are reduced to retain body heat. "Pika" is of Asiatic origin and describes the animal's call. Another common name, "coney," may come from the Spanish *conejo*, for rabbit.

Like other rabbits, pikas graze on plants. But because these chunky mammals are active year-round in an environment where plant food is available only for a short summer, they must gather and store food to sustain them through their nine-month winter. During long alpine summer days, pikas harvest prodigious amounts of hay—grasses, sedges, and flowering plants—from the tundra; spread it on rocks to dry, dotting their territory with drying piles; and later stash the hay in their rock-protected homes. Because their food is high in fiber, not calories, they must fill their stomachs nearly hourly to meet their energy needs. Like ruminants, pikas wring the maximum protein and energy value from their food by digesting it twice; they excrete and reingest special mucus-coated fecal pellets. They also conserve scarce moisture by concentrating their wastes into uric acid crystals. Nor are these nitrogen-rich wastes squandered. Brilliantly colored red-orange LICHEN colonize the white deposit excreted by pikas on their bouldery perches.

Pikas do reproduce like rabbits. By mating immediately after giving

Pika

birth to their first litter, they manage to produce more than one litter even in the short high-mountain summers. Also like rabbits, the young are born blind and furless.

A variety of predators, including HAWKS, eagles, and members of the weasel family, prey on pikas. The shrill, whistling call or thin, abbreviated bleat of a sentinel on a rocky perch alerts the colony to an intruder, sending the group dashing for the rocks. Pikas' fur, usually light gray to pale cinnamon, effectively camouflages them against the local rock formations. A population living on dark volcanic rocks in New Mexico's Jemez Mountains has evolved nearly black fur.

See also VOLCANO.

PIÑON AND OTHER JAYS   Piñon jays (*Gymnorhinus cyano-cephalus*), one of six jay species found in the Southwest, are the most conspicuous bird in PIÑON-JUNIPER woodlands, their preferred habitat. Traveling in flocks that number up to several hundred, these blue-gray, robin-sized jays frequent the foothills of the southern Rocky Mountains, interior plateaus, and the Great Basin. Like all jays, members of the crow family, piñon jays are bold-natured and noisy; their distinctive, high-pitched mewing calls carry long distances through their forest habitats. Piñon jays are less omnivorous than most jays, however, eating one food—piñon nuts—almost exclusively. The birds' association with piñon nuts is so strong that their local population varies from year to year with the abundance of the piñon crop. They normally breed in spring, but if the nut crop is small, they delay breeding until the next good crop.

Piñon jays spend late summer and fall collecting the large, wingless seeds of piñon pines. They search open cones for mature, dark brown nuts, tap them to test their weight and soundness, pack up to twenty in their bulging esophagus, and fly to the flock nesting area, often miles away. Burying the seeds in leaf litter at the soil surface, a flock can cache as much as a ton of the fatty and nutritious seeds each year, guaranteeing ample food for spring nesting season. The seeds feed the jays, and the jays in turn aid the trees. Uneaten caches of otherwise immobile seeds are left to sprout far from their parent trees. Piñon pines and other conifers probably reached isolated mountain ranges via jay transport.

The larger Clark's nutcrackers (*Nucifraga columbiana*), residents of high mountain forests from southern New Mexico to Canada, cache seeds from whitebark and limber pines, carrying up to thirty-eight nuts at a time in a special cheek pouch as well as in their beak. Like piñon pines, whitebarks have evolved to depend on jay-nut caches for reproduction. In years of poor pine nut crops, these noisy jays, named for William Clark of the Lewis and Clark Expedition, emigrate to lower elevations and as far west as the Pacific Coast in search of food.

Piñon jays' association with piñon nuts is so strong that the birds' local population is tied to the abundance of the piñon crop.

The gray-breasted jay (*Aphelocoma ultramarina*, formerly Mexican jay), a resident of OAK and piñon-juniper woodlands in the foothills and mountains, lives from Mexico and Central America into the extreme southern Southwest. Gray-breasted jays practice altruistic breeding, whereby young jays of breeding age delay mating for several years, gaining experience by helping their parents raise new broods. They live in extended-family flocks of up to two dozen birds.

Gray jays (*Perisoreus canadensis*) are denizens of spruce-fir forests in the northern Southwest and the northern United States. Because their habitat lacks large pine nuts, gray jays are scavengers. To survive the long mountain winters, they cache animal fat, meat scraps, and seeds, rolling up small packets of food and gluing them to tree twigs with their saliva. These quiet jays are not afraid of robbing bacon scraps or other choice tidbits from human camps—sometimes right from people's plates. Because of their boldness and stealth, gray jays figure as "tricksters," heroes endowed with all of humans' wisdom and foolishness, in many northeastern Native American stories.

See also PIÑON PINE.

POORWILL Common poorwills (*Phalaenoptilus nuttallii*), named for their ascending, two-note call, are nocturnal counterparts of swallows and swifts. They flit about silently, scooping night-flying moths and other insects from the air with their wide mouths. Large eyes and special tactile bristles lining their mouth help them detect insects in poor light. They even drink on the wing, fluttering open-mouthed over the surface of ponds and slow-moving streams.

At 7 inches long, common poorwills are the smallest North American member of the nightjar family (Caprimulgidae, nighthawks and whippoor-wills). The family name, "goat-milk-suckers," refers to an old belief that these nocturnal insect-catchers drank from goats' teats. Poorwills winter in the Southwest and Mexico and summer in the upland deserts and dry shrublands throughout the western United States. They roost and nest right on the ground, perfectly camouflaged by their mottled, gray-brown plumage, revealing their presence only by the flash of their pink eyeshine in the beam of headlights or a flashlight.

Like some HUMMINGBIRDS and swifts, poorwills become torpid when food is not available, lowering their heart rate, breathing rate, and metabolism to barely perceptible levels. However, only poorwills actually hibernate. When night-flying insects disappear in late fall, poorwills "sleep" on the ground or in a rock crevice until the spring insects hatch, remaining immobile for up to three months with no detectable heartbeat or breathing, and dropping their body temperatures as much as 40 degrees below their usual 106°F. Captive poorwills used less than a half-ounce of stored fat in 100 days. Not surprisingly, some Southwest Native Americans call poorwills *holchko*, "the sleeping one."

PRAIRIE DOG In 1904, Vernon Bailey, a naturalist surveying the flora and fauna of the United States–Mexican border, inventoried a huge black-tail prairie dog (*Cynomys ludovicianus*) colony in southern New Mexico. He estimated that the underground colony contained 6.4 million of the tan, stub-tailed animals and that their network of tunnels covered 1,000 square miles in the Animas and Playas valleys. Today prairie dog alarm whistles are no longer heard in these valleys and most of the GRASSLANDS and shrub-lands of the Southwest. Victims of decades of systematic poisoning to "improve" the range for livestock, *perritos* (Spanish for "little dogs") nearly went the way of the bison and the black-footed ferret. Large colonies remain only where they have been protected from poisoning, for example in Bryce Canyon National Park in southern Utah.

Blacktail prairie dogs' once-enormous colonies were bound by an elaborate social structure. Landforms such as ARROYOS or hills divide the colony into geographic units; these units are further subdivided socially into "coteries"—territorial units occupied by extended families consisting of a male, several females, and their young. Coterie members defend their territory with barks and other vocal and postural signals, and greet each other by touching incisors. In each coterie, individual prairie dogs occupy burrows marked by doughnut-shaped mounds encircling the entrance hole—dikes to prevent torrential surface water flow from flooding the hole during summer thunderstorms.

North America's other prairie dog species, the whitetail or Gunnison's (*C. gunnisoni*), lives in much smaller colonies, consisting of as few as a handful of individuals. Whitetails, which look just like blacktails except for the white tip of their tail, have developed one of the richest animal vocabularies ever studied. Their dozens of squeaks and whistles not only warn fellow prairie dogs of approaching predators, but can specifically describe the individual predator. Whitetails, once common in the SAGEBRUSH and GRASSLAND ecosystems of the COLORADO PLATEAU, are now scarce and federally listed as a threatened species.

See also OWL, COLORADO PLATEAU.

PUPFISH Pupfish (*Cyprinodon* species), chubby, 1- to 2-inch-long, minnowlike fish, live in springs, sinkholes, ponds, and quiet streams scattered throughout the Southwest's deserts. Though playful and puppylike in their behavior, these tiny fish are amazingly hardy, capable of tolerating saltier and hotter water than any other known fish. The eleven species of pupfish endemic to deserts in the West thrive in water up to five times as salty as sea water, with the lowest oxygen concentrations known to support any fish. And pupfish can survive extreme fluctuations in the temperature of their water, from 34°F, just above freezing, to 112°F. Pupfishes' ability to protect their renal systems from salt accumulation may provide clues to preventing kidney disease in humans.

Pupfish have not always lived in such harsh conditions. During the last glacial era, they swam in the freshwater lakes that then filled many Southwestern basins. Several thousand years ago, increasingly warm and arid climates dried up the huge lakes, forming the Southwest's amazingly flat PLAYAS and stranding the tiny fish in isolated springs and outflow streams. Pupfish not only adapted quickly to the stressful new environments, but, cut off from others of their kind, evolved into eleven distinct species specifically adapted to their particular locales.

More species of pupfish occur in the Chihuahuan Desert region than anywhere else. These include the recently discovered White Sands pupfish (*C. tularosa*), unique to Malpais Spring, near White Sands National Monument, New Mexico.

In 1976, a U.S. Supreme Court ruling made the tiny Devil's Hole pupfish (*C. diabolis*) famous and protected water levels in its only home, an isolated limestone sinkhole in Death Valley National Monument, California. Peat extraction from the neighboring valley followed by groundwater withdrawals for agricultural development had lowered water levels in Devil's Hole, threatening the tiny fishes' survival. The National Park Service took the farming company to court, winning a minimum allowable water level for the fish.

Other pupfish populations are similarly threatened by human-engineered changes. For example, the Comanche Springs pupfish disappeared from one spring near Fort Stockton, Texas, in 1952, after groundwater pumping for irrigated agriculture caused a 61 percent decline in the water flow. (The springs dried up completely in 1961.) At a neighboring spring, leftover bait fish dumped by fishermen nearly wiped out the remaining pupfish populations.

See also PLAYA.

Pupfish

QUAIL The Southwest is quail country. Five of six North American quail species live in the Southwest's deserts, shrublands, and woodlands. Chunky ground-dwelling birds, quail look striking close up, with their heavily streaked, spotted, and striped plumage. But from a distance, these small birds fade into the shadows, concealed from aerial predators such as HAWKS and falcons.

Both gregarious and loquacious, quail live in small, family-group coveys during breeding season and congregate in flocks of up to several hundred during winter, filling the air with loud whistles, soft clucks, and plinking sounds. Like chickens, they graze on new green vegetation, eat seeds and fruits, and sometimes catch insects and other small arthropods. When disturbed, they run for cover; if pursued, they explode into flight, startling and confusing pursuers with the flurry of rapid, noisy wingbeats and plump bodies hurtling in various directions. Quail chicks are precocious, hatching fully feathered, with eyes open and legs ready to run.

Like other arid-country animals, quail reproductive activity is tied to the amount and timing of rainfall. In years of abundant winter and summer rains, quails may lay several dozen eggs (providing abundant food for egg-eating GILA MONSTERS); in exceptionally dry years, none. The mystery of quails' widely varying clutch size was solved recently when researchers discovered that in dry years, quail graze heavily on legumes called locoweeds. These plants accumulate high levels of selenium and other heavy metals; large doses of these toxic substances cause spontaneous abortions.

Gambel's quail (*Callipepla gambelii*), plump birds with nodding, apostrophe-shaped black head plumes, the most widespread and most desert-adapted quail, are commonly seen from the southern Southwest to the COLORADO PLATEAU in central Utah. Gambel's quail can tolerate extreme dehydration, losing up to half their body weight in water loss. They eat green, succulent plants when available and conserve water by de-watering their droppings, timing their activities to the coolest parts of the day, and allowing their body temperature to rise as much as 8 degrees when the air temperature exceeds 104°F, their normal body temperature. Gambel's quail drink water when the plants they eat are dry, especially in winter, when huge coveys of up to 200 birds can be observed drinking at waterholes.

Overgrazing of arid GRASSLANDS has endangered two quail species endemic to the Southwest. Masked bobwhite (*Colinus virginianus ridgwayi*) disappeared from southern Arizona earlier this century but were recently reintroduced to the restored Sonoran grasslands of southern

Arizona. As bunchgrasses disappear from foothills oak and pine-oak woodlands in the southern Southwest, so too do Montezuma quail (*Cyrtonyx Montezuma*), also called Harlequin quail for the male's striking black-and-white face pattern.

RATTLESNAKE Eleven species of rattlesnakes live in the Southwest, more than in any other single region of the Americas. Southwest rattlers range in size from the tiny, foot-long, twin-spotted rattlesnake (*Crotalus pricei*) to the western diamondback (*C. atrox*), which can grow to 7 feet long.

Rattlesnakes bite about 1,000 people a year in the United States. Still, the risk of being killed by one is 20 times less than the risk of being struck by lightning.

Rattlers have broad triangular heads, widely gaping, articulated jaws, and hollow fangs through which they dispense their highly toxic venom. Along with cottonmouths and copperheads, they belong to the pit viper subfamily (Crotalinae), named for their loreal pits—heat-sensitive depressions on either side of the head behind the nostril. Loreal pits can measure temperature differences as small as 0.2°F in nearby objects—a rattler can detect the heat of a human hand up to 12 inches away—helping rattlers precisely locate and strike prey, even in complete darkness. Rattlesnakes can also sense approaching animals by picking up air or ground vibrations or flicking their tongue in the air to catch scents.

Pit vipers have the most sophisticated mechanism for injecting venom of any snakes. Hollow, folded fangs at the front of the upper jaw swing forward when the snake bites, stabbing and dripping venom into the bite in a single swift thrust. They use their venom, a complex and highly toxic compound, both to subdue their prey and to protect themselves from predators. When the prey is small, the rattler strikes, bites and holds the prey until it dies—from two to five minutes, depending on size. When catching larger animals, such as a COTTONTAIL RABBIT or a PRAIRIE DOG, the rattler strikes and releases, so that the struggling animal cannot wound the snake. The snake then tracks the wounded animal, following its scent and body heat, and after the animal succumbs to the venom, the snake swallows it whole, head first. With jaws that unhinge to nearly 180 degrees (human jaws open about 40 degrees), loose jawbones, and flexible ribs, rattlers can gulp prey several times larger in diameter than themselves.

Rattlesnake

Unlike smaller, quicker snakes and lizards, heavy-bodied rattlesnakes cannot slither away at the first sign of danger. Instead, they confront their foe. Wrapping their body in a coil, they lift their head, ready to strike. Holding the end of their tail vertically, they vibrate the rattles quickly. Their buzzing warning says clearly: "Back off!" The rattles that give the snake its name are actually a series of loosely interlocking horny segments ending its tail. The volume and quality of the sound produced by the vibrating rattles varies with the snake's size, age, species, and amount of disturbance; it can resemble dry leaves rustling, a burst of steam, clacking castanets, or the clicking of a cicada. Rattlesnakes are also called buzzworms, or, in Spanish, *cascabeles*, meaning "small bell" or "rattle."

Rattlesnakes bite about 1,000 people a year in the United States—but less than 1 percent of those bitten die. The seriousness of the bite depends on a variety of conditions: the location of the bite; amount of venom injected (in at least one-quarter of the bites, no venom is injected); size and species of the rattler (the venom of the Mojave rattlesnake, the most poisonous rattler, is sixteen times more potent than that of the sidewinder); and the victim's size and health. Elderly people and those in poor health are most likely to be seriously affected. Children and small adults are next most likely because they receive more venom in proportion to body size. Still, the risk of being killed by a venomous animal in the United States is 20 times less than the risk of being struck by LIGHTNING and 300 times less than that of being murdered.

Rattlesnake bites are preventable. People get bitten when, intentionally or not, they pose a threat to the snake. If a person locates the snake before moving, then backs away carefully, the rattler will usually retreat also. A rattlesnake's reflex action persists after death and it can still deliver a fatal bite, so all rattlers, even dead ones, should be treated with caution.

Rattlesnakes are ovoviviparous—literally "giving birth to live eggs." The two to twenty-five eggs develop within the mother's body and the young are born alive. Young snakes have only one rattle button, or segment, and cannot rattle. As soon as they shed, and each time thereafter, they gain another button, adding to their noise-making ability. However, the number of buttons does not equal a snake's age. Rattlers shed from zero to five times a year, depending on age, nutrition, and temperature, but the strings of rattles usually break off after six or eight are formed.

Rattlers are poikilothermic (cold-blooded). They bask in the sun or on warm rocks or pavement on cool mornings and evenings, and seek shade during the heat of the day. A rattler dehydrates quickly if caught out in the hot sun. It hibernates for at least part of the winter in rodent burrows, rock crevices, or other sheltered spots.

The most usual Southwest rattler may be the sidewinder (*Crotalus cerastes*), a small, 17- to 33-inch-long, pale-colored, nocturnal rattlesnake. Named for their unique locomotion, sidewinders ripple sideways, using static friction for traction in soft sand, minimizing contact between their body and the burning-hot sand, and leaving parallel, J-shaped tracks at an oblique angle to their direction of travel. Hornlike scales shield their eyes from blowing sand and blinding sun.

The western rattler (*C. viridis*) is the most widely distributed rattlesnake in the West, found in nearly every ecosystem from prairies to high mountain forests. Widely differing environmental conditions throughout its range have resulted in a wide variety of subspecies, ranging in size from 14 inches to more than 5 feet. Even their color varies with their location. One subspecies, the GRAND CANYON rattlesnake, lives only in and around the Grand Canyon and is colored pale salmon to match the canyon's sandstones.

The Southwest's largest rattler is the 3- to 7-foot-long western diamondback rattlesnake (*Crotalus atrox*). Also called the "coontail" rattler, this snake has eye-catching white-and-black rings encircling its tail. Big and aggressive, coontails are active at night throughout the southern West, south of the COLORADO PLATEAU, from deserts and plains GRASSLANDS into open pine forests in the mountains.

See also GRAND CANYON, LIGHTNING.

RAVEN The Southwest is an unlikely environment for animals with black coloring. Black absorbs up to 25 percent more heat in full sun and stands out in sharp contrast to the light-colored backgrounds. Nonetheless, two species of ravens live in the Southwest. One, the 2-foot-long common raven (*Corvus corax*), is the world's largest perching bird. Widely distributed, it inhabits Southwest ecosystems from the Sonoran and Mojave deserts up to the alpine. Common ravens living in the Arctic have evolved thick-soled feet for insulation from snow and ice—the skin on the bottoms of their feet is up to six times thicker than that of ravens of the warmer Southwest! The smaller Chihuahuan raven (*C. cryptoleucus*) is endemic to the Chihuahuan Desert region from Mexico north into the southern Southwest. Ravens can tolerate the intense Southwest sun because their stocky bodies do not gain or lose heat quickly. Also they eat a water-rich diet dominated by carrion and insects and so can "waste" water for cooling.

Common ravens roost communally in flocks of several hundred to several thousand in the winter; Chihuahuan ravens often nest communally as well. Early in spring, pairs court exuberantly. The male soars, wheels, and tumbles for the female, and the pair soars together, with the male above the female. When they perch, the two preen each other. Chihuahuan males fluff up their long neck ruff, flashing the white feathers underneath. They spend several weeks gathering and piling up sticks and weaving them together with string and sometimes barbed wire, into a large, untidy-looking nest in a tree or on a phone pole. Since pairs mate for life, nests are often reused year after year. Once abandoned, they may be colonized by HAWKS and OWLS.

RINGTAIL Ringtails (*Bassariscus astutus*), named for the striking black-and-white rings encircling their 15-inch-long, bushy tail, are the least seen but most common members of the raccoon family in the Southwest. (The other two types are tropical COATI and familiar raccoons.) Ringtails inhabit rocky areas from the deserts to the lower mountain forests. These big-eyed, catlike animals are nocturnal and solitary, spending their days in a den padded with moss, grass, or leaves tucked in a crevice in the rocks. They emerge at night to hunt, seeking out insects, other small animals, and fruit. Like cats, ringtails ambush their prey, pounce on it, and, holding it down with their front paws, break its neck with a powerful bite.

Ringtails possess exceptional climbing skills. By partially retracting the claws on all four feet, they gain such good traction that they can shinny up vertical crevices with ease. Ringtails traverse narrow ledges by rotating their front and hind feet outward. If a ledge runs out, they can truly turn on a dime, reversing direction, and powerful legs allow them to leap in a ricocheting path to reach good holds.

See also COATI.

ROADRUNNER John Bartlett, a surveyor mapping the United States–Mexico border during the First Boundary Survey of the 1850s, wrote of a "most voracious bird," said to attack fearlessly and feed on all manner of "hideous creatures," including RATTLESNAKES. The greater roadrunner (*Geococcyx californianus*), a 2-foot-long, crested bird with an oversized bill, flashy black-and-white speckled plumage, and long tail, does indeed attack small rattlesnakes. Using its short, wide wings like a matador's cape, the bird deflects the striking fangs until the reptile tires. Then the roadrunner kills the rattler and swallows it whole. New Mexico's state bird, roadrunners are year-round inhabitants of the deserts and other hot, arid country of the Southwest and southern Great Plains.

True to their name, roadrunners prefer to run rather than fly. With their long legs, they can sprint as fast as 15 miles per hour. Their speed is a good defense, allowing them quickly to outdistance most predators. It is also a good offense, since they hunt on the run, chasing and catching insects, lizards, SCORPIONS, and other small animals.

Roadrunners use sophisticated adaptations to cope with the harsh climate, since, unlike other desert residents, they are active in both the hottest and coldest months. In cool weather, roadrunners heat their body with solar energy, reducing their caloric needs by as much as 40 percent. Turning their

Roadrunner

back to the sun, they spread their wings wide, drop their tail, and raise the speckled feathers on their back, exposing a "solar panel" of jet black skin. During hot summer days, roadrunners take to the shade during the hottest midday and compress their plumage to retain less heat. But when air temperatures climb above their 100+°F body temperature, roadrunners—like humans—turn to evaporative cooling. Vibrating their throat lining to move air past moist tissues in their respiratory systems, they cool themselves from within.

Roadrunners and most other desert dwellers time their breeding to seasonal rains, when food is most abundant. Roadrunners frequently nest twice in the Sonoran Desert, where rains occur in both winter and summer. The birds lay a larger clutch of eggs in summer, taking advantage of higher numbers of insects. Both parents incubate the eggs, but the male usually takes the chilly night shift. Their three to six eggs hatch at different times, yielding nestlings of varying ages. When food is short, the younger nestlings starve and are eventually eaten by parents or siblings, whose survival is ensured.

SALAMANDER Tiger salamanders (*Ambystoma tigrinum*), the world's largest land-dwelling salamanders, up to a foot long, are stout amphibians with a broad head, small eyes, and long tail. The banded or mottled tiger-stripelike pattern of their smooth, shiny skin gives them their name. Because salamanders lack protection against desiccation and require water for breeding and nurturing their larvae, most species live in moist climates. But not tiger salamanders. North America's most widely distributed salamanders, tigers are found in wet places from the East Coast to the western Rockies, in central California, and from southern Canada south to central Mexico. In the Southwest, these big salamanders inhabit wet places from the deserts to the alpine.

Tiger salamanders avoid the Southwest's aridity. The adults spend much of the year underground in cool, damp burrows. They emerge at night for brief periods during the rainy season—which varies, depending on elevation and latitude—to feed on earthworms, insects, mice, and other amphibians. Pushed by their sexual urges, they head for water to breed, beginning the aquatic part of their life cycle.

Tigers' breeding season varies with the different environments inhabited by these adaptable amphibians. In the Southwest's middle elevations, they breed after heavy spring or summer rains create temporary pools and fill streams and ponds. In the mountains, tigers must wait for the ice to melt. In southern deserts where winters are warm, they lay their floating egg masses in stock ponds and stream backwaters as late as early winter.

The larvae, which hatch some two weeks later, are curious creatures indeed. Tiger salamander larvae look something like tadpoles—except for their big head, four spindly legs, and bushy, bright-colored, external gills. Often called water dogs or mudpuppies for their preferred habitat, they spend their juvenile days swimming, eating smaller animals, avoiding fish and other predators, and growing. The larvae eat and grow as long as possible, making the transformation to air-breathing, land-dwelling, sexually mature adults only when death—in the form of their pond drying or freezing—threatens. But in man-made stock ponds in the hot, dry parts of the Southwest, tiger salamanders' lives take a new twist. The larvae—apparently taking advantage of the abundant food resources and scarcity of predators in these artificial habitats—grow sex organs and can breed in the water as larvae. Only when long droughts dry up their ponds do the larvae transform, crawling out of the water to take their chances on land.

The Southwest's other two salamanders are among the most limited in range of any North American salamanders. Both the Jemez Mountains salamander (*Plethodon neomexicanus*) and the Sacramento Mountain salamander (*Aneides hardii*) live only in moist, high-elevation forests in the mountains for which they are named. These two species of tiny (less than 5.5 inches long), slender salamanders are relics from more temperate climates thousands of years ago, when salamanders were widespread across the Southwest. Warmer, drier climates have isolated them on their SKY ISLANDS.

See also SKY ISLANDS, SPADEFOOT TOAD.

SCORPION   Scorpions (order Scorpionida), arthropods closely related to spiders, look like miniature lobsters with two long, clawed pincers. Their 1.5- to 3.5-inch-long segmented "tail" curves up over their body, ending in a poisonous stinger. About twenty of the seventy North American species, including the largest, the 5.5-inch-long giant hairy desert scorpion (*Hadrurus arizonensis*), are found in the arid Southwest.

Elegantly adapted to desert conditions, scorpions' "shells" are covered with several layers of wax so that they lose water at rates lower than

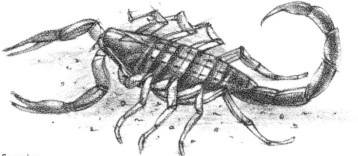

Scorpion

any other desert animals. They can also withstand severe dehydration—losing up to 40 percent of their body weight without ill effects (after losing only 12 percent of their body weight to dehydration, humans usually die). And scorpions can tolerate extreme heat, surviving body temperatures as high as 115°F.

Strictly nocturnal, scorpions emerge to hunt in large numbers on warm nights and are nearly invisible in the dark except under ultraviolet light, which makes them glow eerily. Although most scorpions have at least three pairs of eyes, they hunt by touch: sensory structures on their legs and sensory organs embedded in their body hairs precisely locate prey in the darkness. (Web-spinning spiders have similar structures to detect and locate prey on their web.) Scorpions prey on other ground-dwelling invertebrates, grasping their victims in serrated pincers and paralyzing them by flicking their stinger over their back with a quick downward thrust. In an instant they inject, with a squeeze of their muscles, a fatal dose of neurotoxic venom from two glands located below the stinger.

Scorpions sting humans only in self-defense. Most species' stings simply cause a painful swelling, like a bad bee sting. But, ironically, one of the smallest scorpions—Arizona's 2.75-inch-long bark scorpion (*Centruroides exilicauda*)—possesses the only venom dangerous to humans. A sting from a bark scorpion can cause convulsions, paralysis of respiratory muscles, and heart failure in rare fatal cases. Despite scorpions' potent sting, nocturnal desert predators like elf OWLS and BATS consume them readily.

Scorpions engage in a courtship ritual that may last several hours. The male grasps his prospective mate's pincers in his own, and, interlocked, they twist and circle like two dancers contesting the lead. Finally the male deposits a sperm mass on the soil and maneuvers the female's genital opening over it so that she can vacuum the sperm up. Gestation lasts a few months to more than a year, depending on the species, after which the ten to fifty young, looking like miniature adults, are carried on their mother's back, protected by her potent stinger until their first molt.

SPADEFOOT TOAD The welcome arrival of summer rains in the Southwest triggers the sudden nighttime emergence and clamorous calling of spadefoot toads (genus *Scaphiopus*). These paradoxical animals are dependent on water, yet are most abundant in the Southwest's driest country—deserts, dry GRASSLANDS and shrublands, and arid woodlands.

Spadefoots spend the dry parts of the year dormant in self-dug burrows, or those of gophers, squirrels, or KANGAROO RATS, near where water ponds after summer storms. In extremely dry parts of the Sonoran Desert, spadefoot toads may spend two years underground waiting for the vibrations of thunder that signal summer rains, then emerge for only a few days to feed and mate frenziedly. Exposed toads dehydrate quickly in dry air—they literally mummify if unable to find shelter in time—since they exchange gases and water through their spongy skin. Below ground, however, their porous skin can absorb water from the moist soil of their burrow walls. As the soil dries out, they shed several layers of skin, forming a desiccation-resistant cocoon. And they have the extraordinary ability to pull water from the soil into their body by storing urea in their tissues (at concentrations that would kill a human), thus raising the level of soluble particles in their body fluids. Because water moves across a membrane to an area with a higher concentration of soluble particles, spadefoots can pull water from the soil through their porous-skin membrane. Like DESERT TORTOISES, they store water—up to 30 percent of their weight—in their bladder.

Spadefoots remain within a few inches of the surface during monsoon season, dig as deep as 3 feet down for the winter, then gradually move toward the surface in spring. These small toads are named for their digging tools, black, sharp-edged scrapers ("spades") on the underside of each hind leg that they use to "swim" quickly backward into the soil. Their body wiggles from side to side as each powerful hind foot alternately pushes dirt outward.

When the *Sturm und Drang* of summer thunderstorms rouses these amazing amphibians, they tunnel upward at night from their solitary burrows and congregate by the thousands. Once on the surface, they head for the nearest water and rehydrate, absorbing water directly through a highly porous skin patch on their bellies. Males float in the water and call to attract females, their curious trills and bleats carrying for miles in the night air. In an embrace called amplexus, the male grasps the female from behind and above, ejecting sperm over the mass of eggs which she exudes. The toads feed and breed with abandon through the brief wet nights; the rains also bring other animals out, including massive flights of TERMITES, the toad's major food. In just a few nights of feasting on fat-rich termites, the toads ingest enough energy to carry them through twelve months of dormancy. Each dawn, the tiny toads take shelter in the top layer of damp earth, reappearing again after sunset. When dry fall weather ends the brief rainy season, the spadefoots dig themselves deep into the soil for the more solitary winter months.

Spadefoot toads may spend two years underground, then emerge for only a few days to feed and mate frenziedly.

But the race just begins for the new generation of spadefoot toads. The eggs must hatch and the aquatic tadpoles must metamorphose into air-breathing toads before their ephemeral aquatic environment vanishes. In order to beat the drying puddles, spadefoot toads have a rate of development among the speediest of any amphibian. The eggs of one Southwest species hatch within twelve hours; its tadpoles hurtle to adulthood, transforming in as few as seven days. (By contrast, bullfrog tadpoles take *two years*.)

As space and resources grow scarce in their shrinking world, spadefoot tadpoles feed rapaciously on plants and small aquatic animals, and sometimes on each other. The first tadpoles hatched produce a hormone that slows the growth of later hatchlings, giving the oldest the best chance to live and perpetuate the species. The presence of dead tads stimulates those remaining to grow faster. Those that survive hop out of the drying pond, gulping air and still dragging their tadpole tail, and commence digging their solitary burrow.

Unfortunately, off-road vehicle travel in the desert produces sound waves similar to those of reverberating thunder, stimulating spadefoot toads to expend precious energy and moisture digging to the surface when conditions are not hospitable. Also, roadside drainage ditches, like any other temporary ponds, attract large local toad populations. When thousands emerge after summer thunderstorms, some desert highways grow slippery with toads smashed by passing cars.

The Great Basin spadefoot toad (*S. intermontanus*), the only spadefoot adapted to cold climates, depends on air temperature as much as on rain to cue its emergence. It does not appear until heavy rains come and air temperatures are above 52°F. Great Basin spadefoots breed around more or less permanent ponds and springs from northern Arizona to British Columbia, in habitat ranging from SAGEBRUSH and other arid shrublands to spruce-fir forests as high as 9,200 feet elevation in the mountains.

See also MONSOON, TERMITE.

SPHINX MOTH Sphinx moths (*Hyles* species), named for a hornlike projection that makes the larva look like a sphinx, are the hummingbirds of the insect world. The bright-colored, heavy-bodied adults have wingspans up to 6 inches and are active after dusk throughout North America, including in the Southwest's deserts, hovering while they sip flower nectar through their tubular tongue. After ample winter or summer rainy seasons in the desert, sphinx moth larvae are sometimes so abundant in the resultant plant growth that the sound of their chewing is audible from many yards away.

Sphinx moths fuel their high-energy metabolisms by feeding on flowers with nectar containing about 60 percent sugar—twice that required by bees, half again that needed by butterflies. Hovering generates intense heat, most of which is dissipated through their tissuelike wings; since their food is high in water, they use water to cool themselves evaporatively by circulating air through their respiratory system. Few other arid-environment organisms (besides humans) can afford to waste water for evaporative cooling.

See also BUTTERFLY, YUCCA MOTH.

SQUAWFISH The Colorado squawfish (*Ptychocheilus lucius*) is a giant in its family. While most members of the minnow family measure less than 5 inches, this largest of North American minnows grows to 6 feet long, and weighs up to 80 pounds. These handsome, gray-green and silver fish frequent pools of medium to large rivers and feed on smaller fish. Once found throughout the COLORADO RIVER drainage from Wyoming to the Gulf of California, Colorado squawfish were an important food source in New Mexico, and, before 1910, the basis of a commercial fishery on the lower Salt River in Arizona. A victim of rivers shrunk by water withdrawals for irrigation and DAMS, the Southwest's largest fish is now a federally listed endangered species. The remaining squawfish are found in portions of the Colorado River in Utah and in Colorado, and in the San Juan River in northern New Mexico.

See also EEL, STURGEON, and TROUT.

STURGEON Shovel-nosed sturgeon (*Scaphirhynchus platorynchus*), an odd-looking fish with an exterior skeleton of bony plates, a shovel-shaped snout (hence their name), and pale, edible flesh, once swam in the turbid waters of the RIO GRANDE as far north as northern New Mexico. But after overgrazing aggravated further the Rio Grande's tendency to flood and then retreat, and after irrigators began sucking its often low flow down to a trickle, the shovel-nosed sturgeon disappeared from the Rio's waters. The last record of the Southwest's only caviar-bearing fish was one caught in the Rio Grande near Albuquerque in 1874.

See also EEL, SQUAWFISH, TROUT.

TARANTULA Tarantulas (family Theraphosidae) are North America's largest spiders. With a legspan of up to 6 inches, big, hairy, brown bodies, long fangs, and a row of beady black eyes lining the front of their body, tarantulas look ferocious. Their looks are deceptive. Their fearsome appearance and venomous bite notwithstanding, the twenty-some tarantula species common throughout the Southwest's deserts and arid lowlands are harmless to humans. Their venom is mild and their nature gentle—they do not bite people unless handled very roughly. And, despite the multiple eyes, tarantulas are nearly blind, "seeing" the world through smell and touch.

Tarantulas save their venom and aggressions for their prey, mainly large insects and small lizards, and sometimes other tarantulas. Rather than spinning webs to snare food, these nocturnal spiders emerge from their silk-lined burrow and hunt randomly, sniffing and tapping about, or wait just inside the burrow entrance, ready to rush out and pounce when they sense passing prey. A bite with their quarter-inch fangs dispatches their victim; the combination of venom and the spider's digestive fluid liquefy the animal's soft tissues. Then the spider simply sucks the body dry, leaving an empty shell.

Tarantulas survive both extended drought and winter's cold in their burrows. By plugging the entrance and going dormant, they can survive without food for more than two years, without water for seven months. Fall, tarantula mating season, is when these big spiders are most often encountered. Tarantulas are late bloomers—neither sex is mature until eight or nine years old. And no wonder, for the males must be cautious or the larger females may eat them during mating. The long-legged, active males cruise for mates after sunset or near dawn. When a male locates a female, he taps the ground, enticing her closer. She raises her body and displays her fangs. He carefully grasps her fangs with special spurs on the side of his front legs, and once she is so disarmed, inserts a seminal fluid–impregnated limb into her genital opening. After a few minutes, he carefully withdraws and goes his way to seek another mate.

The following spring, female tarantulas lay a cluster of 500 to 1,000 eggs, wrap them in a silken cocoon, and hang them in their burrow. The spiderlings hatch about a month later and leave the burrow after a couple of days. Not many survive to maturity—tarantulas are relished by a variety of desert hunters, from SCORPIONS to ROADRUNNERS, and are parasitized by large, solitary wasps called TARANTULA HAWKS. After their one season of sex, the male tarantulas die. The females, our longest-lived terrestrial invertebrates, live up to thirty years in captivity.

TARANTULA HAWK   Tarantula hawks (genus *Hemipepsis*) are named for their prowess at fighting and subduing even-larger TARANTULA spiders. In this wasp genus, the larger females, up to 4 inches long, are the hunters; male tarantula hawks sip nectar from flowers. Both sexes are slender and handsome, with metallic-black bodies and striking, translucent, mahogany-colored wings. They frequent the Southwest's lower elevations, wherever tarantulas are found.

After mating, female tarantula hawks run about on the desert surface, searching for tarantulas, the preferred food of their grublike larvae. Once the female wasp finds an active spider burrow, she lures the big, slow-moving spider out, swiftly climbs on its back, and thrusts her half-inch stinger into the spider's abdomen, paralyzing it. The wasp then laboriously drags the comatose but still-living spider off to her burrow, lays an egg atop the spider, and seals the burrow. Soon the tiny, grublike larva hatches, devours the still-fresh spider, and grows. It eventually pupates,

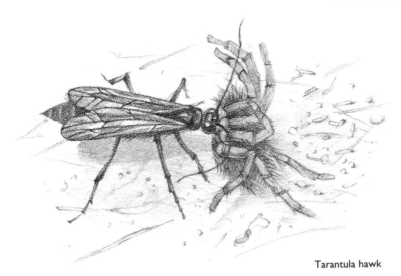

Tarantula hawk

metamorphosing the following spring into an adult wasp. If the offspring is a female, she sets off tarantula hunting; if a male, he hies himself to a lookout post in a tree or shrub atop a promontory and scans for passing females to mate with. Such "hilltopping" is a common insect strategy for locating mates where females are widely dispersed.

TASSEL-EARED SQUIRREL The Kaibab squirrel (*Sciurus kaibabensis*), a large squirrel with a dark, grizzled, gray body and a brilliant white tail, is endemic to the PONDEROSA PINE forests of the Kaibab Plateau, north of Arizona's GRAND CANYON. Its close cousin, the Abert squirrel (*S. aberti*), which lacks the all-white tail, is more widespread, inhabiting ponderosa pine forests throughout the Southwest. The two tassel-eared squirrels—named for the fur tuft protruding from the top of their ears—apparently evolved from two populations of one species isolated by the growing chasm of the canyon.

Tassel-eared squirrels are tied to ponderosa pine. The long-needled pines furnish their major food: ponderosa pine seeds, buds, and the vanilla-scented cambium that grows just under the bark of small twigs. The squirrels build their nests—domes about a foot in diameter and lined with shredded ponderosa pine bark—high in the crotch of a ponderosa pine tree. Some ponderosas have apparently developed chemical defenses against tassel-eared squirrel predation since squirrels will feed intensely on particular ponderosas and leave others alone. But the squirrels benefit the tree too. The rich humus of squirrel middens makes the perfect nursery for sprouting seedlings from uneaten caches of ponderosa pine seeds.

See also GRAND CANYON, PONDEROSA PINE.

TERMITE Termites (order Isoptera) are small (most are less than a half-inch long), soft-bodied, social insects with biting mouth parts and, with ANTS, are the most abundant insects in the Southwest's hot, arid ecosystems. Southwestern termites live underground or in dead wood, in colonies that may contain millions of individuals, and are instrumental in maintaining soil fertility in arid ecosystems. A few species attack wood in buildings, causing serious damage.

> Termites, with ants, are the most abundant insects in the Southwest. Termites live in colonies that may contain millions of individual insects.

Like ants, termites live in colonies with different castes: workers and soldiers, each of which is both sterile and wingless, and fertile reproductives. New colonies are founded after the first few big thunderstorms of the summer rainy season, when the winged reproductives fly from the colony and swarm by the thousands in twilight mating flights. Newly emerged SPADEFOOT TOADS, also summoned above ground by the rains, consume the fat-rich termites. If they survive to mate, the fertile female—now a queen—and the males shed their wings and dig a nest. The first generation of the new colony is sterile workers that collect and distribute food and maintain the nest. Soldiers, individual termites with fearsomely enlarged jaws designed to crush ants and other predators, are born in subsequent generations. Soldiers station themselves at the entrances of the nest or alongside columns of foraging workers. When danger threatens, they herd the workers back into the nest. For further protection, termite species that forage above ground have developed potent chemical defenses such as irritants, contact poisons, toxicants, and even glues. Soldiers of one Sonoran Desert species (*Tenuirostritermes tenuirostris*) squirt a chemical from nozzles on their head to immobilize predators like ants at close range.

Without the recycling activities of termites and other arid-country insects, desert soils would become infertile, with all of the nutrients stored in dead, undecomposed plant litter on the soil surface. In some arid ecosystems, termites eat as much as 90 percent of the dead wood, dried cow and horse dung, and other organic debris on the soil surface, that, without termites, persists in arid environments for many years. With the help of symbiotic protozoa, bacteria, and fungi that live in their intestines, termites digest the cellulose (plants' structural fiber), "unlocking" nitrogen and other nutrients in the organic debris and returning them to the soil. Subterranean termite tunnels and galleries help soils absorb water, especially important in deserts, where violent summer thunderstorms pound the soil surface and erode it, and the water runs off without sinking in. Soil with termite galleries absorbs water for three times as long as soil without termites. Further, the bacteria in termites' intestines capture atmospheric nitrogen, making termite droppings a rich fertilizer.

Tube-formers (*Gnathamitermes* species) are subterranean termites that extend their habitat by building tube-shaped galleries above ground. The mud galleries, constructed around their food—dead branches of desert shrubs, surface litter, and forbs and grasses—protect the feeding termites. (But not completely—cactus WRENS and ROADRUNNERS sometimes turn over cow pies and break open earthen galleries to feed on tube-forming termites.) Built particle by particle and cemented with saliva, the rough tubes of mud are common sights in the Chihuahuan and Sonoran desert areas of the southern Southwest.

See also ANT, SPADEFOOT TOAD.

THICK-BILLED PARROT
Noisy, chattering flocks of thick-billed parrots (*Rhynchopsitta parchyrhyncha*), North America's single remaining native parrot species, once migrated regularly from Mexico into the southern Southwest. However, excessive logging in the long-needled mountain pine forests of Mexico's Sierra Madre shrank the bird's population and pushed its range farther south. The last flock was seen in southern Arizona's CHIRICAHUA MOUNTAINS in 1936. (The Carolina parakeet, our only other native parrot, was hunted to extinction in the southeastern United States by the 1920s.)

Since 1986, thick-bills confiscated from tropical-bird smugglers and birds raised in captivity have been acclimatized and reintroduced to the southern Southwest's mountains in the hope that thick-billed parrot flocks will again enliven central and southern Arizona's PONDEROSA PINE forests.

Thick-bills' vivid, tropical coloring—olive-green with scarlet on their forehead and wings—is a lively contrast to the somber colors of their evergreen forest habitat. Fifteen- to 16.5-inches long from head to long, pointed tail, thick-bills are strong fliers. These parrots forage in flocks and coast from tree to tree, pulling seeds out of pine cones and cracking open acorns with their stout bills. Their earsplitting alarm screeches and squawks can be heard up to a mile away. Thick-bills nest in cavities excavated by other animals in the trunks of tall, dead pines.

See also CHIRICAHUA MOUNTAINS.

THRASHER Five of the eight North American thrashers, relatives of the MOCKINGBIRD, live in the Southwest's deserts. All are pale (the color of desert soil), robin-sized ground dwellers that run rather than fly. All feed by raking surface litter with their down-curved bills in search of small insects and seeds and also eat fruits and even small lizards. But their niches do not overlap—each species inhabits a different desert ecosystem.

Curve-billed thrashers (*Toxostoma curvirostre*), gray-brown birds with a long, down-curved bill and bright orange eyes, are common year-round in cactus-dominated habitat of the Sonoran and Chihuahuan deserts. Curve-billed thrashers and cactus WRENS compete for food and nesting sites. Both build their nests in the protection of the spiny cholla cactus—thrashers sometimes tear up wren nests. And the two birds search the soil surface for similar prey, including insects and small arthropods.

Crissal thrashers (*T. dorsale*), the largest of the five species and named for their bright russet undertail coverts (*crissa* is Latin for "undertail covert"), live in dense stands of MESQUITE and other shrubs in riparian ecosystems and densely vegetated ARROYOS of the Sonoran, Chihuahuan, and Mojave deserts. Crissals are secretive—the rich, varied phrases of their mimicking songs are often heard, but the birds are rarely seen.

The palest of the desert thrashers is Le Conte's (*T. lecontei*). Their light, sand-colored plumage blends perfectly into the pale soils of the sparsely vegetated cholla and CREOSOTE BUSH shrublands in the driest parts of the Sonoran, Mojave, and southern Great Basin deserts.

Bendire's thrashers (*T. bendirei*), the best mimic, are the most likely to fly, rather than run. Bendire's winter in the Sonoran Desert; in summer they move north and east into the PIÑON-JUNIPER woodlands of Utah and northern New Mexico.

The only desert thrashers lacking a curved bill are sage thrashers

(*Oreoscoptes montanus*), named for their preferred nesting grounds, the SAGEBRUSH ecosystems of the Great Basin Desert, COLORADO PLATEAU, and areas farther north.

All of the desert thrashers build cuplike nests low in shrubs—sage thrashers in sagebrush and juniper, crissals in mesquite, the other three among the fortresslike spines of the cholla cactus. Other birds—Gambel's QUAIL, Abert's towhee, and mourning and white-winged DOVES—sometimes appropriate abandoned thrasher nests.

See also WREN.

TROUT Three species of trout are native to cool, clear Southwestern streams and lakes: cutthroat trout (*Oncohrynchus clarki*), Gila trout (*O. gilae*), and Apache trout (*O. apache*). The latter two, unique to the Southwest and once common in their mountain habitat, are now listed as endangered or threatened under the federal Endangered Species Act, as are several dozen other Southwestern fish. Introduction of nonnative fish, including other trout, and loss of stream habitat—due to overgrazing and logging, water withdrawals for irrigation, and DAMS—have nearly exterminated these endemic trout. But a cooperative effort between Arizona state, federal, and White Mountain Apache biologists to capture, breed, and restock Apache trout in its native streams is proving so effective that Apache trout eventually may be removed from the endangered or threatened species list.

Gila and Apache trout are both small trout, and both are "island species," geographically isolated in one or two drainage areas. Gila trout, olive-brown with a heavily freckled body and a yellow stripe under their lower jaw, are native to and named for the Gila River of western New Mexico and eastern Arizona. Apache trout, bright yellow trout with large black freckles sprinkling their body, are native to the upper Salt River and Little Colorado River drainages of northern Arizona.

In contrast, cutthroat are large trout (to 39 inches), and because of their impressive adaptability to a variety of aquatic habitats, are widespread across the northern West. Fourteen distinct local subspecies were once found in coastal drainages from northern California to Alaska; mountain drainages, small rivers, and lakes throughout the Rockies from northern New Mexico and Arizona to Alberta, Canada; and saline desert rivers in the Great Basin in Utah and northern Nevada. A 41-pound Lahontan cutthroat caught in western Nevada's Pyramid Lake stands as the official record for the largest western trout. A 62-pounder was also taken there but not officially recorded. Unfortunately, thoughtless hatchery cross-breeding, introduction of nonnative trout and loss of habitat have caused a loss or blurring of many of the distinctive, locally adapted cutthroat, including some record ones. By 1938, for example, agricultural irrigation had sucked so much water from Pyramid Lake and the lower Truckee River that the huge Lahontan cutthroat had disappeared. Cutthroat are named for the red or orange gashlike stripe under their long lower jaw.

See also EEL, SQUAWFISH, STURGEON.

VELVET-ANT Velvet-ants (family Mutillidae) are actually hairy, parasitic wasps named for the wingless female's resemblance to an ANT. Shaped like an ant, with a big abdomen and narrow, waistlike constriction in the middle of her body, she scurries across the ground in broad daylight. But like many wasps, she possesses a long stinger that packs a severely painful, but not fatal, sting. Males, also hairy, are winged and stingerless. Both sexes are brightly colored—their 0.25- to 1-inch-long bodies are often red, yellow, or orange—and are common throughout the hottest, driest parts of the Southwest, from deserts to semiarid foothill and mesa shrublands.

Adult velvet-ants feed on nectar and are active during the day. Males fly near the ground in search of mates, females comb the ground for wasp or BEE pupal chambers in which to lay their eggs. (Each species feeds on a different species of wasp or bee.) Once the female finds a pupal chamber or burrow, she inserts her ovipositor and lays an egg inside. After hatching, the grublike larva feeds on the host and on any provisions stored by the host's parent. After eating and growing, the larva metamorphoses, emerging as a hairy adult.

The Southwest's two most common velvet-ants are named for their appearance. Thistledown velvet-ants (*Dasymutilla gloriosa*) are named for the long, downy white hair covering their half-inch-long black bodies. They feed on sand wasps in all of the Southwest's deserts. Red velvet-ants (*D. magnifica*), true to their scientific name, are magnificently colored: their heads and upper bodies are wine-red with black hairs; the male's abdomen is also wine-red; the female's is rusty red or bright yellow-orange. Red velvet-ants are found in the southern Southwest and Mexico, most commonly in the Mojave, Sonoran, and Chihuahuan deserts.

VULTURE Vultures, ungainly on land, can soar gracefully for hours without beating their wings, riding thermals—rising columns or bubbles of warm air. With relatively short, broad wings and a low wing loading (the ratio of body weight to wing area), these birds of prey can soar at very slow speeds without sacrificing maneuverability. Vultures counteract the large amount of drag produced by their wide wings by soaring with their primaries (wingtip feathers) widespread. This reduces wingtip turbulence and lowers their stalling speed. To maintain forward thrust, they actually glide downward, but continue to rise because they sink as slowly as 2 feet per second; the warm air rises faster.

Vultures get bad press, mostly for their diet of carrion (rotting carcasses). But they have a crucial role in Southwest ecosystems: they dispose of potential sources of disease and recycle the nutrients contained in the carcasses. Their scientific family name, Cathartidae, from the Greek word for "cleanser," commemorates their sanitation function. Vultures are well designed for their role. They search for their widely dispersed, randomly occurring food by soaring, riding thermals to upward of several thousand feet, thereby expending very little energy. Vultures also save energy by cooperating, searching in groups, and descending en masse when one spies a carcass. Sophisticated immune systems protect them from disease-causing organisms, and the birds easily clean their unfeathered heads of rotten meat and potential pests. Further, the odor-processing area of vultures' brain is much larger than in other birds of comparable size, suggesting that the stench of carcasses helps them locate their food from long distances.

Two of North America's three vulture species are found in the Southwest. Turkey vultures (*Cathartes aura*), one of America's largest birds of prey, soar with their 6-foot-long wings in a characteristic V angle, seeming to teeter on the air currents. Turkey vultures are widespread in open country from southern Canada to South America. In late winter and early spring, flocks of up to several hundred migrate north from Mexico through the Chihuahuan Desert in southern New Mexico and the Sonoran Desert in southern Arizona.

Smaller black vultures (*Coragyps atratus*), with a 5-foot wingspan, inhabit open country, garbage dumps, and roadsides throughout the southeastern United States, the extreme southern Southwest, Mexico, and Central

> **Vultures get bad press, mostly for their diet of carrion. But they have a crucial role in Southwest ecosystems.**

and South America. Proportionally shorter wings give black vultures a faster sink rate than turkey vultures, restricting them to warmer latitudes with stronger thermals. Pesticide poisoning continues to cause eggshell thinning in both black and turkey vultures, resulting in declining populations.

See also HAWK.

WHIPTAIL LIZARD Whiptail lizards (genus *Cnemidophorus*), medium-sized, slender lizards named for their extravagantly long tails, are widespread in arid Southwest ecosystems. Constantly in motion, whiptails are the hyperactive members of the lizard family. Unlike most diurnal (day-active) lizards, whiptails forage ceaselessly, dashing across the ground—often running upright on their large hind legs like miniature DINOSAURS. As they bustle about, they swivel their head rapidly from side to side, sniffing the air with their slender, forked tongue; they probe under surface debris with their pointed snout and even climb up into lower branches of small shrubs. Whiptails eat ground-dwelling insects and spiders, as well as small SCORPIONS, CENTIPEDES, and lizards.

Whiptails' hyperactivity serves them well as a defense. Their alertness, speed, and agility helps them escape from predators like THRASHERS, ROADRUNNERS, GILA MONSTERS, and blind snakes. They can sprint up to 15 miles per hour, as fast as a roadrunner, and typically dive under the nearest shrub, melting into the shadows. Like most lizards, whiptails can forfeit their tails to escape capture; their tail breaks easily along a fracture plane in the vertebrae, and the disembodied tail wriggles violently, startling and distracting the predator so that the lizard can dash to safety. Imagine a predator's surprise at grabbing for a juicy lizard and instead scoring only an eerily wriggling tail.

Six of the Southwest's twelve whiptail species are unisexual—all female. Originally products of hybridization between two other species, these whiptails reproduce without ever mating. Their eggs, clones of the mother, hatch and develop into more female lizards. Since these whiptails are genetically identical, they are vulnerable to disease and inherited defects. But these "weedy" species are perfectly adapted to colonizing newly disturbed habitats—just one lizard can start a new population. By reproducing incredibly rapidly (they out-reproduce bisexual lizards by a factor of two because each young is capable of producing progeny), the species can survive in habitats such as floodplains, where

Whiptail lizard

other populations are regularly wiped out.

Because whiptails develop cryptic coloration for their particular habitat, they come in a wide variety of earthy colors and patterns—lengthwise stripes, stripes and spots, or checkers. Members of the same species that are isolated geographically may look less alike than members of two different species.

Whiptails dig themselves shallow burrows in the soil in October and hibernate there until about April, when their prey is more abundant again and solar radiation is intense enough to warm their bodies to their 102°F active temperature.

See also GECKO, HORNED LIZARD, MALPAÍS, SAND DUNES.

WOODRAT Woodrats (genus *Neotoma*) are large rodents more closely related to mice than to true rats. Up to 18 inches long, they have strikingly bicolored fur (dark above, light below), long hairy tails, naked ears, and large eyes. These nocturnal plant eaters are among the most characteristic small mammals of the Southwest, living in almost every ecosystem from the high-mountain conifer forests to the hottest deserts.

Woodrats have earned the nickname "pack rats" for their acquisitive nature. They scavenge objects such as branches, spiny cactus pads, cowpies, newspaper, cloth, and aluminum cans. They use these treasures for construction material, piling them up into a conspicuous mound at the base of a tree or shrub, in a rock crevice, or in a building. Woodrats are particularly attracted to shiny objects—watches, jewelry, and coins. One Southwest nest even sported an upper denture plate. An average den of a desert-dwelling woodrat contains about 20 cubic feet of material and may be 4.5 feet high by 2 feet wide. The untidy-looking pile of debris acts as insulation, keeping the interior cool in summer, retaining the woodrat's body heat in winter. Inside one desert nest, the temperature never rose above 88°F, despite searing ground-level temperatures of 167°F. Carefully placed cactus spines, glass, and pieces of aluminum cans cover the nest and line the paths leading to it, protecting woodrats and occasional other occupants—rabbits, snakes, SCORPIONS—against large predators; only badgers tear apart woodrat nests. Away from their fortresses, woodrats are vulnerable to predators such as COYOTES, foxes, OWLS, and RATTLESNAKES.

Woodrats, nicknamed "pack rats," are nocturnal plant-eating rodents and are among the most characteristic small mammals of the Southwest.

No amount of fortification, however, protects woodrats from parasitic insects. Tiny blood-sucking insects called cone-nosed kissing bugs feed on the rats, making them carriers of Chaga's disease, a microbial disease affecting millions of people in the tropics. Bot flies lay their eggs in woodrat nest debris so that their minute larvae can enter the rodent's body and feed on its tissues. Bot larvae grow into penny-size grubs under the woodrat's skin before the larvae burst out to pupate. Neither insect is fatal to its host—a woodrat in captivity survived being fed on by over 1,700 bot fly larvae.

Woodrat nests may be continuously occupied for hundreds or thousands of years, and even when abandoned, the nests and adjacent "trash middens" created when the occupants cleaned house persist in the arid environment. Geologists and plant ecologists have learned to read the layers of plant material in the middens to learn about climate and vegetation patterns dating back as far as 25,000 years ago. Caches of pine seeds found in ancient woodrat nests in what is now desert suggest that North American deserts have evolved relatively recently, within the past 15,000 to 4,000 years. Besides their value as prehistoric records, woodrat nests are also valued for their food caches. Seri and Yuma Indians in the Sonoran Desert once gathered MESQUITE seeds from woodrat caches, and Navajo

PIÑON nut collectors have removed as much as 30 pounds of nuts from one woodrat nest.

Three of the Southwest's six woodrat species—white-throated (*Neotoma albigula*), desert (*N. lepida*), and southern plains woodrats (*N. micropus*)—live in close association with PRICKLY PEAR AND CHOLLA CACTI. The rats use the spiny cactus pads for building material, clambering over the cactuses' formidable, needlelike spines without injury. Succulent cactus flesh provides half or more of their food and all of their water. And they somehow neutralize the plants' chemical defenses. Prickly pear and cholla cactus flesh contain high concentrations of oxalic acid, which, when eaten by most mammals, combines with calcium to form crystals that can cause calcium deficiency, kidney damage, and even death. But woodrats are not affected.

Another Southwest species, Stephens's woodrat (*N. stephensi*), depends on JUNIPER, feeding on juniper seeds and building its nests in and around the trees. It lives on the COLORADO PLATEAU, from northern Arizona and northwest New Mexico into southern Utah.

Bushy-tailed woodrats (*N. cinerea*), named for their squirrellike tail, are the most montane of the Southwestern woodrats, living in coniferous forests throughout the West from northern Arizona and New Mexico to British Columbia. Often called "trade rats," they drop whatever they are carrying for a shiny object like a coin or a spoon.

See also MALPAÍS, SAND DUNES.

WREN Cactus wrens (*Campylorhynchus brunneicapillus*) are named for their habit of nesting and roosting in the protective spiny armor of cholla and PRICKLY PEAR cacti, YUCCA, and MESQUITE. The fortresslike location protects the birds from predators; only a few, including gopher snakes and common whipsnakes, can successfully traverse the wicked spines. Larger curve-billed THRASHERS, although not predators, are competitors and sometimes tear up cactus wren nests. For protection against the harsh climate, the wrens build several bulky, domed roosts and nests, orienting each in a different direction for the season. Spring nests, for example, face away from chill winds, while the nests for summer broods are positioned to catch cool afternoon breezes.

These 8-inch-long wrens, North America's largest, are identifiable by their large size, thrasherlike curved beaks, brown caps, and bold white eyebrow stripes. Cactus wrens are abundant year-round wherever cactus and mesquite grow from southwestern Utah and northwestern New Mexico south to central Mexico. Like most wrens, they are noisy fussbudgets. Their staccato, unmelodious voice, exploding suddenly in a low *chug-chug-chug* . . . or a squawking chatter, is a characteristic desert sound.

Incessantly active, cactus wrens poke about for food—insects, some spiders, the occasional lizard, and fruit and seeds in winter—under leaves and other surface litter. Their clutch size is tied to the abundance of the female's main nesting-season food: banded-wing GRASSHOPPERS. Populations of these grasshoppers fluctuate drastically from year to year with the abundance of the annual plants they eat. Female wrens somehow discern the size of the grasshopper supply before laying eggs and adjust their clutches accordingly.

Two other wrens are characteristic Southwest songsters: rock wrens (*Salpinctes obsoletus*) are small gray-and-white wrens whose scientific name means "hidden trumpeter," alluding to their lovely, trumpetlike trills, which seem to issue from the very rocks of Southwestern canyons and foothills. Rock wren males sing to compete for mates. Those with the biggest repertoires attract the most females; individual males may know more than a hundred songs each. Neighbors counter each other's songs, resulting in exuberant evening concerts. Rock wrens inhabit rocky areas— arid and semiarid canyons, valleys with rock outcrops, and talus—from deserts to 10,000 feet in the mountains, from the western edge of the Great Plains to the Pacific Ocean.

Hearing the clear solo of a cañon wren's descending, flutelike trill echoing hauntingly from bare canyon walls, the notes shimmering like silver in the hot midday air, is an unforgettable experience. These small, mottled brown wrens with striking white throats (*Catherpes mexicanus*) live in canyons and on rocky mountainsides near water throughout the western United States and Mexico.

See also PRICKLY PEAR AND CHOLLA CACTUS, THRASHER.

YUCCA MOTH Yucca moths, also sometimes called giant skippers (family Megathymidae), have evolved a specialized partnership with YUCCA plants. Yucca depend on yucca moths to pollinate their flowers; the moths depend on the plants for food. Adult yucca moths emerge only when their particular species of yucca is blooming. After mating, females gather the sticky yucca pollen from one flower, move to another flower, and lay eggs in its ovary. They then stuff the sticky pollen mass into the flower's stigma, pollinating it and ensuring both a food source for the developing larvae and a new generation of yucca. Since the flowers of different yucca species have evolved different shapes and blooming seasons, each species of yucca is now pollinated by its own moth species.

The larvae of yucca moths feed on yucca and AGAVE leaves and fruits. The "worm" in bottles of mescal, a tequilalike liquor made from agave, is actually a moth larva.

See also BUTTERFLY, SPHINX MOTH, YUCCA.

TWO

PLANTS

WHEN MOST PEOPLE think of the Southwest, they think of CACTI. And rightly so. Succulent plants with leaves modified into spines and fleshy stems that double as water storage tanks, cacti are admirably suited to this arid country. More kinds of cacti grow throughout the Southwest than in any other region of the United States.

But the Southwest is home to many other kinds of plants—from tiny, single-celled algae to tall FIR trees. Different kinds of plants are adapted to different conditions. Some plants need moisture at all times, others grow where drought is the norm; some require cool soils, others can stand the heat of desert summers. Elevation provides one general way to sort out what grows where in the Southwest.

Cacti, other succulents, shrubs, and grasses dominate the lowest, hottest elevations of the Southwest, the deserts. Although all four Southwest deserts share an ephemeral abundance of annual wildflowers, each desert is characterized by different cacti and other perennial plants. Cacti, including the tall SAGUAROS, with their familiar upraised arms, are most common in the Sonoran Desert. AGAVES, YUCCAS, and CREOSOTE BUSH dominate the Chihuahuan, a shrub desert. The driest and hottest desert, the Mojave, is characterized by JOSHUA TREE, a tree-sized yucca. SAGEBRUSH and saltbrush are most common in the cold Great Basin Desert of the northern Southwest.

Grasses characterize the plant communities farther up in elevation from the deserts. Overgrazing exposed fragile grassland soils, which once supported unbroken seas of grass, to wind and water erosion. Now shrubs dominate the grasslands—creosote bush in the southern Southwest, cholla on the eastern plains, sagebrush in the north—or, on salty soils, saltbrush and greasewood.

The Southwest's lower elevations are largely treeless. Trees begin to dominate only on the foothills, high MESAS, and lower mountains, forming scattered woodlands of short, evergreen OAKS, JUNIPERS, and/or shortneedled PIÑON PINES. Above these dry woodlands on most of the Southwest's mountain ranges and high plateaus are cooler and wetter evergreen forests. Tall PONDEROSA PINE and other long-needled pines grow on the lower slopes. Above them grow denser DOUGLAS FIR forests, often with extensive ASPEN groves. Mixed spruce and fir forests, sometimes including long-lived BRISTLECONE PINE, clothe the highest elevations. The different forests often interfinger, with ponderosa pine and oak chaparral reaching to the tops of the mountains on the warmer, drier south- and west-facing slopes, and spruces and firs occurring only as patches on the very coolest north- and east-facing slopes.

Constant winds and frigid temperatures banish trees from the tops of the highest mountains in the Southwest, allowing turf- and mat-forming grasses, wildflowers, and dwarf shrubs to dominate alpine landscapes.

Water-loving plants flourish only along the Southwest's few remaining rivers, lakes, streams, ponds, and springs. Tall COTTONWOODS and spreading MESQUITES form bosques (Spanish for "woods") along desert and grassland watercourses. Fan PALMS, sycamores, and other deciduous trees shade the canyons of desert mountain ranges. MAPLES, willows, cottonwoods, and other trees flourish along mountain streams. Where intact, these lush communities provide crucial habitat for many animals, and help maintain water quality and quantity and control flooding. But excessive grazing, logging, road building, and overuse of water continue to dry up the Southwest's watersheds. Dry, eroded ARROYOS have replaced the riparian forests and running water along 95 percent of Arizona and New Mexico's perennial streams and rivers.

Like the Southwest's animals, plants in the Southwest have evolved a myriad of ways to cope with aridity. Some plants, such as the brilliant carpet of DESERT ANNUAL wildflowers, avoid drought altogether by compressing their life cycle—from sprout to new seeds—into just a few weeks following the seasonal rain. Others, like delicate MARIPOSA LILIES, may "hide" underground for years, sprouting leaves and flowers from their bulbs only in sufficiently moist periods. Many perennial plants, such as CREOSOTE BUSH, grow waxy coatings or dense mats of hairs to screen the hot sun and slow moisture evaporation. Some, like OCOTILLO and MESQUITE, grow leaves only when water is abundant, shedding them when they begin to wilt. CACTI and other succulents store water in their tissues, shrinking in the dry months, swelling again when water floods the soil.

From the delicate blossoms of EVENING PRIMROSES, which sprout as if by magic from desert sand dunes, to the ancient, twisted BRISTLECONE PINES, which stud mountain ridges, the plants of the Southwest tell the region's story.

AGAVE Agaves (*Agave* species), succulent relatives of lilies, spend five to thirty-five years growing a large basal rosette of stiff, several-foot-long, leathery leaves. Once mature, the plant squanders all of the energy and most of the water stored in its thick leaves on a glorious but fatal burst of reproduction, sending a single flower stalk resembling a giant asparagus spear spurting up from the leaf rosette. Agave flower stalks can grow as much as a foot a day; some shoot up as tall as 15 feet. As the stalk grows, the succulent leaves rapidly wither. Swollen buds along the stalk or on candelabralike side branches open into big, tubular flowers that emit strong, often musky fragrances. Pollinators such as BATS and insects flock to the nectar and pollen banquet. By the time seeds are set, the agave plant itself is gray, shriveled, dead. It may come to life again, however—in many species, daughter plants sprout from the roots the next season.

The towering flower stalks of agaves delineate the chaparral or shrub ecosystems of upland deserts and rocky foothills of the southern Southwest from southern Arizona, New Mexico, and Texas south to Mexico. One species, Utah agave (*A. utahensis*), grows farther north around the GRAND CANYON and in the Mojave Desert of southwestern Utah, southern Nevada, and California. The common century plant, a huge agave with wide, drooping, 6-foot-long leaves native to Mexico and areas south, is widely planted as an ornamental.

Agave

Agaves survive the scarce and unpredictable water supply in the desert by storing moisture in their large, fleshy leaves. A waxlike coating with a powdery surface seals the leaves against evaporation and also reflects up to 75 percent of incoming heat. To further save water, the plant keeps its stomates, the pores that pierce the plant's skin through which they absorb carbon dioxide for photosynthesis, tightly shut during the day. (In photosynthesis, plants take up carbon dioxide into their tissue and, using solar energy, combine it with water to make sugars for food. Fortunately for oxygen-breathing animals, plants give off oxygen as a "waste product" in the process. In order to manufacture food and still conserve water, agaves and other succulents use an alternative method of photosynthesis: they open their stomates to absorb carbon dioxide during the night when the air is more cool and moist—thereby losing less water—and store the carbon dioxide to use for daytime photosynthesis.

People in northern Mexico harvest agave. They mash and ferment the pulp to produce pulque, which can be distilled into tequila.

Agaves once supplied food and other necessities for desert-dwelling peoples in the Southwest. Southern New Mexico's Mescalero Apaches are named for their trade in and diet of mescal (Spanish for "agave"). Mescal pits—rock-lined pits built for roasting the young flower stalks and the succulent heart of the leaf rosette—are common Southwest archaeological sites, dating back at least 8,000 years. The big plants also provided emergency water supplies, and soap was made from the pulverized stems. Early Southwesterners knotted or wove the tough leaf fibers into hunting nets, baskets, mats, ropes, and sandals.

People in northern Mexico still harvest and roast agave to make alcohol. They mash and ferment the sugary pulp to produce pulque, which can be distilled into mescal and tequila. Northern Mexico's bootleg mescal makers, attempting to meet a growing demand for the drink, are stripping whole hillsides of agaves. Fortunately for wild agaves' survival, some Mexican farmers are beginning to cultivate agaves for the mescal industry.

Agaves provision other desert dwellers besides people. The abundant nectar in their sudden wealth of flowers attracts nectar-feeding insects, as well as HUMMINGBIRDS and BATS. The latter have a special relationship with large agaves. The bats migrate north just as agaves and SAGUARO cactus bloom and spend their nights feeding on flower nectar; the big plants depend on the bats for cross-pollination, without which they lose diversity. Agave flowers are elegantly designed to attract large, night-feeding bats: they smell like rotten meat, a scent the bats appreciate; grow on tall stalks with wide-branching flower clusters, making access easy for hovering drinkers; their nectar secretions peak between eight and ten o'clock at night, when the bats are most active; and the nectar is high in the proteins and hexose sugars that bats need for fuel.

See also BAT, LECHUGUILLA.

ARIZONA CYPRESS Arizona cypress (*Cupressus arizonica*), locally common in mountain riparian woodlands of the southern Southwest, is the only true cypress native to North America outside of California. This medium-sized (up to 40 feet tall) evergreen is one of many Mexican species that barely reach into the Southwest. Arizona cypress grows at elevations of 3,500 to 8,000 feet in mountain canyons along the border, and north to central Arizona. It is also widely planted as an ornamental.

Arizona cypress's scalelike, blue-green leaves look like juniper leaves, but its red-brown, globular cones are bigger than juniper fruits. The cones are hard and split open in characteristic polygonal sections, shedding hundreds of tiny seeds.

ASPEN Aspen (*Populus tremuloides*), also called quaking aspen or *alamillo* ("little cottonwood" in Spanish), paint Southwest mountain and MESA slopes gold in autumn, announcing the change of seasons with a glorious burst of color. Decreasing day length and nighttime freezes trigger the pigment changes that color aspens, as well as MAPLES, OAKS, COTTON-WOODS, and other deciduous Southwestern trees. The trees stop making chlorophyll, the pigment that normally paints leaves green. As the chlorophyll drains away, the yellows, golds, oranges, and reds once masked by it blaze through. The autumn color show begins in mid-September in the northern Southwest, mid-October farther south. Spectacular displays occur in southern Utah's mountain ranges; northern Arizona's GRAND CANYON area, Flagstaff Mountains, and MOGOLLON RIM; southern Colorado's MESA VERDE National Monument and San Luis Valley; northern New Mexico's upper RIO GRANDE Valley; and Guadalupe Mountains National Park near southern New Mexico's CARLSBAD CAVERNS.

Aspen in the Southwest grow in beautiful, many-acre groves, or "clones," which form distinct splotches on hill and mesa sides. Each clone comprises several dozen to thousands of nearly identical trees. All are closely spaced and of a similar height; their bark is either white or olive-colored, satiny smooth or marked by the bumpy black calligraphy of a fungus specific to aspen, and their trunks grow gracefully straight or crooked as a lightning bolt. Each tree is literally no different from its neighbor, since aspen in such clones all sprout from a common root system and are genetically identical. Although all the trees in one clone leaf out and lose their leaves at the same time, neighboring clones' schedules vary widely, delineating clone boundaries in a colorful map. Spring paints one clone pale green with new leaves, while a neighboring clone is still bare, the trees ghostly gray. In autumn, each clone flames a distinct shade of gold on its own schedule.

Sprouting from their roots, aspen can appear as if by miracle where fires and logging have bared the soil. Often shade-loving trees, such as pines, DOUGLAS FIRS, true FIRS, and spruces, which germinate in the cooler, moist microclimate of the tightly packed aspen, will overtake and replace a clone. Or the relatively short-lived stems—which survive up to 250 years—will simply die of old age. Because hormones manufactured by the standing trunks inhibit a new generation of root sprouts, no replacements grow while the clone is still standing. The tops often die and fall within a few years of one another, and the clone disappears as abruptly as it sprouted. After another fire, however, the aspen can sprout again.

Aspen are the only northern, high-altitude trees with "green" trunks. The trunks photosynthesize with the chlorophyll just under their thin, transparent bark, producing only about 2 percent of a single tree's food needs but giving it the energy needed to leaf out early in spring. Photosynthesizing trunks are much more common in trees of the Southwest's deserts and semideserts, including MESQUITES and PALOVERDES.

A multitude of high-country animals depend on aspen for food and cover. Deer, elk, moose, and domestic sheep and goats browse the bark and twigs year-round. The straight trunks make ideal scratching posts for deer and elk to rub the velvet from their antlers. Aphids suck the sap of the tender shoots, tent caterpillars periodically denude the trees of leaves, leaf miners' distinctive translucent tracks scrawl across the leaves they "mine," borers live in the trunks. Cavity-nesting birds such as woodpeckers and OWLS nest in large aspens, as do platform nesters such as sharp-shinned HAWKS. In winter, grouse and QUAIL feed on the buds. Beaver cut and store aspen logs in their ponds for winter food.

People are attracted to aspen, too. The soft bark is easily carved and often records the names of early travelers and shepherds. (But such carving lets in borers and infection and may kill the trees.) Aspen bark contains salicin, the original aspirin, and has long been chewed to treat fever and inflammation. In the Southwest, the light but tough wood is favored for *latillas*, the slats between large roof beams in adobe houses, and for honeycomb dividers, since it is taste- and odor-free. It is also shredded to make the excelsior for evaporative cooler pads.

Aspen is the most widely distributed tree in North America, growing from Alaska to Newfoundland, and south into the mountains of Mexico. Southwestern aspen flourish on moist, sandy soils on the higher mesas and in the mountains up to the spruce-fir forests, from about 6,000 to 11,500 feet elevation. The Southwest's largest aspen, 70 feet tall, 3.7 feet in diameter, grows in the Pecos Wilderness of the SANGRE DE CRISTO MOUNTAINS in northern New Mexico.

See also MAPLE.

BARREL CACTUS Barrel cacti (*Ferrocactus* and *Echinocactus* species), also called compass cacti or *bisnaga* in Spanish, are North America's largest single-stemmed, unbranching cacti. These stout, barrel-shaped cacti are strongly ribbed and can reach heights up to 10 feet (2 to 4 feet is more common), with 2-foot diameters. Growing faster on the shaded side, barrels lean toward the south, hence the name "compass" cactus. *Ferrocactus* comes from the Latin *ferox* or "fierce," for the formidable clusters of spines that sprout from the ribs. The central spines in each cluster are red, yellowish, or golden, several inches long, and often flattened. Some end in a recurving hook, giving those barrels the name "fishhook barrel" (*F. wislizenii* and others).

Like most CACTI, barrels grow incredibly slowly. A 4-year-old barrel may only be 3 inches high and 2.5 inches around. Once established, they may thrive for 100 years, nearly as long as SAGUAROS. Barrels also share with the tree-sized cacti extensive, shallow root systems, which allow them to take up large amounts of water quickly and to store enough water to survive long droughts. One large barrel taken from the ground survived six years, using a total of 24 pounds of stored water. Barrels should not be cut apart for emergency drinking water—most contain bitter, unpalatable juice.

After seasonal rains in spring or summer, barrels sprout a gaudy

Barrel cactus

crown of large yellow, orange, or rose-pink flowers, each with numerous satiny petals. Fleshy, egg-shaped fruits succeed the flowers, maturing by late fall or early winter, when they are avidly consumed by deer and rodents.

Barrels grow in sandy or gravelly soil of washes and dry south slopes up into the mountains and on canyon walls throughout the desert regions of the Southwest, generally from south-central Arizona and central New Mexico southward into Mexico. Fishhook barrel or candy barrel, which grows from southern Arizona to western Texas and northern Mexico, is the source of a chewy confection made by boiling the fleshy inner parts with sugar.

See also CACTUS.

BEANS Dry beans (*Phaseolus* species) are one of the Southwest's most important contributions to agriculture worldwide. So many dryland beans were grown in eastern New Mexico before the dust bowl days of the 1930s that the tiny community of Mountainair, New Mexico, proclaimed itself the "Pinto Bean Capital of the World." Pinto beans, also called frijoles, are one of New Mexico's state vegetables. Although beans are no longer an important commercial crop in the Southwest, hundreds of kinds of dry beans were bred from wild bean species native to the

Southwest, Mexico, and Central America.

Native peoples throughout the Southwest grew beans without irrigation, planting after the first heavy summer rain in fields watered only by runoff from surrounding higher ground. The Papago (whose name comes from *Papavi Kuadam*, "tepary eaters" in Papago) and Pima peoples of the Sonoran Desert cultivated the most desert-adapted of all cultivated beans—tepary beans (*P. acutifolius*)—small, white, brown, and tan beans tolerant of drought, heat, and alkaline soils. In recent dry-farming trials, tepary beans planted after a 2-inch rainfall germinated and grew despite daytime temperatures as high as 118°F, and produced the equivalent of a ton of beans per acre with no irrigation and only a scant inch of additional rainfall.

Once widely cultivated, tepary beans are now being rediscovered as water becomes scarcer and expensive. These beans may save the lives of the very people who nurtured and bred them, the desert Papago, now called Tohono O'odham, and the Pima. As the former "bean eaters" shifted from desert foods to a diet of supermarket and fast foods, diabetes and related problems skyrocketed. The O'odham now have among the highest incidence of diabetes of any population in the United States—one in eight people on the O'odham reservation is a diabetic. Yet consumption of legumes such as beans protects diabetics from dangerously rapid rises in blood sugar after meals and helps reduce cholesterol levels. And teparies have higher iron, calcium, and protein content, higher digestible fiber, and less fat than other beans. Nutritionists have shown that a diet of the small beans, along with native desert foods such as MESQUITE-seed gum, PRICKLY PEAR pads, and plantago seed, can control blood sucrose levels and reduce or eliminate the need for insulin shots.

See also CORN.

BOSQUE DEL APACHE
Bosque del Apache or "Apaches' woods," is one of a few remaining bosques (pronounced BOHS-kays, meaning "thicket" or "woods" in Spanish) in the Southwest. A complex of marshes and COTTONWOOD, willow, SALTCEDAR and MESQUITE thickets along the RIO GRANDE in central New Mexico, Bosque del Apache was once a camping place for Apaches. Later, it became a base for their raids on travelers along *El Camino Real*, "The Royal Road," between Mexico City and Santa Fe.

Today, 57,000 acres of the bosque and adjacent uplands comprise Bosque del Apache National Wildlife Refuge, established in 1936 to protect endangered CRANES. Thousands of sandhill cranes and a handful of whooping cranes winter at the refuge from November through mid-February, along with huge flocks of wintering snow geese and many kinds of ducks. Some 295 bird species and more than 115 other animal species, including herons, eagles, RAVENS, COYOTES, and deer frequent the refuge at various times of the year.

See also CRANE, SALTCEDAR.

BRISTLECONE PINE Gnarled and twisted bristlecone pines grow on windswept, rocky slopes and ridges, from 7,500 to 12,000 feet (upper tree line), in the highest mountains of the southern West. Scarred and shaped by constant winds and blowing ice and snow, bristlecones grow very slowly, adding as little as a half-inch to their girth in a century. Although painfully slow, their growth continues for hundreds, even thousands, of years. Great Basin bristlecones (*Pinus longaeva*), found in the mountain ranges of Nevada, in a few ranges in western Utah, and in eastern California, are known to live more than 4,600 years. One Great Basin bristlecone lived to be more than 4,900 years old, the world's oldest known tree. Sadly, this matriarch, which germinated at about the time the Egyptian pharaohs were establishing their first dynasty, met a tragic end: it was cut down by a thoughtless researcher. Rocky Mountain bristlecone pines (*P. aristata*), of the southern Rockies in Arizona, New Mexico, and Colorado, are mere youngsters by comparison, living only upward of a thousand years.

Named for the recurved bristles on their purplish-brown cone scales, bristlecones are squat trees, growing as tall as 70 feet (20 to 45 feet is more common), with enormous girths. The largest Great Basin bristlecone is *40 feet* in circumference. Their short needles, bunched tightly like a fox's tail at the end of the long spreading branches, also give them the common name foxtail pine. (However, foxtail pine, *P. balfouriana*, is an entirely different species, which grows in California's Sierra Nevada and the Klamath Mountains.) Rocky Mountain bristlecone needles are often marked with "dandruff"—whitish dots of resin on their outer surface; Great Basin needles are not.

Bristlecones' extraordinary longevity was discovered in the 1950s by tree-ring researcher Edmund Schulman. Studying tree rings to chart past climate changes, he heard stories of twisted and possibly ancient bristle-cones in California's White Mountains. When he traveled there and cored some (rings can be read without killing the tree by carefully extracting a slim core with an increment borer), their rings showed them to be upward of 4,000 years old.

See also BRYCE CANYON.

BUFFALO GOURD
Buffalo gourd (*Cucurbita foetidissima*) is one of the desert's summer surprises. Its sprawling stems and large, gray-green triangular leaves appear suddenly in spring from a huge underground root, grow swiftly to lengths up to 20 feet, then die back and disappear with the first frost. A wild relative of squashes, buffalo gourd blooms from April to July, producing 2- to 3-inch-wide, yellow-orange, trumpet-shaped flowers, which, like squash flowers, are unisexual. When pollinated, usually by solitary bees, female flowers produce softball-sized green- or yellow-striped gourds.

> Buffalo gourds contain cucurbitacins, the bitterest substances known to humans. Eating the bitter fruit results in intense nausea.

The desert's many grazers and browsers avoid buffalo gourd and its cousin, coyote gourd (*C. digitata*). Both plants contain cucurbitacins, the bitterest substances known to humans, rendering the plants foul-tasting and inedible. Cucurbitacins are so bitter that their fetid flavor can be detected even in dilutions as minuscule as one part per billion parts of water. Eating the bitter fruit results in intense nausea for people, followed by several days of severe stomach cramps and diarrhea. Small mammals are not so lucky: ingesting just a millionth of their body weight in cucurbitacins kills them.

In northern Mexico, these gourds are called *chichicoyotas*, "trickster breasts," because, the story goes, mothers rub the intensely bitter pulp on their breasts when it is time to wean their babies. When the young ones try to suck, they taste the stomach-wrenching foul juice and turn away.

The wild gourds' very bitterness, although repugnant to most animals, is what attracts one group of insects—the adult luperinid beetles, which include the crop pests cucumber beetles and corn rootworm. Once these small beetles taste the bitter cucurbitacins, they become addicted and feed ravenously on the gourds, ignoring other plants. Luperinid beetles' prodigious appetite for the malodorous chemicals may make buffalo gourd valuable for biological control. By using buffalo gourd plants or their bitter extract to attract luperinid beetles, farmers could avoid millions of dollars of yearly crop damage without harming the environment.

Southwestern researchers view buffalo gourd as a valuable crop for other reasons. The edible seeds are rich in oil (25 percent) and protein (30 percent), and the massive roots (which can reach 5 feet long and weigh over a hundred pounds) are high in starch. Although buffalo gourd has been grown experimentally as an arid-land crop, no market has yet developed for the oil, protein-rich animal meal, or starch.

People and wild gourd plants have a long history. Nine thousand years ago, Mexico's Maya Indians honed their pitching skills with the gourds. Before pottery reached North America, the hard gourd rinds served as bowls, buckets, and storage containers. Gourds are still used for artwork and ceremonial rattles.

Buffalo gourd grows along roadsides, ditch banks, and other open areas from the desert to the PIÑON-JUNIPER woodlands throughout the Southwest and west to southern California, east to Missouri, and south into Mexico. Coyote gourd grows in the hottest parts of the Sonoran Desert, where buffalo gourd cannot survive, from the shores of the Sea of Cortez in Mexico to central Arizona.

CACTUS To survive the Southwest's unpredictable supply of moisture, cacti have evolved external forms to armor themselves against drought and spongelike internal reservoirs to store water. The part of a cactus plant visible above ground is modified stem, coated with a waxy layer, thickest on the sunny side of the plant, which prevents evaporation and protects the tissues from sunburn. Toothpick-thin and wickedly pointed spines—modified leaves—cover the stem. Spines not only lose less water than leaves, they also protect the plant from many grazers and help shade the stem surface. The plant stores water in its own reservoir, the pulpy interior, which is supported by a skeletal column of woody cells. Cacti swell after rains, taking in water through their shallow, broadly spreading root system, and shrink in times of drought.

Like AGAVES, YUCCAS, and other succulent desert plants, cacti even save water during photosynthesis. They photosynthesize during the day, but keep their pores closed to minimize water loss. During the cooler, moister night, these plants open their pores and absorb carbon dioxide, storing it for daytime use.

The many species of cacti (not even cactus researchers agree on the exact number) found in the Southwest range from tree-sized, columnar SAGUARO and organ pipe cacti to PRICKLY PEAR AND CHOLLA the size of large shrubs and tiny Mammillaria just a few inches tall. Larger cacti often branch; smaller ones sometimes grow in clumps of many stems. Cacti are most characteristic of the Southwest's deserts—Arizona's Sonoran Desert has the most species—but also grow in dry GRASSLANDS and shrublands, woodlands of OAK and PIÑON-JUNIPER, and even in dry mountain pine forests.

The first cacti to bloom in spring are small *Echinocereus*—hedgehog or strawberry cacti. Growing in open clumps, their 2- to 12-inch-tall stems resemble spine-covered cucumbers standing on end. The large flowers— 2- to 5.5-inches wide and colored lavender, purple, or rich red—dwarf the small plants. The dark, mahogany-red, juicy fruits are rich in sugar and may be eaten like strawberries once the spines are singed off. Rainbow cactus (*E. pectinatus*) is named for its colorful banding: pink, gray, pale yellow, brown, or white spines ring the stems, marking the growth of different seasons and years. Rainbow cacti grow on rocky slopes and flats between 4,000 and 6,000 feet, from central and southern Arizona to west Texas and northern Mexico. Claret cup cactus (*E. triglochidiatus*) is named for the brilliant 2-inch-wide scarlet flowers that top the spiny stems in April and May. Old, many-stemmed plants are especially spectacular in bloom. Claret cup blooms in April and May on rocky desert slopes and dry woodlands in the mountains of the Southwest and northern Mexico.

Another small cactus, also called a hedgehog for its spiny, nearly spherical stems, Simpson's hedgehog (*Pediocactus simpsonii*) characterizes the sagebrush basins and piñon-juniper woodlands of the northern Southwest (northern New Mexico and Arizona, southern and central Utah), and the Great Basin as far north as eastern Washington state. Like many small cacti, Simpson's hedgehog and its relatives have been overcollected by cactus fanciers and nurseries; they are becoming rare.

Mammillaria cacti—also called nipple cacti for the nipplelike bumps that crowd the stems of fishhook cacti (not to be confused with fishhook barrels) for the slender, recurved spine in each cluster—are small, multi-stemmed cacti common on sandy soils from southern Utah to west Texas, southern California, and northern Mexico. Their small flowers bloom in a crownlike ring around the stem at least an inch from the top. Unlike with most cacti, each flower bloom lasts for several days and the bright red fruits are spineless. Mammillaria fruits, which look like small red chile peppers, are edible.

See also BARREL CACTUS, NIGHT-BLOOMING CEREUS, PRICKLY PEAR AND CHOLLA CACTUS, and SAGUARO.

CHILES Chiles are one of New Mexico's state vegetables—properly so, since the state leads the nation in producing the fiery fruit. In 1990, New Mexican farmers produced 46,781 dry tons of chiles, valued at $53.5 million, the state's third most profitable crop. Many of the commercial chile varieties grown in the United States were developed in New Mexico State University's chile breeding program, begun at the turn of the century.

> **Chiles were cultivated and traded throughout the Southwest and Central America long before they were "discovered" by Christopher Columbus.**

Chiles were cultivated and traded throughout the Southwest and Central America long before they were "discovered" and misnamed a pepper by Christopher Columbus (but then he thought that he had arrived in India, not the Caribbean). Technically a fruit, chiles belong to the Solanaceae family, along with tomatoes, potatoes, tobacco, and deadly nightshade. Columbus took the New World native plant back to Spain with him, and within 200 years chiles had been traded as far away as China.

Chiles get their fire from capsaicins—odorless, colorless, flavorless compounds unique to chiles. These compounds stimulate pain receptors, as anyone who has ever rubbed the eyes with a chile-powder–laden finger can testify. Perhaps because of the nerve-tweaking effects of capsaicins, chiles lower blood and liver triglyceride levels. The hot fruits are also high in vitamin C and may one day be used to treat a variety of diseases. Red chiles lend their fiery color to cosmetics, including lipstick.

Most cultivated chiles are descendants of wild chiltepines (*Capsicum annuum*), the hottest chiles known. These shrubs, bearing pea-sized red fruits called *piquin*, grow wild from the southern United States (where they are probably relicts of earlier cultivation) south into the tropics. Humans can detect capsaicin in amounts as minuscule as one part in 15 million;

piquins set off fire alarms in human nervous systems with 2,600 parts per million, or *39,000 times* that needed to tell your taste buds that you've bitten into a chile!

Chiltepines probably developed capsaicins to dissuade mammals from eating the fleshy fruit and destroying the seeds with their grinding teeth. But the bright red fruits attract fruit-eating birds like MOCKINGBIRDS, which eat them avidly. Not only do the seeds pass through the birds' guts uninjured, they germinate best after the chemical and physical scarifying, and are disseminated by their winged consumers, enclosed in a pat of fertilizer—bird scat.

Wild chiltepines' fire is so highly sought after for traditional Mexican cooking that the tiny chiles fetch high prices in Southwestern and Mexican markets. Tons of the wild fruits are harvested from northern Mexican hills each fall, endangering wild populations. Fortunately for wild chiltepines, chile breeders at New Mexico State University are working on breeding machine-harvestable cultivars, and Mexican farmers are experimenting with them as a drought-tolerant crop.

See also MOCKINGBIRD.

COLUMBINE There is no mistaking the graceful, long-spurred flowers of columbines, named for their resemblance to a cluster of five doves (*columba* means "dove" in Latin). The colorful, outer parts of columbine flowers are actually sepals. The petals, enclosed in the sepals, are elongated into an inches-long spur, ending in a tiny, bulb-shaped nectar sac. Long-tongued animals like BUTTERFLIES and HUMMINGBIRDS reach down the tubular spur to sip the sweet fluid; other insects simply cut holes in the tube.

Found in mountains and canyons from northern Arizona and New Mexico north to Montana, the blue or Colorado columbine (*Aquilegia caerulea*) is Colorado's state flower. Its huge blossoms, up to six inches across, open in June and July and vary from deep blue to lavender and even white in the western parts of its range in Utah.

Farther south, the bright yellow flowers of the golden columbine (*A. chrysantha*) replace the blue columbine, growing around springs in canyons as low as 3,000 feet and in moist places up to 11,000 feet from southern Colorado south through New Mexico, Arizona, and West Texas, into northern Mexico.

CORN Although the Southwest no longer grows the bulk of the nation's supply, corn (*Zea mays*) remains a traditional Southwest crop. Domesticated in the Rio Balsas region of southern Mexico, corn, along with BEANS and squash, has been a staple in the Southwest for at least 2,000 years and remains a traditional part of both Hispanic and Native American cuisine and ceremonies. Corn is eaten fresh, roasted, and dried, and is also ground into meal and flour. Tortillas and special breads such as Hopi *piki* are made from the flour; meal is cooked into mush for dishes such as the traditional Hispanic *chaquegue*, or drunk as *atole de maiz*, a creamy high-energy drink. Many Southwesterners consider corn sacred—a gift from the earth and a symbol of nature's fertility. They still collect corn pollen and corn silk for both ceremonial and medicinal uses.

Hundreds of corn varieties were developed to suit specific Southwest ecosystems, and dozens of these are still cultivated by small farmers and home gardeners. For example, Yaqui Blue, a blue flour-type corn, is well adapted to the hot conditions of the Salt River Indian Reservation in the Sonoran Desert in Arizona; and Santo Domingo Mix, a high-elevation variety with white, red, blue, and speckled kernels, grows in the high-elevation fields of northern New Mexico's Santo Domingo pueblo.

Some of the old corn varieties are finding new devotees: commercial farmers. The growing popularity of Southwestern cuisine has made blue corn one of the Southwest's promising new specialty crops. In New Mexico alone, commercial blue corn acreage grew from only about 100 acres in 1982 to 2,500 in 1990. Supermarkets across the country sell blue corn chips, flakes, and popcorn, and mixes for blue corn muffins and pancakes. Even New York's venerable Bloomingdale's department store started offering blue corn from northern New Mexico's pueblos. Long preferred for its coarser, sweeter, and nuttier-tasting flour, blue corn is higher in lysine than other corns, making it a more complete protein source.

Growing blue corn is not easy. Although relatively pest-resistant, the plant is difficult to harvest mechanically because the stalks fall over; yields are less than half that of most commercial corn. Further, growers along the Rio Grande flyway in New Mexico have to cope with the appetites of an unusual crop pest—sandhill CRANES migrating south for the winter prefer to graze in the fields of blue corn.

See also BEANS, CASA GRANDE, CHACO CANYON.

COTTON Cotton (*Gossypium* species) was first cultivated by desert Southwesterners around 2,000 years ago, probably using seeds from native Mexican species. Central Arizona's Hohokam and Salado cultures developed a silky, short-staple cotton for weaving and other uses; the modern Tohono O'odham (Papago) and Pima bred and grew many varieties, weaving fine, tight cloth from the strong, smooth fibers. But when small-scale Native American farming disappeared with the loss of water to irrigation in the early 1900s, so also vanished the strains of silky-fibered, drought-adapted Pima cotton.

Ironically, the irrigation developments that killed Native American farming made cotton an important commerical crop in the Southwest later in the century. Cotton farming shifted from the humid Southeast to the arid Southwest, which offered abundant, artificially cheap water and a dearth of crop pests such as boll weevils. Today, Arizona leads the nation in production of Pima cotton—a modern long-staple variety, not the original grown by the Pima—producing over half of our national crop. New Mexico is the fourth-largest producer (behind Texas and California). In 1990, the two Southwest states produced over 52,000 tons of Pima cotton.

A shrub of the mallow family and cousin to hibiscus and hollyhocks, cotton is native to southern Mexico and other tropical environments worldwide.

See also CASA GRANDE.

COTTONWOOD Cottonwoods (*Populus* species) once dominated the Southwest's riparian forests from desert rivers to lower mountain streams. The frequency of place names that incorporate the word cottonwood, or *álamo* (Spanish for "cottonwood"), hints at their former abundance. (Alamogordo, New Mexico, for instance, means "fat cottonwood.") Now, after more than a century of livestock grazing, clear-cutting for agriculture, dam building, and stream channelization, over 90 percent of the Southwest's magnificent cottonwood bosques (Spanish for "woodlands") are gone.

These tall, spreading trees grow naturally only in wet soils along streams, rivers, and irrigation ditches. Crucial to lowland riparian ecosystems, their deep roots hold stream-bank soils against erosion and keep the soil porous so that runoff sinks in. Their shady canopies provide a cooler, moister environment for a wide variety of plants and animals. Cottonwoods' broad branches support the heavy nesting platforms of great blue herons,

RAVENS, VULTURES, and HAWKS. The holes formed when their branches fall shelter OWLS, raccoons, and many other cavity dwellers. ORIOLES hang their pendulous nests from their upper branches, tiger swallowtail caterpillars munch their leaves. Berries from gray-green clumps of parasitic MISTLE-TOE, which grows on the trees' limbs, feed PHAINOPEPLAS.

Many Southwesterners revere cottonwoods. The Hopi carve their beautiful kachinas, sculptures of supernatural beings, from cottonwood roots. Pueblo dwellers hollow the logs for two-headed ceremonial drums. Navajos use cottonwood for prayer sticks, rug looms, and hogan logs.

Three of the Southwest's five species of cottonwoods are broad-leafed cottonwoods of the plains, deserts, and MESAS. Fremont cottonwood (*P. fremontii*), named in honor of John C. Frémont, an early Anglo explorer, is the common cottonwood of Arizona and the western Southwest, found up to 6,500 feet elevation from southwestern New Mexico west to California and north to southwestern Utah. Rio Grande cottonwood (*P. wislizensii*), named after Frederick Adolphus Wislizenus, a German naturalist who traveled the Southwest in the 1830s, dominates the central Southwest. Plains, or Sargent's, cottonwood (*P. sargentii*), the stream-bank cottonwood of the western Great Plains, reaches eastern New Mexico and West Texas.

The three broad-leafed cottonwoods grow to heights of 80 or 90 feet, supporting broad, open crowns of large, widely spreading branches. Gray, deeply furrowed bark clothes the fat trunks (2 to 5 feet in diameter). The largest Fremont cottonwood, on a ranch in western New Mexico, has an enormous trunk, nearly 38 feet around—12 feet across—with a crown spread of 102 feet.

Rio Grande cottonwood is a gypsophile, that is, a plant uniquely adapted to soils that are nearly pure gypsum. Rio Grande cottonwood is the only tree, and one of the few plants, growing in the glittering white sea of gypsum SAND DUNES at White Sands National Monument in New Mexico, where it draws on the water stored in the dunes.

Cottonwoods are commonly planted for shade trees throughout the Southwest. Usually, only male trees are planted; females loose clouds of the "messy," cottony down to disperse their seeds. But male trees also have their drawbacks: wind-pollinating, they release tons of tiny pollen grains onto the breezes, wreaking havoc on allergy sufferers' respiratory systems.

See also BOSQUE DEL APACHE, SAND DUNE.

CREOSOTE BUSH The creosote bush (*Larrea tridentata*), an unpretentious evergreen shrub with shiny, yellow-green leaves, is the most widespread, characteristic, and perhaps least-appreciated shrub of North America's hot Sonoran, Chihuahuan, and Mojave deserts. Creosote bush so successfully colonized the deserts that evolved in drier post–Ice Age climates that it now covers a quarter of Mexico and nearly 70,000 square miles (an area larger than the state of Washington) of the southwestern United States. Creosote dominates well-drained, gravelly soils of plains and slopes below 4,000 feet, forming seas of olive-green shrubs.

These unpretentious but tough plants outlive all other desert dwellers. A creosote bush called "King Clone," growing in the sere Mojave Desert northeast of Los Angeles, is the oldest living plant known, older than the oldest-known BRISTLECONE PINE. Radiocarbon dating sets its age at 9,400 years. Creosote's toughness was demonstrated by a thermonuclear explosion at Yucca Flat, Nevada, in 1962. One of the few perennials growing at the extremely arid site, creosote bush—like everything else—seemed to have been blasted to oblivion. But ten years later, twenty of the original twenty-one creosote shrubs at the center of the blast had resprouted.

> A creosote bush called "King Clone," growing in the sere Mojave Desert northeast of Los Angeles, is the oldest living plant known.

Creosote bush sprouts numerous, scraggly stems from its base, producing a scant canopy of small, shiny leaves that do not yield much shade. Yellow, inch-wide flowers dot the shrub after rains, followed by fuzzy, white cotton ball–like fruits. Because it is the dominant plant over such a large area, creosote bush has its own insect fauna. A variety of endemic insects, from GRASSHOPPERS and praying mantises to moths and beetles, take shelter on creosote bush, all camouflaged to look like parts of the shrub.

Creosote bush is also called greasewood for its armor of resins—a complex mix of flavinoids, lignins, volatile oils, saponins, and waxes. Resins fill its tissues and are exuded as an amber, sticky sap on its stems, repelling grazers, from cattle to the tiniest insects, by tasting terrible and by forming indigestible masses in most animals' guts. Only one grasshopper, a tiny creosote cryptic that lives out its entire life on the shrub, is known to be able to digest the protective compounds. Resins also coat the leaves and twigs, forming a varnishlike layer that acts as a combination sunscreen and moisture barrier, shielding the delicate inner tissues from ultraviolet

Creosote bush

light and heat, and reducing moisture loss.

Besides manufacturing the complex resinous armor, creosote bush also protects itself with odors. A single creosote bush stand may contain forty-nine kinds of volatile oils. After rains, the desert air fills with the characteristic resiny, medicinal odor of creosote, hence the common name "creosote bush." In northern Mexico, the bush is called *hediondilla*—"little stinker."

Perhaps because of the medicinal smell, desert dwellers have long used creosote as a cure-all. Teas made by steeping its aromatic branches and leaves are drunk to cure colds, intestinal discomfort, and stomach and menstrual cramps. Its pungent smoke is inhaled for chest infections and lung congestion. Poultices are applied to cleanse wounds, reduce swellings caused by congested circulation, and alleviate rheumatism and arthritis. Not surprisingly, researchers have found a scientific basis for many of the traditional uses: extracts of the resins act as antimicrobials and fungicides, dissolve kidney stones, act as painkillers, and have vasodepressant properties. One particular compound, nordihydroguaiaretic acid, a powerful antioxidant, is currently being investigated for its anti-aging effects and its ability to help control the growth of cancer cells.

See also BLISTER BEETLE.

DATURA Sacred datura, or Jimsonweed (*Datura meteloides*), is one of the Southwest's main drug plants. All parts of the plant, particularly the seeds, contain high concentrations of narcotic alkaloids accumulated from the soil. Datura has been used to induce visions and for divination, for relaxation, as an anesthetic for setting bones, and to prevent miscarriage. The name "sacred" datura comes from the plant's ceremonial use by Native Americans. But, like other members of the Solanaceae family, especially nightshade, it is deadly. Eating datura causes giddiness, dim sight, hallucinations, and stupefaction—even blindness, or death. All parts of the plant are poisonous. "Jimsonweed" commemorates the poisoning of a group of soldiers sent to Jamestown to put down Bacon's Rebellion in 1676. They ate datura and, the story goes, had to be locked up for several days in order not to harm themselves.

Currently, scientists are attempting to use datura in a different way. They hope to harness datura's ability to accumulate toxins in order to clean up soil contaminated by nitroglycerine wastes from past weapons-testing programs.

Only one insect, the larva of the striped datura beetle (related to the potato beetle) munches datura's stems and leaves with gusto. Ironically, the larvae are not immune to the alkaloids and are sometimes poisoned by their food. Harvester ANTS are especially attracted to datura's seeds because of the seeds' sticky "handle." The ants carry the seeds away from the plant, helping to disperse them, but eventually abandon the seeds—even a harvester ant's powerful jaws cannot penetrate the hard seed coat.

Datura is an arresting sight when it blooms. Its spreading mound of large, gray-green leaves is topped by 6-inch-long, trumpet-shaped white blossoms from May to October. The spectacular flowers, which open in the evening and wilt the following morning, exude a faint lemon fragrance and attract a variety of night-flying nectar seekers and pollinators, such as SPHINX MOTHS. The small, spherical fruits, green and covered with spines, inspired another common name: "thorn apple." Various species of datura grow throughout the Southwest between 1,000 to 6,500 feet in sandy soils of ARROYOS, along streams and roadsides, on plains and hills.

DESERT ANNUAL WILDFLOWERS The hot deserts of the Southwest—especially the Sonoran and Mojave—are famous for their spectacular though short-lived spring and summer wildflower displays, resulting in extravagant seas of color in years with abundant winter rains.

Desert annuals avoid drought and intense heat by surviving as seeds stored in the soil, sometimes for decades. Many of the millions of seeds produced in a good year are eaten by insects, rodents, or birds; the remainder stay dormant until conditions are just right, then sprout, grow quickly, and burst into bloom, compressing their lives into the short period that soils are moist.

The timing of the flower show depends on the rains. In the hot, winter rain–dominated Mojave Desert, annual flowers may bloom as early as February or as late as April. Because its most reliable rains come in winter, the Mojave Desert experiences severe drought through the normal growing season, making it hard for perennial plants to survive. Hence, the Mojave has the highest proportion of annual, grow-swiftly-and-die species. In some parts of the Mojave, over 80 percent of the plants recorded, an astounding 250 species, are annuals. Winter rains paint the ground with a panoply of colors—yellow, gold, pink, magenta, blue, and deep purple—with 70 to 400 plants crowded into a square yard.

> **Desert annuals avoid drought and intense heat by surviving as seeds stored in the soil, remaining dormant until conditions are just right.**

Dependent mainly on summer rains, the higher-elevation, cooler Chihuahuan Desert climate favors perennials and has fewer annual species than either the Mojave or the Sonoran. In especially wet summers, from July to September, travelers on Interstate 25 south from Albuquerque to El Paso, Texas, or on Interstate 10 from El Paso west to the Arizona line are treated to a sea of bright yellow chinchweed (*Pectis papposa*) and other wildflowers. In May, the flowers of the Arizona poppy (*Kallistromia grandiflora*) sometimes tint the desert floor orange-yellow, causing travelers to wonder if the highway department planted them.

But it is the Sonoran Desert, with both a winter and a summer rainy season, that is justly famous for its spectacular spring wildflower displays. Annual species from both the Mojave and the Chihuahuan deserts, and species unique to the Sonoran, bloom in April and May. About every ten years, the rainfall and temperature patterns are just right, and wildflower seeds germinate by the billions. The ground blazes with the tiny yellow, daisylike blooms of goldfields (*Lasthenia californica*) and the brilliant orange flowers of goldpoppy (*Escholtzia* species). Magenta spikes of owl clover (*Orthocarpus purpurascens*) and blue-purple lupines (*Lupinus* species) splotch the yellow background, as do fragile pink desert five spots (*Malvastrum* species), magenta sand verbena (*Abronia villosa*), and deep blue-purple larkspur (*Delphinium* species). Many perennials bloom also, from the pale trumpets of desert lilies to the magenta flowers of beavertail cactus. Good places to see the Sonoran Desert's spring wildflowers include Organ Pipe Cactus National Monument in southwestern Arizona, Saguaro National Monument around Tucson, and Picacho Peak State Park between Tucson and Phoenix.

DESERT-MARIGOLD

Desert-marigold (*Baileya multiradiata*), a grayish, woolly biennial plant, produces one of the most noticeable of the desert's "composites," or daisylike flowers. Its sunny yellow flowers appear from April to October, often in such profusion that they form solid yellow ribbons along roadsides. Desert-marigold grows throughout the Southwest's deserts and arid shrublands from southern Utah south to Mexico, and from southeastern California to west Texas. Its common name, "marigold," shared with other yellow-flowered plants in the sunflower family, comes from "Mary's Gold," flowers thought to bloom in honor of the Christian Virgin Mary.

Like many desert plants, desert-marigold is covered with a mat of woolly hairs that screen the plant's delicate inner tissues against both heat and ultraviolet light, and help it retain water. Also like those of many desert plants, desert-marigold's leaves are small, grow on the lower half of the plant, and consist of many separate small surfaces—adaptations to reduce heat gain and water loss.

The bright yellow flower heads, nearly 2 inches across, produce a large quantity of chalky white seeds like tiny sunflower seeds. Flocks of seed-eating birds such as BLACK-THROATED SPARROWS, goldfinches, and house finches clamber over the plants in the fall, chattering while they extract and eat the seeds.

DEVIL'S CLAW

The trailing, 2- to 5-foot-long stems and big, shiny green scalloped leaves of devil's claw (*Proboscidea* species) appear in the deserts and dry grasslands of the southern Southwest after seasonal rains. A spike of snapdragonlike flowers in brassy colors—red-purple, copper, yellow with rust—opens above the leaves in summer, producing the

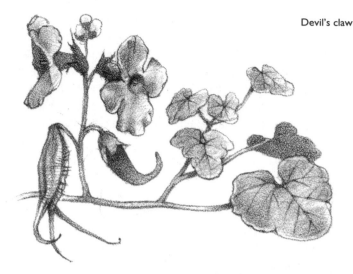

Devil's claw

dramatic seedpods for which the plant is named. Greenish and okralike at first, with a hooked horn up to 5 inches long, the pod dries, turns black, and splits from one end into two long, wickedly hooked "devil's claws." These twin prongs catch on passersby, distributing the seeds as they are carried along.

Southwesterners have gathered and eaten green devil's claw pods for at least 1,000 years, but today the dry, black pods are even more prized for basketry. Weavers gather them, strip the hooks and outer covering, and weave the tough, inner fibers into distinctive black designs on light-colored YUCCA and beargrass baskets. Traditionally a signature of Arizona Tonoho O'odham (Papago), Pima, and Havasupai baskets, devil's claw is now grown and used by fiber workers throughout the West.

Devil's claw grows in sandy soil from southern California's Mojave Desert region east through Arizona's Sonoran Desert to the Chihuahuan Desert region of southern New Mexico and West Texas.

DOUGLAS FIR The oldest-known Rocky Mountain Douglas fir (*Pseudotsuga menziesii* var. *glauca*), a runt only 30 feet tall growing on the black basalt of a MALPAIS near Grants, New Mexico, sprouted in 1062 and has survived 930 years. Often growing as tall as 100 feet, Rocky Mountain Douglas fir, one of the characteristic trees of Southwest mountain forests, is a giant in the region. Still, Rocky Mountain Douglas fir is short stuff compared to its sibling, coastal Douglas fir of the Pacific Northwest, which towers over 200 feet. Rocky Mountain Douglas fir also grows much more slowly and is a less important timber tree in the Southwest than PONDEROSA PINE.

Neither a true fir nor a hemlock, Douglas fir, with drooping branches, resembles both—hence its scientific name and its common name (*Pseudotsuga*, "false-hemlock"). Its downward-hanging cones are distinctive: each cone scale sports a long bract that looks remarkably like the hind end of a tiny mouse disappearing beneath the scale, with only the "tail" and two "hind legs" protruding. Mature Rocky Mountain Douglas fir bark is reddish brown, deeply furrowed, and thick, helping the trees withstand the heat of ground fires caused by lightning in summer thunderstorms.

Douglas fir grows throughout the Rockies, from Canada south to the Sierras of northern and central Mexico, on rocky soils from elevations of about 7,500 feet to just below timberline, generally above ponderosa pine and below true firs. North-facing slopes often support dense stands of Douglas fir with little undergrowth; adjacent warmer and drier south-facing slopes are startlingly different, supporting open, grassy stands of ponderosa pine. Elk and deer use the dense Douglas fir stands for hiding and resting cover, and move to the ponderosa pine stands to graze and browse.

ELEPHANT HEAD Half-inch-long pink flowers exactly resembling miniature elephant heads give this plant (*Pedicularis groenlandica*), a member of the figwort family, its name. The flowers, complete with a long curving "trunk," side petals like big earflaps, and a petal curled over into a domed, elephantine forehead, crowd together along the flower stalk. Elephant head's elaborate flower shape is designed to aid cross-pollination. The blossoms, precisely shaped to fit nectar-seeking bumbleBEES, arch forward under the bee's weight, opening to admit the bee. Inside the flower, pollen from the anthers dusts the bee's hairy body, and the flower's trunk, which encloses the female flower parts, brushes the exact spot on the bee's back where pollen from other flowers has accumulated. Elk also graze the sweet flowers.

The pink pachyderms bloom from June through August, casting a magenta tint on wet mountain meadows, boggy areas, and stream-banks up into the alpine, from 8,000 to 12,000 feet in the Southwest's mountains. It grows throughout the western mountains, from Alaska and Canada south to New Mexico, eastern Arizona, and California.

EVENING PRIMROSE Evening primroses (*Oenothera* species) bloom throughout the Southwest after seasonal rains, from deserts, especially on sand dunes, to high mesas. Thousands of their four-petaled, white or yellow tissue paper–like flowers cover the ground in years of ample rains, like myriads of butterflies. Each delicate flower lasts only one night, opening in the evening to minimize water loss and wilting when touched by the morning sun. Night-flying nectar sippers, especially SPHINX MOTHS, attracted by the flowers' sweet scent, pollinate them.

> Evening primroses were once cultivated in Europe for salad greens. Traditional Hispanic healers prescribe teas of evening primose leaves and dried roots; flowers are applied like a poultice for throat and chest ailments.

Desert evening primroses hug the ground, growing dense basal rosettes of silvery-hairy leaves from thickened taproots, which store water and food. Other species, living where water is more abundant, stretch upward—tall yellow evening primrose (*O. longissima*), common along the roadsides in the PONDEROSA PINE forests on the North Rim of the GRAND CANYON, can reach 10 feet tall.

Birdcage evening primrose (*O. deltoides*) sprouts in profusion on SAND DUNES and sandy soils in the Great Basin, Mojave, and Sonoran deserts after good rainy seasons. Its white, 3-inch-wide flowers open in the evening from March to May, shining palely on desert sands. When the soil dries out, the plants die, their stems curving upward and coming together at the top like a lacy bird cage—hence their common name.

Evening primroses were once cultivated for salad greens in Europe. The leaves and shoots were grown under paper to blanch them and were picked young. Young shoots and roots of Southwest species are edible, but bitter; the young podlike fruits are good eaten raw. *Curanderos*, traditional Hispanic healers, prescribe teas of evening primrose leaves and dried roots to relieve spasms and pain in the bladder and urethra, and for menstrual cramps. The flowers are applied like a mustard poultice for throat and chest ailments.

See also DESERT ANNUALS.

FIR White fir (*Abies concolor*), the largest true fir in the Southwest, grows in the warmest and driest environments of any true fir. It is found as low as 5,500 feet in canyons in the Southwest's mountains, from the PONDEROSA PINE savannas up into mixed conifer forests. Although white fir often forms pure stands in wetter environments, in the Southwest it is usually solitary, growing in cool, moist microenvironments.

Mature white firs are a spectacular sight. They are tall—up to 120 feet in the Southwest, taller in Pacific coastal forests—and are shaped like a symmetrical, bluish green cone. Their straight, pale-gray trunks swell to 4 feet across at the base. White firs' seed cones sit upright on the branches like fat green or purple candles. The tree's graceful shape and dense, aromatic foliage make white fir a popular Christmas tree, and millions are grown in plantations and harvested annually.

White fir grows from southern Oregon and Idaho south through California's mountains and into northwestern Mexico, and east throughout the Southwest's mountains to eastern New Mexico.

Corkbark fir (*A. lasiocarpa* var. *arizonica*), the Southwest's only endemic fir, is a variety of subalpine fir. Named for its thick, spongy, ash-colored bark, corkbark fir grows higher in the mountains than does white fir, up to tree line, where it often codominates with Engelmann spruce. Its range covers Arizona and New Mexico and extends into southern Colorado. Farther north, subalpine fir (*A. lasiocarpa*) takes over. Although the most widespread western fir, subalpine fir is less common in the Southwest than corkbark fir. Subalpine fir, often found at upper timberline, grows in the subalpine zone from southeast Alaska and the Yukon to southern Utah and southern Colorado.

Both subalpine and corkbark fir are narrowly spire-shaped, with a wide "skirt" of branches spreading out and often rooting in the ground around the base, underneath the winter snow. However, corkbark is larger; has thick, corky bark instead of thin bark punctuated by resin blisters; and has distinctly blue needles. The largest known corkbark fir, 111 feet tall and nearly 4.5 feet in diameter, grows in the Lincoln National Forest near Ruidoso, New Mexico.

FUNGUS Hundreds of kinds of fungi grow in the Southwest, including fly amanita (*Amanita muscaria*), one of the world's deadliest mushrooms. Amanitas are responsible for most of the deaths attributable to poisonous mushrooms. Although people's susceptibility to poisonous mushrooms varies, fly amanita, named for its use as a fly poison, is so toxic that just a few bites can kill most people. Other Southwest fungi include edible truffles (*Tuber* species), relatives of the gourmet truffles dug by pigs in France, and the largest edible North American fungus, the football-sized western giant puffballs (*Calvatia booniana*).

Fungi are not plants, but fungi and plants are inextricably linked. Unable to photosynthesize, fungi nourish themselves from plants, growing their threadlike hyphae (analogous to stems and roots) into both living and dead plant tissue. Fungi can be saprophytes, feeding on dead plant tissue; parasites, eating living plant tissue; or mycorrhizae, sucking food from living plants but benefiting the host by extending its root system so the plant can obtain additional water and nutrients from the soil. Mycorrhizae are very widespread. Nearly every species of vascular plant cooperates with at least one species of mycorrhizae. The hyphae or mycorrhizae are hidden in the soil, in decaying logs, or in plant tissue. The visible portion of the fungus—the mushroom, puffball, or bracket fungus—is the fruiting body, full of seedlike spores.

Because they are dependent on moist conditions, Southwest fungi either grow in moister ecosystems such as woodlands and forests, or sprout after seasonal rains. Perhaps the most common fungus to grow in the Southwest's hot deserts and arid shrublands after seasonal rains is false shaggy mane (*Podoxis pistillaris*), a sac fungus named for the resemblance of its closed, shaggy cap to a shaggy mane mushroom. This tough fungus appears in spring along desert roads, even pushing up through the asphalt. Another Southwest fungus, *Battarea phalloides*, has a foot-plus-tall, erect stalk capped by a globular top. The weathered white fungus, accurately described by its specific name, *phalloides*, persists in the sagebrush grasslands long after the spore mass has been ejected. Another Southwest fungus, *Phallus impudicus*, looks just like its scientific name—"unbashful penis"—with its 10-inch-tall, thick stalk and small, slightly pointed cap.

Deciduous riparian forests, mixed pine and OAK stands, and PONDEROSA PINE and DOUGLAS FIR forests in the northern Southwest are home to edible truffles. Truffles form mycorrhizal relationships with trees, growing under the surface litter near tree roots. As with all fungi, we eat the fruiting body. For truffles, this is a spore-filled underground sac resembling a potato, complete with dark, dimpled outer skin and pale inside. Some truffles are as small as new potatoes, others as large as baking potatoes; Southwestern species tend to be small. Truffles mature in late fall and early winter and release distinctive odors, attracting insects and small mammals to dig up and consume the truffles, dispersing the spores in their scat. Truffles save moisture and can reproduce even in drought times by growing their fruiting bodies in the moist soil.

See also MICROBIOTIC CRUST.

GLOBEMALLOW
Globemallows, members of the hollyhock or mallow family with bright scarlet to peach flowers shaped like miniature hollyhocks, are common throughout the Southwest, from the low deserts up into the PIÑON-JUNIPER and PONDEROSA PINE woodlands of the MESAS and lower mountains.

Globemallow

Globemallows are covered with a dense, grayish, and slightly sparkling coating of short hairs, which branch like stars from a central stalk. The hairs, visible with a hand lens, help the plant reflect sunlight and retain moisture. In some parts of the Southwest, globemallows are called *mal-de-ojos*, or "sore-eye" flowers, in the belief that the hairs can injure the eyes. The Pima name, however, translates to "a cure for sore eyes." Hispanic *curanderos* (traditional healers) prescribe a globemallow tea for a hair rinse and conditioner, as well as to soothe raspy, dry sore throats.

The white pith inside globemallow stems can be chewed like gum. Marshmallows were once made from the roots of an eastern mallow, which grows in marshy places.

After ample winter rains, Coulter's globemallows (*Sphaeralcea coulteri*) tint the desert landscape red-orange with millions of flowers. Named for John Coulter, the early explorer, Coulter's globemallows open their orange-red blossoms as early as January in the lowest elevations of the Sonoran and Mojave deserts, and bloom through the spring. Other species, which grow at higher elevations, begin blooming in May and June and continue through October if summer moisture suffices. Some are small plants, less than a foot tall, such as scarlet globemallow (*S. coccinea*), named for its bright scarlet flowers and common in SAGEBRUSH and dry GRASSLANDS from the COLORADO PLATEAU and the Great Basin to the western Great Plains. Others, like desert globemallow (*S. ambigua*), grow in many-stemmed clumps up to 5 feet tall.

GRASSLANDS In 1598, Juan Oñate trailed 7,000 head of livestock along El Camino Real ("The Royal Road") from Chihuahua, Mexico, through El Paso, Texas, to Santa Fe, New Mexico, bringing the first big herd of domestic animals to graze the Southwest's once-abundant dry grasslands. Nearly three hundred years later, between the end of the Civil War and the late 1880s, millions of cattle, sheep, and horses were trailed into the Southwest, denuding most of the region's millions of acres of grasslands in less than two decades. Between 1882 and 1884, 60,000 cattle were brought to Socorro County, New Mexico, alone. With no grasses to hold it, the fine soil washed or blew away. Summer cloudbursts poured off the MESAS, hills, and plains instead of soaking in, eroding ARROYOS in once-stable stream and river channels, dropping water tables so low that COTTONWOODS and willows lining the streams died. Where early ranchers baled hay from native grasses growing "high as a horse's belly," now only shrubs that cattle abhor—SAGEBRUSH, saltbrush, CREOSOTE BUSH, MESQUITE, PRICKLY PEAR cactus—grow.

Mile upon mile of olive-green creosote bush line Interstate 25 and the RIO GRANDE Valley from El Paso to Socorro, New Mexico, instead of the black grama-sacaton grassland that once flourished on the plains of southern New Mexico and the Rio Grande Valley. (The Nature Conservancy's Gray Ranch in extreme southwestern New Mexico still contains beautiful expanses of this grassland, a mix of southern Great Plains and northern Mexican species.) Fertile grassland dominated by grama grass once bordered the upland Sonoran Desert in southern and central Arizona at elevations between 4,000 and 5,000 feet; at the Audubon Society's Research Ranch near Sonoita, Mexico, and the University of Arizona's Santa Rita Experimental Range south of Tucson, remnants of grassland with dense, 2-foot-high grasses contrast sharply with the bare soil of adjacent, over-grazed shrublands.

The Southwest's largest remaining grassland is the blue grama–buffalograss prairie, which once covered the western Great Plains, includ-ing the eastern third of New Mexico and Colorado. Although some of the western Great Plains has been plowed for crops such as cotton, winter wheat, cantaloupes, and, before the drought of the 1930s, pinto beans, miles of grassland remain. Interstate 25 between Colorado Springs and Albuquerque, and Interstate 40 between the LLANO ESTACADO of the Texas panhandle and Albuquerque traverse the shortgrass prairie, offer-ing sightings of pronghorn antelope, golden eagles, PRAIRIE DOGS, and horned larks.

Llanos (yah-nos), or grassy plains, occur in the midst of the desert in basins of southern New Mexico, Texas, Arizona, and northern Chihuahua, Mexico, where drainage is poor and soils are flooded seasonally. These tussocky grasslands often consist of pure stands of big galleta (*Hilaria mutica*), a tall bunchgrass that thrives in fine-textured, salty soils. The grasslands are particularly striking in northern Chihuahua, where they cover thousands of acres, surrounded by desert.

See also COLORADO PLATEAU, PRAIRIE DOG.

> **Between the end of the Civil War and the late 1880s, millions of domestic animals were trailed into the Southwest, denuding millions of acres of grasslands.**

IRONWOOD Ironwood (*Olneya tesota*), a short, spiny tree of the Sonoran Desert, has wood so heavy that it sinks in water. Called *palo de hierro* (Spanish for "wood of iron"), ironwood weighs 78.4 pounds per cubic foot and is one of our heaviest native woods—only lead-wood (*Krugiodendron ferrum*), from southern Florida, is heavier. Ironwood is so hard that desert dwellers once used it for arrow points. The Seri Indians and other residents of southern Arizona and northern Mexico carve the fine-grained, dense wood into graceful sculptures of desert animals. Unfortunately, cutting trees to provide wood for carving and to heat homes and fire cookstoves is decimating northern Mexico's old-growth (400- to 700-year-old) ironwood trees.

Ironwood bursts into bloom in late May or early June, its spreading, rounded crown covered with violet clusters of wisterialike flowers. Seen against the morning sun, the tree glows with a blue-gray or lavender light, like a puff of smoke rising from a desert wash. The fragrant and nectar-filled flowers attract hundreds of female DIGGER BEES, foraging for pollen and nectar to stock their brood chambers. Cylindrical pealike pods, each bearing shiny, brown beanlike seeds, grow after the flowers fade and are avidly eaten by desert animals. Rock squirrels, normally ground-dwellers, climb into the trees to pick the pods. Unpicked pods eventually dry and drop to the ground, seeds and all, where javelinas (small wild boars), WOODRATS, and pocket mice graze them. People also gather them; roasted ironwood seeds taste like peanuts.

Like many desert trees, ironwood sprouts its tiny leaves only when soils are moist, shedding them in the driest months of late spring and early summer to save water.

Ironwood grows in sandy and gravelly washes, often with MESQUITE and PALOVERDE, fellow members of the pea family, below 2,500 feet in the Sonoran Desert of southern Arizona, southeastern California, and north-western Mexico.

JOJOBA Jojoba (*Simmondsia chinensis*), a shrub of the Sonoran Desert, is a valuable desert crop: its brown, acornlike nuts contain a high-quality liquid wax that is a promising substitute for the oil from endangered sperm whales. The unsaturated wax is a familiar ingredient in hair conditioners, lotions, and cosmetics. It also has potential uses in medicines, lubricants, as a wax for cars, and, since it does not spoil like other oils, in cooking. Jojoba (pronounced "ho-HO-bah") cultivars recently developed are now being planted by farmers to substitute for wild gathering.

Jojoba shrubs, 2- to 3-feet tall, are easily recognized by their ever-green, leathery, oval leaves, which grow in pairs. The flowers are yellow-green and inconspicuous; male and female flowers grow on separate shrubs. The dark brown nuts hang down from the stems and are reputed to taste rather like bitter filberts. Still, the oily nuts were an important food of native desert dwellers and early settlers. Ground squirrels and rock squirrels gather them avidly.

Jojoba shrubs are common on arid, rocky slopes below 5,000 feet in the Sonoran Desert of central and southern Arizona, southeastern California, and northern Mexico.

JOSHUA TREE Tall, many-branched Joshua trees (*Yucca brevifolia*) are the largest of the YUCCAS, members of the lily family with stiff, stiletto-like evergreen leaves and stalks of waxy white flowers. Big Joshua trees grow to 35 feet tall, with a single trunk and branches spreading outward as much as 15 feet from the trunk. They are among the oldest plants in the desert; some are over 1,000 years old.

Forests of these queerly shaped trees, which look like giant human figures with waving arms, are characteristic of the Mojave Desert, just as SAGUARO cacti are of the Sonoran Desert. Joshua tree forests grow where annual rainfall averages 8 to 10 inches in southern California, southern

Joshua tree

Nevada, southwestern Utah, and northwestern Arizona. In west-central Arizona, Joshua trees grow with saguaros where the Sonoran and Mojave deserts overlap. Joshua Tree National Monument in southern California was established to protect a Joshua tree forest.

Joshua trees put out their first branches when they reach 10 feet tall, and like saguaros, grow slowly. Their foot-long leaves are covered with a waxy cuticle to retard evaporation, and tipped by stiff spines to discourage grazers (hence another common name, "dagger trees"). ORIOLES weave their nest pouches in the shelter of Joshua tree leaf rosettes, and WOODRATS climb the stems to harvest the leaves for food and midden-building materials. In years of good winter rainfall, each branch sprouts a flower stalk laden with dense clusters of small, waxy, bell-shaped, greenish-yellow flowers. The masses of flowers, appearing between February and April, make a beautiful counterpoint to the colorful DESERT ANNUAL WILDFLOWERS. Each flower only opens for one night and is pollinated by a female YUCCA MOTH, which lays its eggs in the ovary. The moth larvae feed on the fruit and seeds, leaving some to mature into new Joshua trees. The flowers, which smell dank and musty, also attract nectar-feeding BATS.

Joshua trees are the largest of the yuccas, growing to 35 feet tall. They are among the oldest plants in the desert; some are over 1,000 years old.

Mormon settlers named Joshua trees for their resemblance to the supplicating posture of the Biblical Joshua. Kawaiisu Indians, however, say that Joshua trees are enemies who were pursuing Coyote, the trickster figure in Southwest Indian tales, and his brother. The pursuers were eventually turned into Joshua trees; Coyote and his brother found their way eastward to the end of the world, where they turned into two stones. When the stones move, say the Kawaiisu, they cause earthquakes.

See also YUCCA, YUCCA MOTH.

JUNIPER Junipers (*Juniperus* species) are the most common small trees and shrubs in the Southwest. Of five tree-sized Southwestern junipers, oneseed (*J. monosperma*), a multi-stemmed juniper, and Utah juniper (*J. osteosperma*), named for the state where it is most common, are the two most abundant species. Cedar Breaks National Monument and the town of Cedar City in southern Utah are both named for Utah juniper (junipers are often erroneously called cedars). Alligator juniper (*J. deppeana*), the giant of Southwest junipers, grows in the southern Southwest and got its name from its checkered, alligatorlike bark. Centuries-old alligator junipers reach 50 feet tall, with stout trunks as thick as 10 feet in diameter.

Junipers grow in woodlands of widespread trees, often with equally scrubby PIÑON PINES, their closest associate, at lower tree line on the MESAS, foothills, and plains, in the most arid environments of all conifers. In order for junipers to survive with low average annual precipitation and frequent months of drought, their leaves, which they retain year-round, are reduced to tiny, waxy scales covering their twigs and small branches. Even their fruits, fleshy cones with one or several seeds inside, are coated with water-retaining wax.

Slow-growing, rot-resistant, and pleasantly fragrant, junipers' twisted wood—often the only wood for miles—is used for everything from fence-posts to firewood. Navajos still use juniper logs to construct traditional hogans, or eight-sided houses; prayer sticks; and weaving tools. Spicy juniper smoke is widely used in medicine and in traditional Southwest Native American ceremonies.

See also PIÑON-JUNIPER, WOODRAT.

LECHUGUILLA Lechuguilla, a small, narrow-leaved agave, is endemic to the Chihuahuan Desert of southwest Texas, southern New Mexico, and northern Mexico. (It is especially common around Big Bend National Park in southwest Texas.) Lechuguilla, diminutive for Spanish *lechuga*, "lettuce," is a most inappropriate name for this plant. Its close-packed, rigid, and slightly curving leaves are not lettucelike: each is stiff and termi-nated by a finger-length needle strong enough to pierce a car tire. Another common name, "shin dagger," is more apt.

Like all agaves, lechuguilla blooms but once in its life, sending up a tall, slender flower stalk, then dies. But lechuguilla depends on vegetative reproduction more than most agaves. New plants bud from the parents' roots whether the parent blooms or not, forming shin-high, impenetrable thickets on desert slopes.

Lechuguilla sap contains poisonous compounds, including a strong muscle contractor. The Tarahumara of Mexico's Sierra Madre use lechu-guilla sap to poison their arrows and in water to kill fish.

See also AGAVE.

LICHEN   Neither plants nor animals, lichens are composed of fungi and algae: the FUNGUS, the visible portion of the lichen, provides a home and shelter for the alga; the alga, able to photosynthesize, feeds the fungus. This pairing has been seen as a cooperative venture, but some scientists now believe that the fungus "captures" the alga. Crucial soil builders, lichens fix nitrogen for plant growth, break up rocks, and decompose dead wood, making them vital to desert ecosystems, where they grow abundantly on the soil surface and, in foggy locations, on plants. Their varying colors furnish dyes for Southwest rug weavers.

Lichens come in three forms: crustose, foliose, and fruticose. Crustose lichens are more common in the deserts and other moisture-limited sites; foliose and fruticose types are more common in the moist, shady forests.

Crustose, the common lichens on rocks, are so closely attached to the rock that prying them off inevitably harms them. Brilliant lemon-yellow *Acarospora chlorophana* is a common crustose lichen of Southwest deserts. It often paints whole rocky hillsides and cliff faces with its eye-catching color, sometimes along with *Xanthoria elegans*, a fluorescent-orange crustose lichen.

Foliose lichens, common on the surface of forest soils, have lobed, almost leaflike margins. The wavy upper surface of *Peltigera maleacea*, a common foliose lichen, turns deep green when wet, like a liverwort. It grows on the soil surface in open areas of mountain conifer stands from the Douglas fir forests upward.

Fruticose lichens, the most conspicuous of the three kinds, grow large, hairy bodies often mistaken for dry mosses. "Spanish moss," the wispy, gray "moss" that drapes trees in the humid Southeast, is the name used for both a fruticose lichen and a plant related to pineapple. Two Spanish moss–type lichens are common in Southwestern forests. *Pseudevernia intensa*, a dark-gray lichen, often completely covers the dead branches of spruce and fir trees. *Usnea arizonica*, endemic to southern California and the Southwest, looks like a mound of pale green hair.

Because lichens succumb readily to air pollution, they provide an early warning for the deterioration of entire ecosystems. Long before acid rain was recognized as a killer of forests in Europe, the forest lichens began dying, and with them, fungi essential to the trees' growth.

See also FUNGUS, MICROBIOTIC CRUST.

MAPLE The Southwest's sugar maple, bigtooth maple (*Acer grandi-dentatum*), has thin, sweetish sap that is sometimes tapped for maple sugar. A single-stemmed tree that can grow 50 feet in height, with a short trunk, spreading, rounded crown, and five-lobed leaves that turn brilliant orange or scarlet in autumn, the bigtooth maple even looks like a small sugar maple. The two trees are, in fact, closely related. Some botanists believe that the two species may have split as recently as the end of the last glacial era, less than 15,000 years ago, when deciduous forest retreated from the West as the climate grew warmer and drier. On the eastern edge of the bigtooth maple's range in west Texas, its leaves are intermediate between sugar maple and typical bigtooth leaves.

Also called canyon maple because it grows most commonly in canyons, bigtooth maple is found between 4,000 and 8,000 feet, the upper limit of the PONDEROSA PINE forests, from Mexico north to extreme south-eastern Idaho, west to California, and east to southwest Texas.

The other Southwest maple, Rocky Mountain maple (*A. glabrum*), is the northernmost North American maple species, growing from Arizona and New Mexico's mountains north to Alaska and western Canada. It forms a multistemmed tall shrub in Southwest forest understories. Rocky Mountain maple's numerous three-lobed leaves turn lemon yellow to bright red-orange in the fall.

See also ASPEN.

MARIPOSA AND SEGO LILIES Mariposa and sego lilies' scientific name, *Calochortus*, means "beautiful grass." Their tuliplike flowers, composed of three satiny petals, each with a nectary at the base, are carried atop slender stems bearing a few narrow, grasslike leaves. These graceful lilies survive the Southwest's long dry periods as bulbs buried deep in the soil, and bloom only in years of ample winter and spring moisture. In extremely dry years, the plants remain dormant, not sprouting as much as one slender leaf.

Mariposa and sego lilies grow from the Mojave and Sonoran deserts in the southern Southwest to the SAGEBRUSH shrublands and PONDEROSA PINE savannas of the COLORADO PLATEAU and the Great Basin. Arizona state law makes it illegal to collect mariposa and sego lilies, as well as all other wild lilies or cacti.

Of the several *Calochortus* that grow in the hot deserts of the southern

Southwest, desert mariposa (*C. kennedyi*) is most common. When winter rains are ample, the vermilion, orange, or brilliant yellow flowers of the desert mariposa dot the desert floors and PIÑON-JUNIPER woodlands from March to May. The most common *Calochortus* of the sagebrush country in the northern Southwest is sego lily (*C. nuttallii*), the state flower of Utah. Yellow tinges its satin-white petals, and a purple crescent marks each at its base. Shoshonean people taught the Mormons to dig and eat the thin-skinned, walnut-sized bulbs ("sego" is the Shoshonean name). The sweet and nutritious bulbs are full of starch—like potatoes—and proved important food during the Mormons' first years in Utah. Now, bears emerging from hibernation are the primary consumers of sego lily bulbs, sometimes leaving meadows pockmarked with holes.

Mariposa and sego lilies

MESQUITE Mesquites (*Prosopis* species), small, spreading trees with edible, beanlike pods, once had a limited range in the Southwest, confined to valley and ARROYO bottoms and floodplains, forming dense woodlands, or bosques (pronounced BOHS-kays). Now these thorny small trees or large shrubs dominate over 130,000 square miles of deserts and semidesert GRASSLANDS in the southern Southwest, Texas, and Mexico—equal to half the size of the state of Texas.

Mesquites began expanding their range in the 1680s when Padre Eusebio Kino, a Spanish missionary, introduced *criollos*, free-ranging Spanish cattle, encouraging widespread ranching in the Southwest. Cattle and horses readily graze the mesquite's sweet, beanlike pods, but do not digest its stony seeds. As many as 1,600 germinable mesquite seeds have been found in a single cow chip. Because the seeds germinate twice as well after passing through an ungulate's digestive system, herds of domestic stock spread these tough, well-armored trees throughout the Southwest and west Texas. Further, domestic stock eliminated grasses—the competition to mesquite on the drier uplands.

Millions of cattle, horses, and sheep were trailed into the Southwest after the Civil War; in the Arizona Territory alone, cattle herds swelled from 35,000 in 1880 to well over 720,000 in 1891. The huge herds of domestic stock soon wiped out the grasses and, browsing on whatever they could find, left billions of mesquite seeds behind them, ready to take over. While mesquite was hitching a ride up into the grasslands with cattle, valley-bottom bosques were being clear-cut. A mining boom in the 1880s in the mountains of Arizona and New Mexico consumed thousands of acres of OAK, JUNIPER, and mesquite woodlands for ore processing. The elimination of the grass cover and cutting of the valley-bottom bosques later caused widespread flash flooding and arroyo downcutting.

Mesquites once had a limited range in the Southwest. Now the tree dominates over 130,000 square miles of deserts and semi-desert grasslands.

Three kinds of mesquites grow in the Southwest: honey (*P. glandulosa*), velvet (*P. velutina*), and screwbean (*P. pubescens*). The first two are the most widely distributed. Honey mesquite, a large shrub or small, multitrunked tree growing no taller than 20 feet, covers much of the Chihuahuan and Mojave desert areas. Velvet mesquite, a single-trunked, spreading tree that reaches 40 feet tall, is the largest of the three, and is found throughout the Sonoran Desert. Screwbean, also called *tornillo*, or "little screw," for its tightly corkscrewing pods, is scattered throughout the southern Southwest and northern Mexico, mostly along streams or valley bottoms.

Mesquites' numerous branches are armed with up to inch-long, stout spines; the plants form dense, well-nigh impenetrable thickets. Mesquites' extraordinarily deep and heavily branched root systems—reaching as far as 60 feet down—allow them to survive extreme droughts and to outcompete other, more shallowly rooted plants, especially grasses. Because cattle only browse on mesquites when they have grazed out the more favored grasses and herbs, the trees increase with heavy livestock grazing. However, their thorny tangle of branches often protects remnant grasses and other plants from being completely grazed out. In sandy soils, especially those eroded by overgrazing, low, spreading honey mesquites form hummocky dune fields. Each mesquite traps windblown soil and continues to grow within its dune, despite often being buried up to the tips of its thick, zigzagging branches.

Contrary to what many ranchers think, mesquites are not worthless.

Rather, these small, thorny trees harbor a myriad of lives. In spring, mesquites sprout small, pinnately compound leaves and an abundance of catkinlike clusters of fragrant, yellow flowers, attracting nectar feeders such as solitary BEES, TARANTULA HAWKS, beetles, HUMMINGBIRDS, flycatchers, and honeybees. (Mesquite honey brings top dollar for its delicate flavor.) Praying mantises, crab spiders, and assassin bugs, colored like the flowers or foliage for camouflage, congregate to feed on the nectar feeders. At least a dozen animal species and nearly a hundred bird species use mesquite bosques.

Mesquites' stone-hard seeds are embedded in sweet, string-beanlike pods that do not split open, forcing consumers to eat seeds and all. Rich in sugar, minerals, and fiber, the pods are sought after for food. People harvest the pods and grind them to a meal called *pinole*, the base for a beverage, an intoxicating drink, a mushlike cereal, and dried cakes. Mesquite pods were a staple food of many desert-dwelling people, including the Tohono O'odham (Papago), Pima, and Seri Indians of the Sonoran Desert. The Seri of Sonora, Mexico, had different names for eight stages of mesquite pod development. Many other desert dwellers eat the pods, especially WOODRATS, KANGAROO RATS, QUAIL, and DOVES.

Like other legumes, members of the pea family, mesquites fix nitrogen, a nutrient vital to plant growth. Given a boost by mesquite fertilizer, grasses and other plants growing in the shade of mesquites are several times as big as those growing nearby.

See also ARROYO, GRASSLANDS.

MISTLETOE Mistletoe (*Phoradendron* species), the familiar Christmas "kissing ball," is one of the few truly parasitic plants. Instead of producing its own food, mistletoe feeds on trees. It sprouts on a tree branch, grows a root into the tree's vascular system, and draws its food and water solely from the tree. Dense mistletoe growth weakens, and may even kill, its host. Many different species of mistletoe grow in the Southwest, forming conspicuous masses of many-branched, slender stems in the upper limbs of deciduous trees of the deserts, plains, and foothills. Different mistletoe species parasitize different tree species. Those that feed on desert trees, such as MESQUITE, IRONWOOD, PALOVERDE, and acacia, tend to be leafless in order to conserve water. However, other mistletoe sprout leaves. A mistletoe parasitic on COTTONWOOD (*P. tomentosum* spp. *macrophyllum*) is widely used for Christmas decorations because of its large gray-green leaves and glistening white berries.

Although mistletoe foliage is toxic to most plant eaters, great purple hairstreak BUTTERFLY caterpillars consume the foliage voraciously with no ill effects. The bright coral-pink berries of the various kinds of mistletoe that parasitize desert trees constitute the major winter food of many birds; PHAINOPEPLAS and robins consume great quantities. (In fact, phainopeplas are so dependent on mistletoe berries that if the crop is scant, they do not breed the following spring.) Mistletoe, in turn, depends on avian consumers to find new hosts. The hard seeds pass through the bird's gut undigested and are deposited in a pat of fertilizer—bird scat—on a branch.

NIGHT-BLOOMING CEREUS

For most of the year, night-blooming cereus (*Peniocereus greggii*), a cactus, looks like a few sprawling, dead sticks leaning on CREOSOTE BUSH or other desert shrubs. But in late June and early July, fat buds swell on the plant's skinny, lead-colored stems. When night falls, the buds open, revealing beautifully exotic and fragrant cactus flowers. The huge, ghostly white blossoms cast a sweet perfume that attracts moths and other night-flying pollinators. Called *reina-de-la-noche*, or "queen of the night," in Mexico, the flowers unfold in the early evening and last only one night, wilting soon after sunrise.

Night-blooming cereus

Lacking succulent stems, this odd cactus stores moisture and food in a beetlike root weighing from 5 to 85 pounds. Although endangered by collectors, night-blooming cereus still blooms in the Sonoran and Chihuahuan deserts of southern and central Arizona, southern New Mexico, south Texas, and Mexico.

See also CACTUS.

OAK

Oaks (*Quercus* species), called *robles* or *encinas* in Spanish, dominate zones of woodland or shrubby thickets throughout the Southwest.

The most widespread of Southwestern oaks is Gambel oak (*Q. gambelii*), which ranges from the COLORADO PLATEAU and the southern Rockies to northern Utah, extreme southwestern Wyoming, and northwestern Colorado. Shrubby thickets dominated by Gambel oak are called chaparral for the leather *chaps* (pronounced "shaps") worn by horse riders to protect their legs from the tough brush.

Gambel oak is the only Southwestern oak with deciduous, classically oak-shaped leaves. The deeply lobed leaves turn reddish brown in autumn and often cling to the branches all winter, rattling like agitated rattlesnakes in winter winds. In spring, whole hillsides blush purple-brown, colored by swelling Gambel oak buds. The inch-long oval acorns are the sweetest produced by the Southwestern oaks. Ground into meal and leached of the tannic acid that makes them bitter, Gambel oak acorns make fine mush, soup, bread, and pancakes, especially when combined with cornmeal. In the montane oak woodlands of the southern Southwest, Gambel oak grows as a small tree.

In the warm-winter areas of the southern Southwest, several species of taller evergreen oaks from Mexico dominate. Evergreen Emory oak (*Q. emoryi*), a medium-sized spreading tree with a straight trunk, rounded crown, and shiny, yellow-green leaves, is the most common oak in these savannalike woods, but it shares dominance with nearly fifteen other evergreen oaks, and with long-needled pines.

Oak woodlands and chaparral feed and shelter a wide variety of wildlife. Birds such as acorn woodpeckers, band-tailed pigeons, and wild turkeys depend on the fatty and nutritious acorns to sustain them through the winter, as do animals from tiny acorn borers to BEARS. Oak leaves are browsed by Colorado hairstreak BUTTERFLY caterpillars, deer, desert BIGHORNS, elk, and porcupines. Round-tailed HORNED LIZARDS and cougars alike hunt in oak woodlands, as do insect-eating birds like warblers, flycatchers, and HUMMINGBIRDS, attracted by the unusual variety of insects. The diverse oak woodlands of the southern Southwest are also home to Mexican animals like elegant trogons, magnificent HUMMINGBIRDS, and COATIS.

OCOTILLO Ocotillo (*Fouquieria splendens*), a shrub of the hot deserts, is also called "coachwhip" for its bare, 8- to 15-foot-long stems. But within 48 hours after a rain, the slender, thorny branches, now

Ocotillo

sprouting a fuzzy covering of small, green leaves, no longer look like coachwhips. While the soil is moist, the plant transpires and photosynthesizes with abandon; as soon as the soil dries out, ocotillo sheds the leaves until the next rain. The remaining green stems, slightly succulent and covered with a thick, water-resistant cuticle, photosynthesize enough to keep the ocotillo alive.

Each late spring, dense spikes of fiery-red, tubular blossoms flame at the end of ocotillo's long stems, attracting HUMMINGBIRDS and other nectar feeders. The Tohono O'odham (Papago) of the Sonoran Desert in southern Arizona ate the sweet flowers like candy and rubbed the yellow flower stems on their cheeks for rouge.

Because wood is scarce in the desert, ocotillo's relatively straight, long, and tough stems furnish building material. Traditional houses are still constructed of mud-plastered ocotillo limbs, and the thorny cut stems, when planted close together, form impenetrable fences and corrals, sometimes taking root and growing.

Ocotillo grows in the Sonoran, Mojave, and Chihuahuan deserts and adjacent dry, rocky desert mountainsides to 6,000 feet, from western Texas to southern California and south into Mexico. It is most abundant on open, stony slopes above 3,300 feet elevation along the upper edge of deserts and in adjacent hills.

The ocotillo family is one of the few families of flowering plants confined to the desert. Ocotillo is the most northern of the eleven mainly Mexican species. The most bizarre-looking plant in the family is definitely the boojum tree (*F. columnaria*) of Baja California, named by a startled explorer in the early 1900s after the mythical being in Lewis Carroll's *The Hunting of the Snark*. Boojums, shaped like giant, upside-down, gray carrots, grow to nearly 30 feet high; their succulent trunk, 2 to 3 feet in diameter at the base, tapers to 3 to 5 inches across at the top, and is studded with short, thorny branches.

PAINTBRUSH Paintbrush (*Castilleja* species) derives its name from the colorful bracts that make the upper part of the plant look as if it had been dipped into vivid magenta, red, orange, or yellow paint. The flowers are small, green, and often hidden under the brightly colored bracts, which serve to attract nectar feeders such as BUTTERFLIES and HUMMINGBIRDS to pollinate the flowers. Although their leafy stems are green and produce food, paintbrushes are partial parasites. Their roots tap into nearby plant roots, usually SAGEBRUSH or grasses, to suck food and moisture from the host. Their genus name honors the Spanish botanist Domingo Castillejo, and is usually pronounced "cas-til-LAY-yah."

> **Paintbrush derives its name from the colorful bracts that make the plant look as if it had been dipped into vivid magenta, red, orange, or yellow paint.**

Paintbrush flowers are sometimes eaten; the plants are also used to make tea for treating water retention and kidney disorders. However, paintbrushes can be toxic, since they accumulate selenium and other metals from soils bearing those minerals.

Many species of paintbrush grow in the northern Southwest, from SAGEBRUSH shrublands to alpine areas in the mountains. Desert paintbrush (*C. chromosa*), with brilliant orange or red bracts and stems up to 16 inches tall, is among the most common dryland paintbrush. It blooms from April at the lower elevations to August at mid-elevations, usually in sagebrush shrublands, from northern Arizona, northwestern New Mexico, and western Colorado north to Idaho and eastern Oregon. One of the few yellow paintbrushes, sulfur paintbrush (*C. sulphurea*), blooms June to September in moist subalpine to alpine meadows and slopes from Utah and northern New Mexico north to southern Alberta, Canada.

PALM California fan palm, or Washingtonia (*Washingtonia filifera*), named for President George Washington, grows 20 to 80 feet tall and is the largest palm native to the continental United States. Fan palms grow in oases—dense groves around permanent springs or seeps, usually where faults force groundwater to the surface—in southwestern Arizona, through the Salton Sea Basin in southern California, and northern Baja California and Sonora, Mexico. Ironically, Palm Springs, California, named for its once-extensive fan palm oases, is losing the groves because of development and groundwater pumping for lawns and golf courses.

The widely scattered locations of natural fan palm groves reflects the shallow-rooted tree's need for permanent surface water and the wandering habits of the consumers of its seeds. Many desert dwellers—from birds to BATS to COYOTES, and at one time, humans—avidly consume fan palm's small, sweet, datelike seeds. Fan palms depend on such wandering consumers to transport their seeds the many miles between rare desert springs, then deposit the germinable seeds in a pat of fertilizer, perhaps founding a new fan palm grove.

Fan palm groves—verdant islands of shade, water, and food in the hot southern deserts—were vital to early desert-dwelling humans. People once thatched roofs with the leaves and split them into fiber for hats, cloth, sandals, baskets; the buds, flowers, and fruit furnished food. Anthropologists believe that palms were as important to the desert Cahuilla of southern California as bison were to the Plains tribes. Fan palm groves still shelter an abundance of birds, some eighty species, and animals. Palm borers, boring beetles, spend years eating their way through the pithy trunks, while yellow jackets feed on the sweet flowers and fruit. ORIOLES weave their nests under the large, fanlike leaves, and bats roost in the cool shade of the dense skirts of dead leaves. WOODRATS and other rodents forage for fallen fruit.

Fan palm oases depend on frequent ground fire for survival. Such fires recycle nutrients that otherwise take centuries to decay in the dry climate; control the insects that feed on the stocky palms; prepare a seedbed for reproduction; and kill competitors such as SALTCEDAR and other water-loving species. Although the palms' long skirts of dry fronds burn easily in ground fires, their vascular tissue, the cells that carry food and water, is scattered in bundles throughout the trunk tissue, protected from the heat of fire. After ground fires, fan palms produce twice as much fruit and grow more quickly. People once burned palm oases frequently.

PALOVERDE Paloverde trees—small, spiny trees of the Sonoran Desert—are named for their green, photosynthesizing trunks, branches, and twigs. (*paloverde* means "green wood" in Spanish.) In order to survive in the hot, lowland Sonoran Desert, paloverdes save water by remaining leafless most of the year, producing their food in the chlorophyllous tissue that tints their branches and trunk green. In especially dry years, paloverdes shed twigs and sometimes even whole branches for the same reason that other deciduous trees shed their leaves: to save water and survive long periods of drought (winter drought in the case of other deciduous trees).

After rains, paloverdes do sprout small, pinnately compound leaves with minute leaflets, but these provide less total area for photosynthesis than do the stems and branches. The tiny leaflets, shed as soon as the soil dries, are full of nitrogen fixed by the bacteria that live in paloverde roots. Paloverde leaflets, and those of other legume family trees such as IRON-WOOD, acacias, and MESQUITES, fertilize nitrogen-deficient desert soils when they decay.

In April and May, after the winter rains, paloverdes burst into bloom; their thousands of tiny yellow flowers wreathe the tree in yellow fog. The five-petaled flowers attract nectar-seeking beetles, flies, and both social and solitary BEES. Predacious insects such as ambush bugs and crab spiders, camouflaged the exact shade of yellow of the blossoms, in turn arrive to prey on the nectar feeders.

Once pollinated, paloverde flowers develop into small, flat, beanlike seedpods, each containing one to eight seeds. In a good year, paloverdes produce millions of seeds, a bumper crop relished by desert seed eaters: larvae of bruchid beetles, mice, WOODRATS, and other rodents. Surviving seeds germinate only in years with sufficient spring moisture, however, and even then the thousands of tender little seedlings rarely make it into trees. Hordes of rodents and rabbits mow down the succulent seedlings, or they die in the early summer drought. Since paloverdes live 300 or 400 years, a high seedling survival rate is not necessary.

Two species of paloverde are native to the Southwest: foothill, or yellow paloverde (*Cercidium microphyllum*), and blue paloverde (*C. florida*). Foothill paloverdes are common "nurse trees" for SAGUARO cactus seedlings, sheltering them during their first half-century from burning sun and winter frost. Blue paloverde is the state tree of Arizona. Another paloverde, Mexican paloverde (*Parkinsonia aculeata*), reaches the Southwest only in extreme southwestern Arizona, but is widely planted as an ornamental.

See also DIGGER BEE, SAGUARO.

PENSTEMON OR BEARDTONGUE Penstemons, or beardtongues

(*Penstemon* species), a group of showy, snapdragonlike flowers, are named for their hairy fifth stamen (*pent* means "five" in Greek), which curves over the lip of the tubular flower like a golden tongue. All penstemon flowers are tubular, with a nectary at their base. But they fall into two groups, each designed to accommodate their major pollinators. One group produces brilliant red or scarlet, narrowly tubular flowers that just fit HUMMINGBIRDS' needlelike bills. The other group, with swollen blue, violet-blue, or pink flowers and a broad, lobed landing platform, are designed for the chubby bodies of BEES.

Some two dozen species of penstemons of all sizes grow in the Southwest, from deserts to mountaintops. The largest is Palmer's penstemon (*P. palmeri*). Its multistemmed, 5- to 6-foot-tall stalks bloom profusely with fragrant, pale-pink or lavender flowers from May to July in SAGEBRUSH shrublands and PIÑON-JUNIPER or PONDEROSA PINE woodlands, from southeastern Arizona to central New Mexico and southern Utah. Aptly named firecracker penstemon (*P. eatoni*) and scarlet buglar (*P. barbatus*) are common red penstemons. Scarlet buglar grows in OAK and piñon-juniper woodlands and ponderosa pine forests up to 10,000 feet in elevation throughout the Southwest, from southern Colorado and Utah to central Mexico. Firecracker penstemon, with spikes of red tubular flowers as bright as exploding firecrackers, grows from the Sonoran Desert of southern Arizona and California to the dry woodlands of the COLORADO PLATEAU in Utah and southwestern Colorado. Tiny mat penstemon (*P. linarioides*), a Southwest endemic, grows only a foot tall, with crowded spikes of purple flowers above narrow, needlelike leaves. Mat penstemon blooms on the North and South rims of the GRAND CANYON.

PIÑON-JUNIPER Both pioneers of the lower tree line, piñons and junipers are so closely associated in the Southwest that the two short, shrubby conifers are spoken of in one breath: "piñon-junipers." The two trees form characteristic woodlands, patterning the pale soil of MESAS, foothills, and lower mountains with dark polka dots. Piñon-juniper woodlands cover more than 40,000 square miles of the Southwest and the Great Basin—equal to a third of the state of New Mexico—extending west as far as eastern California, east to Colorado's Front Range and west Texas, north to southern Idaho and Wyoming, and south to northern Mexico.

A grassy and shrubby understory grows under the open canopy of piñons and junipers, including desert species such as grama grasses, CACTI, and YUCCAS at the lowest elevations, where junipers predominate. Bluestem grasses, RABBITBRUSH, SAGEBRUSH, OAKS, and other shrubs grow at higher elevations, where piñons take over. The abundant forage, browse, and cover attracts a wide variety of wildlife, including flocks of PIÑON JAYS and wild turkeys—which nest and roost in the trees—deer, and cougars—which hunt the deer.

But the real feast in piñon-juniper woodlands comes every three to seven autumns, when the piñons produce a bumper crop of 2-inch-long, egg-shaped cones holding fat, delicious seeds. Wildlife and humans converge on the woodlands to collect the nutritious, oily nuts. People have eaten them since 4,000 B.C.; Navajo and Pueblo traditions both identify piñon nuts as food of their ancestors. Collecting and selling the nuts remains an important social and economic event for many Southwesterners—in bumper years, Navajos alone collect as much as a million pounds.

Waxy juniper "berries"—the fleshy cones—are also important food for some kinds of wildlife. Thousands of bluebirds winter in juniper and piñon-juniper woodlands, dependent on the fleshy cones for food. Rodents like WOODRATS gather and cache juniper cones, winter black BEAR scats are often packed with juniper berries. People also eat juniper berries, using them to flavor meat, drying and grinding them to form cakes, or using them to flavor gin. Navajo children treasure juniper berries for "ghost beads," believing that they ward off the night-stalking ghosts of dead people.

Historic overgrazing and prevention of natural fires have changed piñon-juniper woodlands, increasing tree density and subsequently decreasing the native grass understory. Junipers have also spread downhill into adjacent shrublands and GRASSLANDS. In an attempt to improve forage for livestock and game animals, millions of acres of piñon-juniper overstory were cleared in the 1950s by "chaining," dragging battleship anchor chains between two bulldozers, or by spraying with herbicides. Between 1950 and 1964 alone, three million acres of piñon-juniper woodland were chained. Now the wisdom of such drastic treatments is in question: forage did not increase permanently, nor did numbers of game animals, and the effects on other woodland inhabitants are unknown. Valuable nut crops and firewood sources were lost. Worse still, heavy equipment damaged the fragile soil, destroying the MICROBIOTIC CRUST of fungi and bacteria in the top layer that naturally prevents soil erosion and helps water infiltrate the soil.

See also JUNIPER, PIÑON PINE, PIÑON AND OTHER JAYS, WOODRAT.

PIÑON PINE
Piñon pines, now a popular Southwest symbol, have long been appreciated by Southwesterners. Their dense, resinous wood burns hot and fragrantly, and still perfumes the winter air of Southwestern towns as it has since early Southwesterners first settled in pueblos and cliff dwellings. Piñon nuts are a staple of traditional Native American and Hispanic cooking and are now finding new popularity as the delicious pine nuts of gourmet recipes. And the slow-growing, twisted shapes of piñon pines stamp a distinctly Southwestern character on the MESAS and foothills.

Piñons grow at a snail's pace. An 80- to 100-year-old tree may be only

Piñon pine

10 feet tall, with a trunk just 4 or 6 inches in diameter. Growing where yearly precipitation averages only 10 to 20 inches and long droughts punctuate the seasons, piñon pines depend on an enormous root system, which is at least as large as the above-ground part of the plant. Piñon pine taproots stretch down 40 or more feet in deep soils; in shallow soils, lateral roots stretch outward the same distance. These extensive root systems determine the regularly spaced pattern in which piñons grow, each tree an island in its bit of open space.

Common piñon (*Pinus edulis*), which grows on the COLORADO PLATEAU and in the southern Rockies, is the Southwest's most widespread piñon and New Mexico's state tree. The champion common piñon, a tree 67 feet tall and nearly 6 feet in diameter, grows near Cuba, a town in northern New Mexico.

See also JUNIPER, PIÑON AND OTHER JAYS, PIÑON-JUNIPER.

PONDEROSA PINE Ponderosa pine (*Pinus ponderosa*), also called *pino real*, or "true pine," is the most widely distributed and common pine in North America. Named by Scottish botanical explorer David Douglas in 1826 for its heavy, ponderous wood, ponderosa pine is also the most commercially important western pine and the major mountain forest tree of the Southwest. About 500 million board feet of ponderosa lumber is harvested annually from New Mexico and Arizona forests, more than all the other species of trees in those states put together. Because its wood is heavy for a pine but easily worked, ponderosa lumber is the major wood used for millwork, cabinets, and interior trim. Southwestern style furniture is usually made from ponderosa pine.

Ponderosa pine, PIÑON PINE, and DOUGLAS FIR are the main species used for dendrochronology, tree-ring dating, the study of historic climate patterns accomplished by reading the width of tree rings. Reading tree-ring widths from roof beams of CLIFF DWELLINGS and other Indian ruins has allowed archaeologists to date their construction precisely.

Ponderosas are found throughout the West, from Canada south to Mexico, west to California and east to the Dakotas and western Nebraska. In the Southwest, ponderosas grow on dry mountain slopes and mesas from 6,500 feet to 10,000 feet—above PIÑON-JUNIPER but below spruce and mixed conifer forest.

The stately size of ponderosas quickly distinguishes them from other conifers. They are usually the tallest, with straight, thick trunks clad in rusty-orange bark that is split into big plates and smells like vanilla. Four- to 8-inch-long, evergreen needles in groups of three droop gracefully from their branches. Although Southwestern ponderosas top out at about 120 feet with 3- to 4-foot-diameter trunks, in moister climates the trees surpass 200 feet. The champion is 223 feet tall, with a trunk 7.6 feet in diameter, growing in California's Sierra Nevada near Plumas. Large trees live for 500 or more years. For their first 150 years or so, young ponderosas have nearly black bark and were once thought to be a separate species called blackjack pine.

Unlike piñon pines, whose heavy seeds are distributed by animals and birds, ponderosa's seeds are winged, dispersed from the parent tree by the wind. They may float as high as 1,000 feet before coasting to the ground. Although small, the seeds are edible and are readily consumed by TASSEL-EARED SQUIRRELS, chipmunks, THICK-BILLED PARROTS, JAYS, band-tailed pigeons, and finches.

The stately size of ponderosas quickly distinguishes them from other conifers. Southwest ponderosas top out at about 120 feet.

Other tall, straight-trunked, long-needled pines with platey, reddish bark similar to ponderosa grow in the mountains of southeastern Arizona, southwestern New Mexico, and northern Mexico. Arizona pine (*P. ponderosa* var. *arizonica*) has five needles per bundle instead of three, shorter cones, and tops out at 100 feet. Apache pine (*P. engelmannii*), so named because its range coincides with part of the Apache homeland, has very long, slender needles—to 15 inches—which droop, making the branches look like parasols. Chihuahua pine (*P. leiophylla* var. *chihuahuana*), the smallest of the ponderosa look-alikes, grows about 80 feet tall, with 2- to 4-inch needles and small cones on long stalks. All four pines grow together in the CHIRICAHUA MOUNTAINS in southern Arizona.

See also TASSEL-EARED SQUIRREL.

PRICKLY PEAR AND CHOLLA CACTUS
Prickly pear and cholla are shrubby cacti with jointed stems. Both belong in the genus *Opuntia*, which has the greatest number of species and shows more variation than any other cactus group. However, all *Opuntias* share certain characteristics: stems of flattened pads or rounded joints, each of which can root a

new plant; leaves modified into spines; and glochids—tiny, barbed bristles. Like all other CACTI, *Opuntias* conserve water by forgoing leaves, instead manufacturing food in green stem joints. Their fleshy stems also store water, growing plump after rains, shriveling in droughts. (In especially dry years, chollas and prickly pears self-prune by dropping off stem joints.) *Opuntia* species with flattened, more or less oval stem joints, are called prickly pears; those with cylindrical stem joints are cholla.

Prickly pear and cholla arm themselves against grazers with spines and with a layer of toxic calcium oxalate crystals just under the skin, which renders their watery flesh poisonous to most mammals. Only WOODRATS and javelina (wild boars) can metabolize the calcium oxalate without harming their kidneys; the canny rodents also delicately munch their way around the spines. Woodrats and others even borrow the spines for their own protection. Woodrats arm their moundlike houses with cholla joints; cactus WRENS and other birds build nests in the fortified shrubs.

Prickly pears and chollas range from shrubs as tall as an adult person and 15 feet in diameter to sprawling, ground-hugging species less than a foot tall. They bloom in the spring, just after the DESERT ANNUAL wildflowers, sprouting brilliantly colored, 2- to 3-inch-diameter flowers. Flies and BEES burrow into the satiny centers, pollinating the flowers as they search for nectar.

Several dozen species of prickly pear and cholla grow in the

Prickly
pear cactus

Southwest, from the deserts to dry mountain slopes. Prickly pears, named for their fleshy, pear-shaped, and spiny fruit, are more widespread than chollas. Plains prickly pear (*O. polyacantha*), a low, mounding prickly pear, occurs farther north than any other cactus, inhabiting the deserts, plains, and PONDEROSA PINE woodlands from northern Arizona north to Canada. Other prickly pears are found as far east as the Atlantic Ocean and south to the tropics.

The Southwest's most common prickly pear is Engelmann prickly pear (*Opuntia engelmannii*), which grows as tall as 6 feet, with bright, lemon-yellow flowers, in the Sonoran and Chihuahuan desert regions. Low, spreading beavertail cactus (*O. basilaris*) is a prickly pear named for the shape of its flat, gray-green pads. Beavertail pads lack the long, stiff spines of other *Opuntia* species, but have nearly invisible glochids, which fester under the skin of anyone who touches them. Beavertail's spectacular rose-red or magenta flowers punctuate the Mojave and the hottest parts of the Sonoran deserts from March to June. Grizzly-bear cactus (*O. erinacea*), common in the inner gorge of the GRAND CANYON, is named for its 4-inch-long, white spines, the longest of any prickly pear. Its rose-pink flowers bloom at the same time as beavertail cactus.

The fruits of some prickly pears, called *tuna*, turn red or purple when they mature and are prized as an ingredient in soups and stews and for syrup and jelly. Many desert animals search out and consume the juicy fruit, including DESERT TORTOISES, white-winged DOVES, cactus WRENS, and WOODRATS.

Chainfruit cholla (*O. fulgida*), the largest of the chollas, can be as tall as a small tree and is named for the clusters of greenish fruit hanging from its stem joints. Flowers form on the fruit clusters of previous years, extending the chains. Chainfruit cholla is common in the Sonoran Desert around Phoenix and Tucson, Arizona.

Teddybear cholla (*O. bigelovii*), a large, single-stemmed cholla with short, stubby joints, receives its name from its shape and dense cover of golden spines. The spiny joints are so easily detached that they seem to jump off and impale unwary passers, hence its other name: jumping cactus. New plants sprout from fallen joints, forming spiny thickets around the parent. Teddybear cholla grows on the hot, dry mountainsides of the Sonoran Desert throughout central and southern Arizona, west to southern California and Nevada, and south into Mexico.

Christmas cholla or *tesajo* (*O. leptocaulis*), a many-branched, scrawny cholla with pencil-thin stems, is named for its bright red fruits, which lend color to the desert in late fall and winter. Christmas cholla grows from the Sonoran and Chihuahuan deserts east in the plains grasslands as far east as southern Oklahoma, and south to Mexico.

See also CACTUS, WOODRAT.

RABBITBRUSH

The intense golden-colored flower heads of rabbitbrush (*Chrysothamnus nauseosus*), a shrub of the composite family, announce fall in the Southwest's higher elevations. Rabbitbrush blooms at the same time as late purple asters on dry slopes, MESAS, and roadsides in shrublands, GRASSLANDS, and PIÑON-JUNIPER woodlands from western Canada to northern Mexico. Its Spanish name, *chamisa*, simply, "brush," reflects its abundance in the northern Southwest—especially the COLORADO PLATEAU and the upper RIO GRANDE Valley.

> The intense golden-colored flower heads that cluster at the ends of rabbitbrush stems yield a yellow dye used by Navajo rug weavers.

Rabbitbrush is a flat-topped shrub with slender, erect branches and narrow leaves covered with a dense, feltlike layer of white hairs that makes the whole plant look gray-green. Rabbits, deer, elk, and sometimes domestic livestock browse the slender, flexible branches; Hopi use them for basket making. Another common name, rubber rabbitbrush, describes their flexibility and the small amounts of natural rubber that they contain. The small flower heads that cluster at the ends of the stems like a bright, flattop haircut yield a yellow dye used by Navajo rug weavers.

RESURRECTION PLANT

Surprisingly, many kinds of mosses, clubmosses, and ferns grow in Southwest deserts. For much of the year, they are shriveled up and dry, dormant. But with the seasonal rains, they revive, turning green and growing new fronds or branches. Resurrection plant (*Selaginella* species), a clubmoss that forms an almost continuous carpet on steep north- and east-facing slopes in the upper elevations of the Chihuahuan and Sonoran deserts, looks gray, dried up, and dead during the long dry seasons. But within hours after the first seasonal rain, the small mosslike plants resurrect themselves, turning a deep vivid green and coming alive.

SAGEBRUSH Big sagebrush (*Artemisia tridentata*) is as characteristic of the cold-winter Great Basin Desert and Rocky Mountain shrublands as CREOSOTE BUSH is of the warm-winter Sonoran and Chihuahuan deserts. Sagebrush ecosystems have the largest range of any ecosystem in the United States, spreading over half the acreage of the eleven western states, nearly 470,000 square miles, an area larger than the states of Texas, Oklahoma, and New Mexico together.

Sagebrush ecosystems support many species of large and small animals as well as one endemic bird: the sage grouse. Over 70 percent of the adult sage grouse's diet consists of sagebrush leaves and buds. Sage grouse also nest beneath small sagebrush and use clearings in extensive stands for their early-spring mating dances. In these spectacular rituals, dozens of males—the size of small turkeys—gather in the early morning to strut for the watching females. The males puff up their plumage, spread their tail feathers, and inflate bright yellow air sacs in their chests. Successful strutters mate with one or more females.

Common in the northern Southwest, especially in the upper RIO GRANDE Valley, and the COLORADO PLATEAU, big sagebrush is the easiest to recognize of the many Southwest sagebrushes. Its many-branched, erect form grows from 2- to 7-feet tall, with a single trunk at the base, and dull gray bark. On deep, fertile soils, it grows to 15 feet, and can live as long as 150 years.

When crushed or wet, big sagebrush's silvery-hairy, wedge-shaped, three-toothed (*tridentata*) leaves release the plant's trademark pungent odor, giving rise to its Spanish name, *chamisa hediondo*, "stinking brush." The distinct aroma comes from difficult-to-digest volatile oils, which deter browsers, such as deer, BIGHORN SHEEP, cows, and elk. Overgrazing by cattle favors sagebrush; the cattle eat the grasses first, removing competition and allowing sagebrush to grow more densely.

The hairy leaves of sagebrush, which remain on the shrub year-round, also give the plant its distinct gray-green color. A dense coat of hairs insulates the leaves against heat, cold, and dry winds. Retaining the leaves year-round costs sagebrush some water and energy, but allows it to manufacture food for more of the year—important in surviving cold, short-season climates. Sagebrush can photosynthesize when temperatures are near freezing, and its leaves point in all directions, allowing the plant to catch sunlight from many different angles.

People often mistake big sagebrush for the "purple sage" of Zane

Grey's novel, *Riders of the Purple Sage*. However, purple sage is not a sagebrush; it is a shrubby mint of the genus *Salvia*. The "sage" frequently used in cooking is also a *Salvia*, but French tarragon is a sagebrush, an *Artemisia* native to Europe. Sagebrush wood and foliage are full of volatile oils and are used for ceremonial fires by Southwest Native Americans.

SAGUARO Saguaro (sa-WAH-row) cacti (*Carnegia gigantea*), tall, columnar CACTI with upraised arms, are giants of the cactus world. The largest cacti in the United States, saguaros grow to 50 feet tall and weigh several tons.

Saguaros epitomize the adaptations that make cacti so successful at desert life. Their heavy trunks and thick arms consist almost entirely of succulent water-storage tissue, supported by a ring of vertical, woody ribs. Between each rib a pleat allows the stem to swell when the saguaro takes on water, and prevents the waxy outer skin, or cuticle, from tearing. A saguaro can absorb up to 95 percent of its total weight in water, an amount that could equal a ton, expanding for three weeks after rains. The cactus shrinks again as it uses its reservoir in times of drought. An elaborate network of ropelike roots just below the soil surface, that extends out as far as the trunk is tall, harvests water within hours after the sporadic desert rains.

The waxy outer cuticle, thickest on the south side of the plant, protects the saguaro from sunburn and slows evaporation of the precious water inside. The saguaro's vertical ridges are deeper on the south side and shade the plant's surface. Stout spines along the ridge discourage grazers.

Despite their massive form and formidable spines, saguaros are surprisingly fragile. Although they can live for 175 years or more, they succumb to a variety of causes, including a microscopic bacteria. A strong gust of wind may send these giants crashing to the ground because they lack a taproot to anchor their bulk firmly. LIGHTNING during summer thunderstorms often injures or kills these tall cacti. Although saguaro tissues "supercool" instead of freezing into crystalline ice at 32°F, allowing them briefly to withstand temperatures into the 20s, prolonged cold explodes the cells, eventually killing the plant. Finally, tiny bacteria, penetrating the saguaro in wounds caused by woodpeckers excavating nest holes or windstorms tearing off limbs, can reduce a saguaro's interior to mush in a matter of days.

A continuing decline in Arizona's saguaro populations has prompted some researchers to worry about what bedevils the giant cacti. Theories proposed range from increasing frost damage to increased exposure to ultraviolet-B rays as the ozone layer thins. Other researchers argue that saguaros, like other long-lived plants, fluctuate in long population cycles.

Although thousands of tiny saguaro seedlings sprout in a good year, most die of drought, are gutted by cutworm larvae, or are mowed down by hungry rodents and rabbits. To survive, a saguaro must sprout under a sheltering "nurse tree," usually a PALOVERDE or MESQUITE. The tree protects the tender, slow-growing seedling from the searing summer sun and frigid winter air until it has established its spreading root network and has manufactured its waxy, waterproof outer coating. Ironically, acting as a nurse is usually fatal for the sheltering tree. After several decades, the growing saguaro often outcompetes its nurse tree and kills it.

At 25 to 50 years of age, a young saguaro stands 5 or 6 feet high and is ready to reproduce. Diverting about half of its energy to reproduction, it sprouts dozens of knobby buds at the end of its stubby stem. In May and June, these open at night, one by one, revealing spectacular waxy-white flowers. The 3-inch-wide, funnel-shaped flowers remain open until the following afternoon, broadcasting a curious, skunky odor to attract their chosen partner: the long-nosed BAT. Flocks of the nectar-feeding bats migrate north to the Sonoran Desert just as the saguaros begin to bloom and, flying at night, search out the pollen and nectar-laden flowers. The bats hover over the saguaro flower while pushing their entire head into the flower to sip the nectar. Carrying a golden mantle of pollen, the bats fly on to fertilize the sticky stigmas of other flowers. Night-flying moths, other insects, and birds also feed on the flowers.

Saguaro fruits mature in July and burst open, revealing a scarlet pulp, filled with tiny black seeds, that is avidly consumed by

Saguaro
cactus

bats, birds, rodents, moths, other insects, and people. Traditional Tohono O'odham (Papago) and Pima Indians still harvest the fruit, knocking it to the ground with long poles and eating the scarlet pulp either raw or preserved. They ferment the juice into wine to celebrate the coming of the summer rains, a time of plenty.

Gila woodpeckers and gilded flickers excavate nest cavities in the flesh of big saguaros. The cacti seal off the wound with thick scar tissue, thereby preventing the entrance of fatal bacteria. Once vacated by their builders, the cavities provide homes for other desert residents: tiny elf OWLS and other birds, as well as insects and reptiles. But gilded flickers can cut large holes through the skeletal ribs and cause structural damage, which can result in the loss of a branch or branch tip in a windstorm, exposing the succulent flesh to saguaro rot.

Saguaro cacti are the giants of the cactus world. The largest cacti in the U.S., saguaros grow to 50 feet tall and weigh several tons.

Symbolic of the Southwest, saguaros are characteristic of the Sonoran Desert, growing only in its 120,000-square-mile area in southern and central Arizona, extreme southeast California, and northern Sonora, Mexico. Saguaro National Monument near Tucson, Arizona, created to protect an extensive saguaro forest, is a good place to see these tree-sized cacti. Saguaros are the state flower of Arizona.

Two other large cacti grow in the Sonoran Desert: organ pipe cactus (*Lemaireocereus therberi*), named for its upright organ-pipe–like clusters of stems, barely reaches north into the United States and can be seen at Organ Pipe National Monument in southwestern Arizona. Cardón cactus (*Pachycereus pringlei*) of Baja California, Mexico, looks like an extra-massive saguaro with more branches coming from lower on the stem.

See also BAT, CACTUS.

SALTCEDAR Between 1899 and 1915, the U.S. Department of Agriculture introduced eight kinds of saltcedar or tamarisk (*Tamarix* species, named for the Tamaris River in Spain), into the continental United States for use in erosion control, as windbreaks, and as ornamental trees. They succeeded all too well. Dense thickets of these small, extremely fast-growing trees crowd out native plants along streams, rivers, and reservoirs throughout the lower elevations of the West and lower stream levels by sucking up groundwater with their deep roots.

Saltcedar has taken over in many places where overgrazing and ARROYO cutting has weakened riparian communities such as COTTONWOOD, MESQUITE, and streambank willow bosques. Although dense thickets of saltceder do control erosion and provide some wildlife habitat, the tree is usually considered a "weed" in need of removal. But saltcedar's tough stems and ability to resprout following fire or cutting make it very difficult to control.

Saltcedar are graceful trees, rarely taller than 20 feet, with numerous slender, upright or spreading branches and a rounded crown. In the fall, the trees shed their tiny, succulent, and needlelike leaves, along with some of the slender twigs. In spring and summer, masses of pink, minute flowers cover the trees, which attract honeybees and other nectar-seeking insects. The fruits contain thousands of tiny seeds, which, spread by the wind, germinate readily on bare, damp soil.

See also BOSQUE DEL APACHE.

TUMBLEWEED
Tumbleweed (*Salsola kali*), or Russian thistle, a symbol of the West popularized by western movies, is actually an immigrant. It hitched a ride to the northern Great Plains with flax seed that Ukrainian farmers brought from their homes in the Russian steppes. Fast-growing—in a few months, one seed can produce a plant 6 feet high, 15 feet across, and containing 200,000 more seeds—well adapted to arid climates, and with no competitors in the New World, tumbleweed spread rapidly across plowed prairies and overgrazed rangelands. Appropriately, a Hopi name for tumbleweed means "white man's plant."

Common throughout the Southwest, this annual sprouts quickly along roadsides, in cracks in pavement, in abandoned fields and developments, or wherever the soil has been disturbed. Browsers and grazers from DESERT COTTONTAILS to BIGHORN SHEEP and cattle find the young, bright green, succulent plants palatable. But tumbleweed quickly changes into a large, globular mass of tough and prickly stems. The frequent winds tug at dried plants, eventually snapping the plants' single stem and causing them to bound across the landscape, spreading seeds far and wide before the dead plants catch on fences or pile up in the lee of buildings. Pima Indians call tumbleweed *votadam shai*, "the rolling brush."

These ubiquitous weeds are high in calories and can provide

emergency forage for domestic livestock. In the 1970s, a project at the University of Arizona manufactured pressed fireplace logs ("tumblelogs") from the millions of tumbleweed growing on abandoned COTTON fields in southern Arizona. But tumblelogs never hit the commercial market; testers said that the smoke smelled foul, and the cost of harvesting, pressing, packaging, and shipping the logs was too high.

WATERMELON SNOW Watermelon snow is the name for the pinkish cast lent to spring and summer mountain snowbanks by the tough, reddish cell coat of a minute green alga. These tiny cryophiles (literally "cold-loving" organisms) are part of an ecosystem adapted to the 32°F temperatures of surface water on melting snowbanks. The algae, along with microscopic bacteria, FUNGI, and protozoa, feed on wind-borne soil particles. In turn, they are eaten by springtails or snow fleas, tiny black arthropods that also live on the surface of the melting snow. When the snow and its meltwater disappear, the tiny algae live on, like FRESHWATER SHRIMP of low-elevation puddles and ponds, in tough, drought-resistant resting cells, distributed by the wind, waiting for next spring's snowbanks.

The red pigment that colors the algal cell coats—and the snow— probably protects the cells from damage by the abundant ultraviolet light at high elevations. Although the algae-tinted snow tastes and smells faintly like watermelon, samplers should exercise moderation: too generous a sample can have a laxative effect. Also, the algal cells concentrate airborne radiation from their diet, a phenomenon discovered by a URANIUM prospector who let his coffee pot boil dry after melting snow water and then heard his Geiger counter begin to click!

YUCCA Yuccas—shrubs or small trees of the lily family with rosettes of stiff, stilettolike, evergreen leaves—grow throughout the Southwest's deserts, GRASSLANDS, and foothills. Some yuccas are tall, the size of small trees, and look like dwarf palm trees with their rosettes of living leaves at the top of the stems and "skirts" of dead leaves hiding their trunk. Others are short, the size of large shrubs, their leaf rosettes growing from the ground like AGAVES. Yuccas are sometimes confused with agaves, but unlike agaves, which bloom only once, yuccas bloom every spring. Their tall flower stalks, laden with clusters of bell-shaped, waxy flowers, punctuate the landscape like giant candles, giving them the name "our Lord's candles."

Soaptree yucca (*Yucca elata*), the state flower of New Mexico, banana yucca (*Y. baccata*), named for its large, fleshy, edible fruits, and plains yucca (*Y. angustifolia*) are the most widespread of the Southwest's fifteen yucca species.

Like the agave, yucca was crucial to early Southwesterners, providing fiber, food, and building materials. These residents split and chewed the fibrous leaves, which lack agave leaves' marginal spines, to make rope, matting, sandals, baskets, and cloth. They ate the succulent buds and young flower stalks as a vegetable; the sweet flowers are still so popular in parts of Mexico that some species rarely grow seedpods. Yucca roots, called *amole*, are still peeled, and pounded or boiled to make a gentle soap for washing hair and for cleaning handwoven rugs and blankets.

All yucca species have evolved a special relationship with yucca moths. Each species of the plant has its own corresponding species of pollinating moth.

Cattle, deer, pronghorn, and other grazers relish the young flower stalks of short yuccas. Most grazers avoid the leaves, which are protected by a thick, waxy cuticle and a sharp tip. Only WOODRATS consume them. They shear the long leaves off at the base with sharp, chisel-tipped teeth so that the nearly leafless yucca looks like it had been given a buzz cut, and tote the leaves off for food and nest-roofing material. Javelinas tear the plants apart with their sharp hooves to eat the succulent leaf bases. ORIOLES and cactus WRENS build their nests deep in the protected heart of the dense leaf rosettes.

All yucca species have evolved a special relationship with pronuba, or YUCCA MOTHS. The yucca depend on the small, pale-colored, night-flying moths to pollinate their flowers; the moth larvae feed only on yucca fruits and seeds. Female yucca moths gather pollen from one flower and work it into a tiny ball before flying to another flower, stuffing the ball into the stigma and depositing their eggs in the ovary. The growing larvae feed on the developing fruit capsule but leave some seeds to mature into new yucca plants. Each species of yucca has its own species of pollinating moth.

Soaptree yucca, a tree-sized yucca of grasslands and deserts, is also called *palmilla*, "little palm," for its resemblance to a small palm tree. Soaptree yucca grows a single, unbranching trunk or a cluster of trunks to 20 feet high and topped with a dense rosette of long, narrow, evergreen leaves. In late spring, soaptree yucca sprouts a flower stalk up to 10 feet tall, the tallest flower stalk of all the yuccas, which is covered with clusters of waxy, ivory-colored, bell-shaped blossoms. The flowers exude a light perfume that attracts nighttime nectar feeders like BATS, and SPHINX and yucca moths. The fruit, a dry, light brown capsule, splits into three parts, remaining on the stalk but releasing many small, flat, black seeds. Yucca stalks provide perches for HAWKS and shrikes to survey the landscape for prey; other birds use them for song posts. People decorate the tall, dried stalks for ceremonial staffs on saint's day pilgrimages. Soaptree yucca dominates the plains of southern New Mexico and west Texas, often in pure stands, forming yucca "forests."

Banana yucca, a trunkless, shrubby yucca, is named for its up to 10-inch-long, fleshy fruit. The cylindrical fruits are edible and were once a staple of native Southwesterners. Baked, the pulpy fruit is supposed to taste like a sweet potato; the fruits were also eaten raw, or dried and ground into meal for the winter. Banana yucca grows on rocky soils in deserts, GRASS-LANDS, and open woods throughout the Southwest.

Plains yucca, a small yucca with narrow, gray-green leaves, is found as far north as Wyoming, farther north than any other yucca species. This aptly named yucca grows across the Great Plains as far east as western Iowa. In the Southwest, it is found on the LLANO ESTACADO of west Texas and eastern New Mexico and in southeastern Colorado.

See also AGAVE, JOSHUA TREE, YUCCA MOTH.

THREE

NATURAL FEATURES

FROM SNOW-SPOTTED MOUNTAIN peaks rising higher than 13,000 feet to searing desert basins near sea level, the Southwest encompasses an astonishing diversity of natural features: bare SLICKROCK plateaus, brilliantly colored MESAS, deep canyons, flat plains. One characteristic that links these landscapes is lack of water. All four of North America's deserts occur here.

But aridity has not always defined the region. Eons ago, shallow oceans covered much of the Southwest. In their salty depths and along their shores were deposited thick layers of limestone, dolomite, and sandstones. The seas receded and continental drift shaped the landforms, pushing up mountains and plateaus, dropping basins, bending thick layers of rock into great folds. Then, during the wetter glacial ages beginning some 15,000 years ago, streams and rivers eroded thousands of cubic miles of material from mountains and other high places, and drowned basins in layers of rocky debris. Today, wind and water erosion continue to mold the land.

People have changed the landscape too. Remnants of ancient cultures that long ago flourished here are still visible in places such as CHACO CANYON and MESA VERDE; their descendents today still occupy traditional pueblos and villages such as the ÁCOMA PUEBLO. In modern times, ranching, industry, and the impact of a growing population have altered the land: water diverted for irrigation has dried up once-flowing desert rivers and streams; other rivers have been dammed, their waters flooding canyons to create reservoirs; mining has gouged mountainsides.

Four North American geologic provinces shape the region's landscape: the contrast of mountain and desert in the BASIN AND RANGE; the richly colored rock wonderland of the COLORADO PLATEAU (the only province to fall completely within the Southwest); the high mass of the southern Rocky Mountains; and the flat expanse of the Great Plains.

The Basin and Range province dominates the southern Southwest and western Utah, where miles of hot desert basins soar abruptly to cool mountain forests, and then drop back just as suddenly into endless desert. The level sea of basins covers 50 to 75 percent of the Basin and Range land surface and contains the Southwest's deserts—the Chihuahuan, Great Basin, Mojave, and Sonoran. Hundreds of small, high mountain ranges called SKY ISLANDS punctuate the desert sea, providing oases of cooler, more northern ecosystems.

The Colorado Plateau, a world of sculptured rock, forms the landscape of the northern Southwest, encompassing 130,000 square miles and stretching from northern Arizona and the northwestern corner of New Mexico into central Utah. Built of sandstone, siltstone, and limestone some 65 to 50 million years ago, the plateau remained largely level and stable while folding and faulting pushed up mountains all around the plateau. Even uplift to elevations as high as 9,000 feet above sea level failed to deform this large surface. Wind and water have since shaped the colorful rocks into a panoply of forms: deep, narrow canyons, undulating SLICKROCK surfaces, sheer-walled MESAS, ARCHES, fins, domes, HOODOOS, and spires.

Mountains bound the Colorado Plateau on three sides. The Rocky Mountains edge the north and east, and the ranges of the Basin and Range province line the west side. The MOGOLLON RIM, a line of cliffs some 200 miles long and up to 2,000 feet high, marks the plateau's southern edge. South of the FOUR CORNERS, the plateau sags in northwestern New Mexico's nearly oval San Juan Basin, a mineral-rich area containing extensive oil and gas reserves, and URANIUM and COAL deposits.

Between the northern edge of the Basin and Range province and the relatively stable Colorado Plateau, a diagonal band of crust compressed from opposite edges into tight folds and wrinkles forms highlands that stretch from western New Mexico's Gila and Mogollon mountains to west-central Arizona. Some of the Southwest's biggest COPPER ore bodies occur in this crumpled transition zone.

Like a long finger extending from the main mass of the Rocky Mountains, the southern Rocky Mountains reach southward into southern Colorado and northern New Mexico, bringing plants and animals from northern latitudes into the Southwest. Although a small part of the Southwest's total area, here, a world away from the Basin and Range deserts, are the region's highest mountains, topped by 13,161-foot-high Wheeler Peak in the SANGRE DE CRISTO MOUNTAINS.

East of the mountain ranges that edge the Rio Grande rift—a great slice of down-dropped crust that splits the Southwest from north to south, are the western Great Plains, encompassing eastern New Mexico and Colorado. A sea of GRASSLAND underlain by flat-lying sedimentary rocks, the plains are dotted in places by small dormant volcanos. Other places, like the LLANO ESTACADO, an expanse of land of eastern New Mexico and west Texas, are so flat and featureless that travelers once drove stakes into the ground to mark their way.

ÁCOMA PUEBLO The sheer, 365-foot-high sandstone walls of a MESA in northern New Mexico provide a dramatic fortress for a tidy cluster of ancient masonry buildings covering the mesa's flat top. The ochre-colored one- and two-story buildings, constructed of the sandstone that forms their isolated mesa, were built between A.D. 600 and 1150 by the Anasazi and other early inhabitants, and are still occupied by their descendants, the people of Ácoma *pueblo* (Spanish for "town"). Ácoma, also called "Sky City" for its high, nearly inaccessible location, may be the oldest continuously lived-in site in the Western Hemisphere. Ácoma was a long-established pueblo when the first European, Hernando de Alvarado of the Coronado expedition, visited the city in 1540.

Oraibi, a Hopi pueblo atop Third Mesa in northern Arizona's Hopi Reservation, may be nearly as old, dating to at least A.D. 1150.

See also CHACO CANYON, CLIFF DWELLINGS.

ARCHES Nearly 150 million years ago, miles of Sahara-like sand dunes covered much of the landscape of what is now the COLORADO PLATEAU. Over subsequent millennia, more layers of sediments compressed the ancient waves of sand into a 300-foot-thick layer of hard sandstone. Much later, the whole region was gradually uplifted, and thick salt layers deep beneath the sandstone deformed, resulting in upward-arching domes and downward-arching valleys. The stress caused the hard sandstone layers to crack in a regular, checkerboardlike pattern of joints. Gnawed by water freezing and thawing in winter and rasped by wind, the rust-colored rock fell away in crescent-shaped chunks along the fine laminations of the old dune slopes, forming the thousands of fins, spires, HOODOOS, and free-standing arches that characterize today's Colorado Plateau landscape. Most of the Southwest's arches stud the Colorado Plateau, in areas such as the Needles of CANYONLANDS National Park, and in Zion National Park. Zion's Kolob Arch, one of the longest, spans 310 feet.

The largest concentration of stone arches in North America is contained within Arches National Park, just north of Moab, Utah. This 115-square-mile SLICKROCK landscape boasts nearly 1,800 arches—more than 200 with openings larger than 3 feet across. Landscape Arch, one of the world's largest, rises 106 feet above the ground and spans 290 feet. Hundreds more small arches, arch-shaped alcoves, HOODOOS, and mazes of canyons between tall fins of pink sandstone dot the park's slickrock landscape.

Angel arch

Arch formation begins when water percolates into sandstone and other porous rock along cracks or joints, slowly dissolving the cement that holds the grains together. As freezing and thawing wedge cracks wider, soil forms from the eroded rock, and plants take root, further prying the rock. Eventually, the erosive forces pierce the rock, creating an arch. Unlike NATURAL BRIDGES, freestanding arches do not span streams or watercourses. They rise upward from the rock surface like dynamic sculptures, growing narrower as erosion shaves their supports away, until they finally fall, returning to dust. Large, arch-shaped alcoves in cliff walls are also sometimes called arches.

Devil's Garden, part of Arches National Park, includes sixty-four arches, the largest group in the park. Landscape Arch is there. So is Double-O Arch, a large arch atop a small, round, eyelike arch. The opening of another, Skyline Arch, doubled in size when a massive block of sandstone dropped out in 1940. One of the most-photographed arches, Delicate Arch, stands alone in another part of the park, appearing taller than its 40-foot height.

Stephen T. Mather, the first director of the National Park Service, promoted Arches's establishment as a national monument in 1929. It was made a national park in 1971. Writer Edward Abbey, undoubtedly the Arches's most famous resident, wrote *Desert Solitaire* from his experience as a seasonal park ranger there.

See also NATURAL BRIDGES, ZION CANYON.

ARROYO Arroyos are water-carved washes, gullies, or small canyons with near-vertical banks that slice through much of the Southwest's arid landscape. Dry most of the time, arroyos can, after a summer thunderstorm, suddenly fill with torrents of rushing water and sediment, funneling the roiling slurry through their narrow channels in flash floods. The violent nature of Southwest thunderstorms causes such flash flooding. The rainfall is so heavy that it quickly saturates the surface of the bare soil and, because the soil cannot absorb more, the remaining water pours downhill. Flash floods are most common from July through September, but can occur any time of year. Obviously, arroyos should be avoided when thunderstorms are nearby.

Many of the Southwest's arroyos were formed in the late 1800s, when overgrazing and woodland clear-cutting stripped the dry soils of the vegetative cover that once intercepted some of the rainfall and prevented severe surface erosion. In 1895, a 12-foot wall of water swept through Silver City, New Mexico, carving a 35-foot-deep arroyo where Main Street had been. After another bad flood in 1903, the arroyo, called "Big Ditch," cut to 55 feet below the original street level. Downtown business owners simply put new fronts on what had been the back sides of their buildings, and Bullard Street, one block west, became the new main street.

BABOQUIVARI PEAK Resembling a huge, pale thumb pointed at the sky, Baboquivari Peak pushes 7,700 feet high above sea level and 1,700 feet above the ridge of the Baboquivari Mountains in south-central Arizona's Sonoran Desert.

Rising high and mysterious above the surrounding sea of desert, Baboquivari Peak is considered sacred by the people who live near it. The Tohono O'odham (Papago), whose homeland is dominated by the dramatic peak, say that the peak is the home of I'itoi ("Elder Brother"), the god who created them. I'itoi, say the Tohono O'odham, lives in a cave deep in the Baboquivari Mountains and does not appreciate disrespectful trespassers. He sometimes appears as a monster with a pig's face and eats those who displease him.

BAJADA Bajadas (bah-HAH-dah), Spanish for "slopes," flow around the bases of desert mountain ranges in the BASIN AND RANGE province of southern New Mexico, southern and central Arizona, and western Utah. These evenly sloping skirts of debris consist of the sand, gravel, and boulders that streams and rivers carry out of the mountains in occasional flash floods. As fast-moving water emerges from the mountains and abruptly slows down, it deposits the debris in fan-shaped alluvial cones. Merging alluvial fans create the even slope of a bajada, the transition between the vertical, bare rock of the mountains and flat-floored, horizontal desert basins.

Besides providing animal residents with a link between mountain habitats and basin habitats, bajadas also support extraordinarily diverse plant communities. Their deep, well-drained soils are more conducive to root growth than the silty, poorly drained soils of basin floors. In the Sonoran Desert more species of perennial plants—including SAGUARO cacti and PALOVERDE trees—grow on bajadas than on any other landform.

See also PLAYAS.

BASIN AND RANGE Nearly two-thirds of the Southwest, including all of its deserts, lies in the Basin and Range province, a stark landscape of flat, arid basins punctuated by narrow, rugged mountain ranges. Named for its appearance from the air, the Basin and Range stretches from southern Oregon to the Big Bend area of extreme southwest Texas and northern Mexico, and represents about 8 percent of the country's land area. In the Southwest, the Basin and Range arcs from the western edge of Utah south and east through Arizona, and across southern and central New Mexico.

Characterized by extreme contrasts, Basin and Range landscapes soar abruptly from miles of searing desert to cool mountain forest, and then drop just as suddenly back to desert. The level sea of desert basins—often dominated by monotonous expanses of olive-green CREOSOTE BUSH—encompasses up to 75 percent of the land surface. Hundreds of SKY ISLANDS—narrow, long mountain ranges rising as high as 13,000 feet above sea level—interrupt the desert sea, providing oases of cooler ecosystems more common farther north and supporting small populations of mountain animals such as BEARS. Lower mountain ranges, sparsely dotted with desert vegetation and home to desert BIGHORN SHEEP, jut from basin floors in stark, angular, rocky spines.

The Basin and Range topography is one of the Southwest's youngest, born between 15 and 8 million years ago when movement of the North American plate caused the crust to stretch and break along numerous short, north–south fault lines. The chunks of crust tilted every which way, like tumbled blocks. Some dropped down between the parallel faults, forming basins, some rose, forming mountains. Others moved horizontally, thrust miles out of place. Subsequent erosion removed many cubic miles of material from the higher pieces of crust (the mountains), and partly filled the basins—many of which even today have no outlets—with sand and gravel.

Intermittent drainages, filled by summer thunderstorms or spring mountain snowmelt, gouge steep, angular canyons in the skeletal mountains, dump their debris at canyon mouths, then sink into porous basin gravels, disappearing below ground. Evenly sloping BAJADAS, built of large debris deposited by mountain streams, smooth the transition between near-vertical mountain slopes and horizontal basin floors. Bajadas support the most diverse desert plant communities, including the SAGUARO-dominated Sonoran Desert of central and southern Arizona. Because they drain inward, many Southwest basins contain PLAYAS, the level beds of shallow, ephemeral lakes.

Frequent, often powerful winds characterize the Basin and Range province, powered by solar heat stored in the enormous expanses of rock and bare soil. DUST DEVILS spin above basin floors from spring through fall. Large rocks sandblasted by the wind form HOODOOS and balancing rocks. DESERT PAVEMENT, a thin layer of pebbles winnowed out by the wind, armors soil surfaces.

BRYCE CANYON
Water, freezing and thawing as air temperatures fluctuate between night and day, has sculpted the slopes of Bryce Canyon in

southwestern Utah into a pastel-colored gallery of spires, pinnacles, HOODOOS, and narrow, deep canyons. Millions of giant rock figures—resembling minarets, crowds of people, various animals, and crenellated walls—clothe the slopes in Fairyland and Silent City, the two most densely carved areas. The Paiute Indians believed the weirdly shaped forms to be birds, animals, and lizards turned to rock by an angry god.

The panoply of bizarre forms crowding Bryce's steep slopes are carved from a thousand-foot-thick series of mud and siltstone sediments that were deposited at the bottom of ancient Lake Falstaff between 35 and 60 million years ago. As the COLORADO PLATEAU rose, faults broke it into smaller segments such as Bryce's Paunsaugunt Plateau. These smaller plateaus shifted vertically—some bobbing up, some sinking—and tilted at odd angles. Bryce's sculpted slopes are on the low side of the fault that created the plateau—erosion on the high side removed the soft mud layers entirely, creating the Paria Valley.

> **The Paiute Indians believed the weirdly shaped forms that crowd Bryce Canyon's steep slopes to be birds, animals, and lizards turned to rock by an angry god.**

Bryce's descending ramparts and crowds of ornate rock figures are newcomers in geologic time—probably less than 500,000 years old. Several small creeks, tributaries of the Paria River, continue to sculpt spectacular landscape as they eat their way into the plateau edge. During spring snowmelt or after a summer rainstorm, the myriad narrow gullies that etch Bryce Canyon's slopes run with a slurry of liquid rock, coating all they touch with pastel-colored "stucco"—mud. Small amounts of minerals in the soft sediments paint the fairyland with an array of colors: iron tints the rocks pastel pink and orange; manganese adds pale blue and purple.

Tree-ring dating, developed to date archaeological sites, has helped geologists measure the speedy erosion of Bryce's slopes. By coring ancient, gnarled BRISTLECONE PINES standing on "tiptoe"—their roots bared by erosion—at the plateau rim, geologists found that various parts of the rim are being nibbled away at the rate of 9 inches to 4 feet per century.

Bryce Canyon is named for homesteaders Ebenezer and Mary Bryce, who raised cattle, cut lumber, and farmed in the area from 1875 to 1880. Remarked Ebenezer Bryce about the scenery that today draws thousands of visitors, "It's a hell of a place to lose a cow."

See also COLORADO PLATEAU, ZION CANYON.

CALICHE Composed of calcium carbonate and other mineral salts, caliche (ca-LEE-chee) forms when water in the soil evaporates. Visible as a whitish crust on the undersides of rocks at the soil surface, caliche can build an impervious, cementlike layer called "hardpan" or "calcrete" at or below the soil surface when salts are abundant. Because caliche is deposited at the level where soils dry out, the depth of the caliche layer depends on how deeply rains penetrate the soil. Some desert soils contain recurring layers of caliche up to 100 feet deep. Caliche develops most readily in the well-drained, gravelly soils of BAJADAS and lower slopes of desert mountain ranges and MESAS.

Caliche prevents groundwater from penetrating deeply into desert soils, and blocks plant roots. Plants with shallow root systems may thrive despite the caliche layers if the cemented layer is deep enough; deeply rooted trees such as MESQUITE rarely grow, or are stunted, in soils with thick caliche layers. Only CREOSOTE BUSH, with a combination of dense surface and deep roots, succeeds in soils with multiple caliche layers and often occurs in monotonous expanses.

See also SALINIZATION.

CANYON DE CHELLY AND CANYON DEL MUERTO Near the town of Chinle in the northeastern corner of Arizona, the desolate, windswept surface of the COLORADO PLATEAU is sliced by two canyons that join to form a great "Y." Protected by spectacular, thousand-foot-high sandstone cliffs, and nourished reliably by dependable water from the small Rio de Chelly, the comparatively lush, flat-bottomed valleys of Canyon de Chelly (pronounced d' shay, a Spanish corruption of the Navajo *tse' gi*, "rocky canyon") and Canyon del Muerto (Spanish for "of the dead," a reference to mummies found in its caves) have sheltered humans for nearly two millennia.

Canyon de Chelly and Canyon del Muerto originated as the sweeping dunes of a Sahara-like desert that some 250 million years ago covered much of what is now the Colorado Plateau. The weight of sediments deposited in succeeding millennia transformed the dunes into the thick layer of salmon-colored Navajo sandstone that today forms the vertical canyon walls. Following joints in the sandstone, the Rio de Chelly and a tributary stream draining from the Chuska Mountains eroded the Navajo sandstone, depositing the fine sediments that form the

Canyon de Chelly

arable soils in the bottoms of the narrow canyons. By undermining the hard rock, the streams cut shelter caves near the bottom of the soaring cliffs.

People came early to these sheltered canyons. Big Cave in Canyon del Muerto holds remains of pit houses (underground dwellings) dating from A.D. 300 to 800. A buried pair of arms and hands wrapped with three abalone shell necklaces was found in one of the pit houses. Between A.D. 1030 and 1300, the Anasazi constructed CLIFF DWELLINGS from the salmon-colored sandstone, tucking the multistoried masonry buildings into the protected shelter caves. Both Anasazi and Navajo rock art, including a herd of half life-sized antelopes above Antelope House, decorate the rust-colored walls. A trail that switchbacks down a 500-foot cliff leads to the sixty-room village known as White House.

The canyons nurtured small settled populations until the thirteenth century, when regional drought caused consolidation of settlements. For several hundred years, the canyons were home to summer people who came to till fields. Around 1700, Navajos settled in the canyons, farming, raising livestock, and planting orchards. Forced in the 1860s by the U.S. Cavalry to move 300 miles away to eastern New Mexico, the Navajos eventually returned and today occupy the hogans (traditional six- to eight-sided log houses), graze flocks of sheep and goats, and tend farms and orchards in the verdant canyon bottoms.

See also CHACO CANYON, CLIFF DWELLINGS.

CANYONLANDS Canyonlands National Park, in southeastern Utah, displays what some consider the wildest side of the COLORADO PLATEAU: a formidable and magnificent SLICKROCK landscape of bare, sculpted rock. The area remained a blank spot on maps of the western United States until Major John Wesley Powell and his group ran the Colorado River in 1869. Even today, the heart of this awesome rock wilderness, protected in the 527-square-mile national park, remains largely wild, accessible mainly by jeep, foot, or raft. For example, the main approach to the Maze district, a full third of the park, is via a 45-mile-long dirt road.

Like a giant layer cake, Canyonlands is composed of some 10,000 feet of nearly horizontal layers of rock. The oldest and most deeply buried are 3,000-foot-thick salt layers laid down by an evaporating shallow sea around 300 million years ago. Above come a succession of thick layers of vari-colored, softer siltstones and mudstones dumped by rivers on their flood-plains. These alternate with pale-colored sandstones formed as shoreline dunes. The topmost layers, orange and rusty-red sandstones, blew in as massive dunes in a Sahara-like desert 200 to 150 million years ago.

Carved by the COLORADO and Green rivers, which meet in Canyonlands to form a great Y, the alternating layers of softer rock and harder rock shape the park's slope-ledge-slope topography. Miles of near-level bare rock plateaus and MESAS rise in stairsteps high above the two rivers, and deep, narrow, side canyons carve intricate loops in hard plateau surfaces, forming steep-walled mazes. Wind sandblasting the massive rock layers and water freezing and thawing in place etch the landscape. Isolated buttes, sheer-walled mesas, and CURVING arches tower over slickrock. Striped rock spires stand in crowds; tall rock fins form orderly ranks like so many dinosaur spines.

Island in the Sky mesa, isolated between the arms of the great Y where the two rivers join, is connected to the main plateau only by a slender, cliff-edged neck. At the southern tip of Island in the Sky, Grand View Point, 2,000 feet above the confluence of the Colorado and the Green rivers, over-looks hundreds of square miles of slickrock and three distant, green, and cool SKY ISLAND mountain ranges. Upheaval Dome, a huge craterlike fea-ture on the west edge of Island in the Sky, was once thought to be a col-lapsed dome. Many geologists now interpret the "dome" as the print of a meteorite impact from the million-year-long meteor shower that some believe led to the extinction of the DINOSAURS and other species about 65 million years ago.

After their confluence, the waters of the Green and the Colorado rivers—often colored differently by varying amounts of eroded sediment—flow side by side, unmixed. A few miles downstream, the rivers plunge into Cataract Canyon, named by John Wesley Powell for fifty-two rapids created as the river drops 425 feet in 40 miles—whitewater every bit as hair-raising as that in the GRAND CANYON. Lake Powell, a downstream reservoir, now drowns the lower part of Cataract Canyon.

East of Cataract Canyon, the main stem of the Y, lies the Needles, a forest of red-and-white-striped pillars, turrets, fins, and arches eroded in sandstone. Nearby are the Grabens, linear canyons as narrow as 9 feet and as deep as 300 feet. These natural avenues were cut not by water, but by the rock itself stretching and fracturing as thick layers of salt deep underneath moved upward under pressure, bending the rock layers above.

The Maze, a labyrinthine confusion of canyons, boasts some of America's finest examples of PETROGLYPHS AND PICTOGRAPHS, most created by the Fremont people after A.D. 1000, a mobile, part farming, part hunter-gatherer culture. The imposing, life-size figures with great shields and headdresses continue to awe modern viewers.

Despite temperatures that range from minus 20°F to 115°F (an annual temperature range of 144 degrees, one of the widest in the world) and a scanty average annual precipitation of only 8 inches, the slickrock landscape of Canyonlands is home to a variety of lives, from endangered desert BIGHORN SHEEP to lush bunchgrass GRASSLANDS. Potholes eroded in the undulating rock surface by the freezing and thawing action of water explode with ephemeral life such as FRESHWATER SHRIMP, gnats, endemic pothole mosquitoes, algae, and other aquatic life-forms when they fill during the rainy season. Mini-ecosystems of bacteria, algae, FUNGI, LICHEN, and moss flourish at the soil surface, forming bumpy, blackened MICRO-BIOTIC CRUSTS—a living mulch.

See also SLICKROCK.

CARLSBAD CAVERNS One of the world's greatest fossil reefs rises above southeastern New Mexico's flat, grassy plains, far from modern oceans. Some 250 million years ago, when a shallow ocean flooded this region, generations of microscopic marine animals built this enormous limestone ridge, creating a reef thousands of feet high and up to a mile wide. Three to five million years ago, the ocean long gone, the area was uplifted, and sediments deposited later atop the reef eroded away, exposing the great reef. Groundwater percolated into cracks and joints and, combining with carbon dioxide from the air to produce a dilute acid, gradually dissolved the limestone. As the reef filled with water, the cracks widened into corridors, and then chambers, hollowing the ancient reef from within. Today, the Guadalupe Mountains—the eroded reef—is honeycombed by about seventy caves, including one of the world's largest, Carlsbad Caverns.

Carlsbad's 24 miles of surveyed passageways and chambers include Big Room, the largest natural cave room in the world, ample enough to hold fourteen football fields. The ceiling of Big Room soars to 255 feet, high enough to fit our nation's capitol in one corner, dome and all. After the water drained out of the reef, the decoration phase began, producing Carlsbad's spectacular array of downward-pointing stalactites and upward-pointing stalagmites, draperies, soda-straws, spiky and hair-thin aragonite crystals, popcorn, and helictites—tiny stalks that grow every which way in defiance of gravity. Millions and millions of drops of water and thousands of years were required to form the 6-story-tall stalagmite in Carlsbad's Big Room.

Carlsbad Caverns' other major attraction, the nightly flight of BATS swooshing from the cave entrance, led to the cave's modern exploration. In 1901, Jim White, a local cowboy, spotted the cloud of bats and from their location discovered the cave. For the next few decades, Carlsbad Caverns

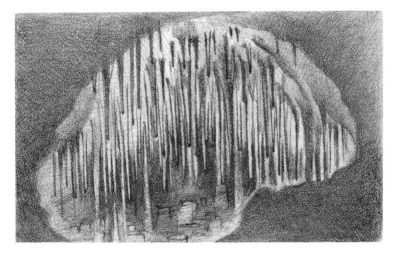

Carlsbad Caverns

was a bat guano miner's dream. More than 100,000 tons of the fragrant natural fertilizer—the droppings from 17,000 years of bat occupation—were hauled out in buckets and shipped to California to enrich citrus groves. In 1930, Carlsbad Caverns became a national park. Now, the caverns into which Jim White lowered tourists by guano bucket are accessible by elevator and lighted walkways, and are visited by over 500,000 people each year.

Although most of the guano is gone, several hundred thousand bats still roost in the caverns from May through September. Each evening, beginning at sundown, the cave's entire population of adult bats exits synchronously, swirling out like a black whirlwind. Each bat first lets go of its upside-down hold on the roof of the roosting cave, rights itself in the air, and flies through the cave toward the entrance. The bats ascend the final 150 feet to the outside in a counterclockwise spiral, exiting at the rate of between five and ten thousand bats per minute. After all-night insect-feeding flights, the bats return before dawn, diving into the cave's mouth from several hundred feet up.

Carlsbad Caverns has 24 miles of surveyed passageways and chambers, including Big Room, the largest natural cave in the world.

Miles of other caves—most unexplored for lack of money and time—pierce the ancient reef around Carlsbad Caverns. New Cave, so named because it was discovered only in 1937, is the only other cave open to the public. National Park Service staff lead rigorous flashlight tours through the undeveloped cave, whose formations include "the Klansman," a huge stalagmite resembling a white-robed, hooded figure. Nearby Lechuguilla Cave has recently been explored to depths of 1,593 feet below the surface of the ground, making it the nation's deepest cave.

CASA GRANDE In 1694, Father Eusebio Francisco Kino wrote in his diary of a magnificent ruin in the central Arizona desert. Naming the ruin "Casa Grande" (Spanish for "big house"), he described it as "a four-story building as large as a castle and equal to the finest church in Sonora." The Indians who guided him knew the building only as a ruin; its builders were called the *Hohokam*, a Piman word meaning "those who have gone." Today Casa Grande endures much as Father Kino saw it nearly three hundred years ago; towering over a flat desert plain, it stands empty, its thick, partly eroded walls now protected by a soaring modern metal roof. Although archaeologists have learned much about the Hohokam people, Casa Grande, their only known "skyscraper," remains an enigma, its purpose unexplained.

Casa Grande's massive walls, constructed by hand of puddled CALICHE, the natural cementlike layer found in many desert soils, are over 4 feet thick at the base, nearly 2 feet thick at the top. More than 600 wood beams, including PONDEROSA PINE and white FIR brought from the mountains 50 miles distant, support the floors of what is actually a three-story-high structure on a tall mud base. The third story, a single room with holes in one wall that line up precisely with sunset at the equinoxes, may have been an astronomical observatory.

The Hohokam, probably northward migrants from Mesoamerica, moved into Arizona around 300 B.C. They lived for more than a thousand years in open villages—clusters of pit houses roofed with layers of branches and mud. In the 1300s, Hohokam architecture suddenly changed. Influenced by Anasazi culture, this people began to build pueblo-style, above-ground adobe houses clustered within walls, including towering Casa Grande. But a hundred years after Casa Grande's massive roof beams were cut, the Hohokam disappeared. Today's Tohono O'odham (Papago) and Pima Indians claim the Hohokam people as ancestors.

See also CALICHE, CHACO CANYON, CLIFF DWELLINGS.

CHACO CANYON From A.D. 900 to about 1200, Chaco Canyon, a wide, shallow, flat-bottomed valley cut in the sandstones of the arid COLORADO PLATEAU in northwestern New Mexico, was the center of Anasazi life and the apex of Southwestern culture. But late in the thirteenth century, the Anasazi, roughly, "ancient ones" in Navajo, abandoned Chaco Canyon, leaving silent eleven large stone pueblos (Spanish for "towns"), some 400 other sites, an extensive irrigation system with terraced croplands, and a 200-mile road network that is still visible in aerial photographs. Like other cultures flourishing in the Southwest at that time—the Hohokam, Salado, Sinagua, and Mogollon—the Anasazi simply vanished. The most outstanding examples of the 2,000-plus ruins in the Chaco area are preserved in Chaco Culture National Historical Park, in the FOUR CORNERS region between Gallup and Farmington, New Mexico.

Incised into the edge of a sandstone plateau during wetter glacial ages some 15,000 years ago, Chaco Canyon possesses a level, 15-mile-long, 1-mile-wide bottom, composed of arable soils delivered by a small stream and by wind erosion. Carved from Cliffhouse sandstone, the same formation that shelters the dramatic cliff houses at MESA VERDE, the canyon walls rise only 100 to 200 feet high and are breached by landslides in many places, providing easy access to the expansive valley floor. The sandstone itself, deposited near the shore of an eastward-retreating sea around 100 million years ago, contains layers of shales, coal, gypsum, and clay, all valuable for building and pottery work.

Today, the partially restored ruins of Anasazi pueblos—apartment house–like communal villages built of hand-cut blocks of Cliffhouse sandstone—dot the deserted valley bottom at the base of the cliffs. The largest, Pueblo Bonito, a precise half-circle in outline and oriented to catch the low-angle winter sun, once rose five stories, contained 800 rooms, and may have sheltered several thousand people. Now partly collapsed, its intricately laid walls still reach several stories high. Its numerous small rooms, once roofed with pine beams, small branches, and mud, are open to the sky, its central, dirt-paved plaza silent.

The remains of kivas—circular, underground chambers, walled by sandstone blocks, and once roofed—pit the pueblos. Modern Pueblo people still use such kivas as social and ceremonial gathering places. Besides the neighborhood kivas, the Anasazi at Chaco built "great kivas," including the largest known, Casa Rinconada (Spanish for "Box Canyon House"), 64 feet in diameter. Its partly rebuilt rock walls today rise in a solitary circle, precisely oriented north-south and east-west, away from the ruined pueblos. Niches piercing Casa Rinconada's stone walls capture the light of the rising sun at winter solstice.

The Anasazi abandoned Chaco Canyon in the late 1200s, leaving its pueblos, kivas, and fields to ruin. Archaeologists now think that the large concentration of people exhausted the area's wood, arable cropland, and wild plants and animals. For example, more than a hundred thousand large PONDEROSA PINES and other trees were felled for pueblo roof beams. Such lumbering, plus fuel-wood gathering, probably deforested the Chaco watershed, eroding arroyos and dropping the small stream system out of reach of the Anasazi's extensive network of dams and reservoirs. A serious drought throughout the Southwest from 1276 to 1299 was likely the final blow.

The Anasazi migrated out of Chaco to build new pueblos and CLIFF

DWELLINGS in unspoiled sites. Eventually these too were abandoned. Their descendants eventually settled along the Rio Grande and at the isolated Zuñi and Hopi mesas, building pueblos like ÁCOMA PUEBLO, still occupied by the Hopi and Pueblo people of Arizona and New Mexico.

See also ÁCOMA PUEBLO, CLIFF DWELLINGS, MESA VERDE.

CHIRICAHUA MOUNTAINS Southeastern Arizona's Chiricahua (cheer-ee-KAH-wah) Mountains were named the "land of the standing-up rocks" by the Apaches for their wonderland of gigantic HOODOOS: towering rock spires, weird figures, and huge, balanced rocks. The extraordinary monoliths—including the Totem Pole, 137 feet high and only a yard thick at its narrowest point, and Big Balanced Rock, weighing 1,000 tons and resting on a base about 4 feet thick—were formed by erosion of volcanic ash layers deposited some 25 million years ago in fiery volcanic holocausts.

> Arizona's Chiricahua Mountains were named the "land of the standing-up rocks" by the Apaches for their wonderland of rock forms.

The eruptions laid nearly 2,000 feet of tuff, rock formed of ash containing pumice fragments, on the Chiricahua area, including a single 880-foot-thick layer from which most of Chiricahua's fantastic rock sculptures are carved. As it cooled, the ash layer contracted, developing intersecting sets of vertical joints. Water gradually widened the joints, eroding the softer and harder layers differentially and resulting in the rock figures. Unusual "volcanic hailstones," formed of ash in the turbulent air of the volcanic clouds, are today visible on the ground in parts of the Chiricahuas.

The Chiricahua Mountains are well known not just for their geology. Rising to 9,000 feet above the surrounding Sonoran and Chihuahuan deserts and grasslands, the Chiricahuas are the largest and most accessible of the Southwest's SKY ISLANDS, isolated areas of cooler and moister climate very different from that of the surrounding landscape. Close to Mexico's major mountain chain, the Sierra Madre, the Chiricahuas harbor "exotic" Mexican species that traveled the mountain corridors north across the border. Mexican chickadees, THICK-BILLED PARROTS, and Apache squirrels feed in tall Apache and Chihuahuan pines on the lower slopes. In narrow canyons, riparian woodlands dominated by spreading sycamores shelter elegant trogons, whiskered owls, berylline HUMMINGBIRDS, troops of raccoonlike

COATIS, three-tailed swallowtail BUTTERFLIES, and green rat snakes.

Once home to the Chiricahua Apaches under Cochise, part of the mountain range, including the most spectacular rock figures, is now protected by the 12,000-acre Chiricahua National Monument, created in 1924.

CLIFF DWELLINGS Cliff dwellings, apartment house–like villages built in the shelter of caves or cliff overhangs, are uniquely Southwestern, having evolved from the multistoried masonry pueblos built by the Anasazi. Economical buildings designed to house small villages in tight, easily defended spaces, cliff dwellings were usually sited in south-facing alcoves in order to harvest the warmth of low-angle winter sunlight. Constructed of rocks quarried from the cliffs that shelter them, the complexes of small, interconnected rooms contain undersized doors, high door sills to keep out drafts, and few windows. Massive roof beams—hewn from trees felled and hauled from tens of miles away—remain intact in many buildings, but the twig and mud roofs have long since fallen. Mortar and plaster of local mud once cemented and sealed the rock walls.

The most dramatic cliff dwellings are those built under the soaring overhangs of dune-deposited or ocean-shore sandstones. These rocks tend to break along the sweeping lines of the ancient dunes, creating huge, arching alcoves like those at Navajo National Monument in northeastern Arizona and MESA VERDE in southwestern Colorado. Sandstones are the most common home of cliff dwellings, but cliff dwellings were also built in niches eroded in limestone—for example, at Walnut Canyon on the MOGOLLON RIM in Arizona—and in layers of welded volcanic ash. At Bandelier National Monument in northern New Mexico, the interconnected alcoves are often only large enough to accommodate individual rooms, with holes for roof beams gouged in the soft volcanic ash layers and masonry front walls.

Some cliff dwellings, like the elegant structures at MESA VERDE, are now partially restored and protected in national and tribal parks and monuments. But hundreds of others, many comprising just a handful of rooms and now a jumble of partly fallen walls, are tucked into canyon walls from the Gila Mountains in southern New Mexico to the SLICKROCK country of CANYONLANDS in southern Utah.

The predominant Southwestern architectural style between A.D. 1050 and 1300, most cliff dwellings and pueblos were abandoned peacefully by

Keet Seel (Navajo National Monument)

1350, after only one or two centuries—or in some cases, only one or two decades—of use. Archaeologists think that the demands of permanent, relatively large settlements soon exhausted local natural resources— wildlife, firewood, water, soil. Severe droughts, perhaps triggered by the human-caused desertification, forced the people to disperse in small groups, searching for new farmland and hunting areas.

See CANYON DE CHELLY AND CANYON DEL MUERTO, CASA GRANDE, MESA VERDE.

COAL Coal beds, deposited as dead plant material in lagoons and swamps at the edge of a shallow sea around a hundred million years ago, occur in many parts of the Southwest. Most of the coal now mined in the Southwest today comes from the Four Corners region, but small seams scattered throughout the region have been important in earlier times.

Around a thousand years ago, Anasazi people gathered coal from the San Juan River area, using it in their jewelry and other art. Between the 1880s and the 1940s, Southwest railroad companies mined many small coal deposits. From the late 1800s until the 1950s, underground mines at the edge of the southern Rocky Mountains near Trinidad, Colorado, and Raton, New Mexico, employed thousands of miners. Raton, now a town of

8,000, once called itself the "Pittsburgh of the West." Today, most Southwestern coal comes from giant strip mines on the COLORADO PLATEAU. The Southwest's largest coal mine, Black Mesa on the Navajo and Hopi reservations, produces 12 million tons per year. Other mines exploit coal in northwest New Mexico's San Juan Basin, which is underlain by one-quarter of the nation's coal reserves accessible to strip mining.

The Southwest's wealth of low-sulfur, bituminous (soft) coal comes from the Mesaverde group of sediment layers in southwest Colorado. Most of the coal is mined to power coal-burning power plants in the area, such as Four Corners Power Plant east of Shiprock, New Mexico, and Navajo Generating Station at Page, Arizona. These giant plants—the Four Corners plant alone burns 7 million tons of coal each year—produce electricity for users as far away as Las Vegas, Salt Lake City, and Los Angeles. Each day, the Four Corners plant pours 252 tons of particulates and 445 tons of smog-producing gases into the once-clear air, reducing visibility so much that at places such as the GRAND CANYON visitors often cannot see from one rim to the other. Four Corners' smoke plume is visible from space.

COLORADO PLATEAU

This is a country that leads one to think in terms of geologic time, which if I am not mistaken is about the same as thinking in religious terms. —Wallace Stegner

The spectacular rock landscape of the Colorado Plateau, covering 130,000 square miles, defines the shape of the northern Southwest. Sandstone, siltstone, and limestone—each hundreds of feet deep—built the plateau, geophysical forces lifted it more than a mile above sea level, wind and water continue to sculpt its surface.

This great raft of rock encompasses what is now the southeastern quarter of Utah, east of the Wasatch Mountains and south of the Uintas; southwestern Colorado west of Durango; the northeastern quarter of Arizona; and northwestern New Mexico north of Gallup. When mountain-building forces some 65 to 50 million years ago were raising the Rocky Mountains and ranges all around, the Colorado Plateau simply floated upward nearly a mile, almost undeformed. Although dipping gently to the north, the stacked sediments still lie essentially horizontal. The current surface is, however, anything but monotonous. Smaller plateaus—Shivwits,

Coconino, Kaibab, Paunsaugunt, Tavaputs, and others—break up the larger plateau. Great folds bend the sediments into miles-long walls, locally called "reefs." Domes pock the surface. Deep canyons like the GRAND CANYON, cut by the Colorado River and its tributaries, incise the layers. And myriad sculptural details decorate the plateau: ARCHES, badlands, fins, goosenecks, HOODOOS, MESAS, NATURAL BRIDGES, potholes, spires, and toadstools.

The deep canyons expose ever-older layers in a stair-stepping geologic history. The plateau's oldest rocks—the dark, contorted rocks of the 2-billion-year-old Vishnu schist revealed at the bottom of the Grand Canyon—speak of immense heat and pressure deforming even older sedimentary rocks in a once-giant mountain range. The youngest rocks—dark basalt flows and layers of ash and cinders—tell of volcanoes and volcanic vents belching as recently as 900 years ago. In between, an array of limestones, sandstones, siltstones, mudstones, and shales paint the landscape with vivid bands of red, pink, orange, purple, olive green, ochre, tan, cream. These layers tell stories of the oceans, evaporating lakes, rivers depositing sediment in spreading floodplains, and wind-blown desert sand dunes that at various times washed over or spread across what is now the Colorado Plateau.

> Myriad sculptural details decorate the Colorado Plateau: arches, badlands, fins, goosenecks, hoodoos, mesas, spires, and toadstools.

From the Arizona–Utah border north lies SLICKROCK country, named for its bare rock surfaces. Here wind and water have scoured a litany of fabulous rock layers: Cedar Mesa sandstones shelter CLIFF DWELLINGS at MESA VERDE and form the spires of the Needles at CANYONLANDS; Kaibab limestone drapes enormous WATERPOCKET FOLD; pastel-striped Moenkopi, Shinarump, and Chinle shales contain URANIUM and multicolored fallen forests of petrified wood. Above them, the great layers—Wingate, Kayenta, Navajo, Entrada, deposited as dunes in a long-gone Sahara-like desert—form the slickrock surface.

Rising like mirages above the arid plateau surface are small island mountain ranges: the San Francisco Peaks north of Flagstaff, Arizona; and the Henry, La Sal, and Abajo mountains in southeastern Utah. Their green, often snow-covered slopes offer a refuge to mountain animals from beavers to BEARS, and tantalize hot and weary plateau travelers.

Isolated by a near-ring of mountains and by its own rugged topography, the Colorado Plateau has evolved endemic plants and animals, species unique to the area. The endangered Gunnison's PRAIRIE DOG numbers among the plateau's endemic animals; others include the plateau WHIPTAIL LIZARD, Painted Desert glossy snake, Mesa Verde night snake, and midget faded RATTLESNAKE, a diminutive, pink form of the western rattlesnake.

An unusual concentration of parks and monuments protects the plateau's spectacular landscape and abundant prehistoric sites. Besides state and tribal parks, the plateau boasts nine national parks and ten national monuments, including ARCHES, BRYCE CANYON, Canyonlands, CHACO CANYON, Grand Canyon, PETRIFIED FOREST, and ZION.

COLORADO RIVER When Major John Wesley Powell and his colleagues explored it in the 1870s, the Colorado was the Southwest's wildest and most inaccessible river. Today, ten major DAMS, including Hoover Dam, the second highest in the United States, block the Colorado, trapping the Southwest's second-longest river in a string of reservoirs. Still, sections of the river, such as Cataract Canyon in CANYONLANDS National Park and the GRAND CANYON, remain wild enough to thrill the hundreds of thousands of people who float the river each year.

On its journey from snowy cirques in Colorado's Rocky Mountain National Park to the desert shores of the Gulf of California, the Colorado River travels 1,450 miles and drops 14,000 feet, or an average of about 10 feet per mile. The Green River, the Colorado's longest tributary, runs 730 miles straight south from Wyoming's Wind River Mountains—bending only to avoid the Uinta Mountains. The two rivers join at the confluence in Canyonlands National Park, flow a few miles as two distinct currents, then mix as they plunge into Cataract Canyon. The Gila River, once the second-longest tributary, originates in New Mexico's Gila Mountains and once flowed 650 miles west across southern Arizona's deserts. Now the Gila, dewatered by agricultural and residential users, disappears under the desert soil 150 miles before it reaches the Colorado.

The Colorado's 244,000-square-mile drainage basin encompasses much of the Southwest, including all of western Colorado and eastern Utah, the FOUR CORNERS and western New Mexico, and almost all of Arizona. But this largely arid country does not yield great quantities of water—except after thunderstorms, which can drop as much as 4 inches of rain in an hour. Spread out evenly over the upper Colorado River Basin, the entire yearly flow of the Colorado would puddle just over 2 inches deep.

Some of the Southwest's bitterest battles have been fought over the Colorado's scanty water supply. In 1922, after years of squabbling, the seven Colorado River basin states—Wyoming, Colorado, Utah, Arizona, New Mexico, Nevada, and California—signed an agreement divvying up every drop of the 16.8 million acre-feet then assumed to be the average annual flow. (An acre-foot is the amount of water needed to flood an acre of land one foot deep.) Unfortunately, the water engineers erred: the average annual flow is only about 13.5 million acre-feet—20 percent less than the amount promised to the states. Because no state would relinquish any of its share, several enormous reservoirs were built on the lower Colorado between 1931 and 1966. Storing water in reservoirs is not without significant problems. In the thirsty desert climate, the huge reservoirs lose around 2.5 million acre-feet of water each year to evaporation. And the river that once created a 12-foot-high tidal bore at the Gulf of California that "roared like thunder" now barely reaches the gulf. Its once-verdant estuary has been reduced to a silent stretch of mudflats and empty channels.

The Colorado's notorious silt content also creates problems for reservoirs. Early Anglo Southwest residents described the river as "too thick to drink, too thin to plow." Before the gates on Hoover Dam were closed in 1935, the Colorado carried an average annual load of 180 million tons of silt past Yuma, Arizona, just above the Mexican border. After the gates were

Colorado River

closed and two other dams were constructed on the lower river, this amount dropped to 13 million tons. Once the flow of water halts behind a dam, it drops its load of sediment. Silt accumulation at the upper end of Lake Mead, the reservoir formed by Hoover Dam, reduces the storage capacity of Lake Mead by 137,000 acre-feet a year.

Despite its scanty flow, more than half the population of the West depends on Colorado River water. More water is exported from the Colorado River watershed than from any river basin in the country. Canals divert Colorado River water hundreds of miles—in some cases water is pumped uphill over a thousand feet—to provide water for agriculture and industry and to water lawns and fill fountains in Phoenix, Los Angeles, and Las Vegas.

See also SQUAWFISH.

COPPER In 1990, mines in Arizona, New Mexico, and Utah yielded 70 percent of the 1,500 million metric tons of copper produced by the United States, the world's second-largest producer of copper. Once mined in underground tunnels, most of the Southwest's copper now comes from open pit mines like the huge pits at Morenci, in eastern Arizona, and Tyrone, south of Silver City in southern New Mexico.

In the upward-faulted mountain blocks of the BASIN AND RANGE province, which covers southern and central Arizona and New Mexico, western Utah, and much of Nevada, copper ores are often found mixed with gold and silver in veins at the edges of cooled "plutons," bodies of igneous rocks intruded into older rocks.

Prospectors scouring the Southwest for silver and gold toward the late 1800s often found and ignored copper veins. In 1875, a gold prospector discovered one of the Southwest's most famous copper deposits at Bisbee, Arizona, and left without mining copper, disappointed he didn't find gold.

Within five years, however, copper suddenly became valuable for electric and phone wires, and the Copper Queen Mine at Bisbee was fueling a spectacular boom. By 1900, Bisbee was Arizona's largest and most prosperous city. The imposing Copper Queen Hotel, built in 1902, attracted the rich and famous. Both the underground Copper Queen and the newer mile-long, 950-foot-deep Lavender open pit mine are now silent, victims of falling copper prices.

Weathering of copper ores produces a variety of beautiful minerals.

Brilliant green malachite is the most common and most stable, forming where copper ore bodies occur near the earth's surface. Bisbee's Copper Queen Mine once produced high-quality malachite, dense and hard enough for carvings and jewelry, but today the finest malachite comes from Africa. The Copper Queen Mine also once yielded fine azurite, a brilliant blue, less-stable form of copper that decomposes into malachite. Azurite, used widely for jewelry, is still mined in Arizona.

DAMS Hoover Dam, completed in 1935, was a triumph for its engineers and builders. It was the first major dam to span the wild COLORADO RIVER and was the showpiece of President Franklin Roosevelt's public works program. One hundred ten workers died before it was finished, many from heat prostration caused by daytime temperatures of up to 150°F at the dam site in a sheer-walled rock canyon.

> **Hoover Dam was the first major dam to span the wild Colorado River. One hundred and ten workers died before it was finished in 1935.**

A cement arc 725 feet high, Hoover Dam is the nation's second-highest dam. Behind it stretch the 108-mile-long waters of Lake Mead, the largest man-made reservoir in the United States. Lake Mead can hold over 28 million acre-feet of water, enough to cover the state of New York with water a foot deep.

Upriver is Glen Canyon Dam, the fourth largest in the United States. Its 708-foot-high arc required 4.9 million yards of concrete to construct, and it backs up the second-largest reservoir in the United States, Lake Powell. The 180-mile-long reservoir drowns Glen Canyon, the longest and one of the most beautiful canyons on the Colorado River.

Lake Powell, designed to store up to 27 million acre-feet of water, is part of the system of dams built to offset the 20 percent deficit between the Colorado River's average annual flow and the amount of water allocated to the seven Colorado River basin states. However, the lake's storage capacity is reduced by about 70,000 acre-feet per year by silt deposited by the river. More water still is lost to evaporation—about 450,000 acre-feet per year. The reservoir's porous sandstone and shale banks absorb another million acre-feet per year. The dam itself leaks upward of 2,000 gallons per minute.

See also COLORADO RIVER.

DESERT PAVEMENT Desert pavement, a veneer of tightly packed pebbles covering the surface of many arid-country soils, gets its name from its pavementlike regular surface. But desert pavement is natural. Frequent winds, aided by runoff from heavy summer downpours, remove the smaller sands and silts from the soil surface, leaving behind the heavier pebbles. Once exposed, the pebbles are polished and rounded by the winds and darkened by DESERT VARNISH, creating the distinctive surface.

DESERT VARNISH Cliffs and boulders throughout the Southwest are often streaked with a thin, shiny, blue-black polish called desert varnish. Composed mostly of clay, desert varnish derives its intense color and slight shininess from small amounts of iron and manganese oxides.

Desert varnish is formed both chemically and biologically. Water seeping from the rock and evaporating into the dry air concentrates clays and tiny amounts of manganese and iron oxides on the surface of the rock, aided by microscopic bacteria like those in MICROBIOTIC CRUSTS. Desert varnish forms over many centuries and is apparently laid down in cycles.

Early Southwest artists used desert varnish as "scratchboard," pecking PETROGLYPHS through the dark varnish to reveal the light rock underneath. Petroglyph National Park and Three Rivers Petroglyph Site, both in New Mexico, are outstanding examples of such scratchboard art.

DUST DEVILS Dust devils whirling across the dry soils of Southwestern landscapes resemble miniature tornadoes. They are not—tornadoes need moist conditions, dust devils need aridity. These whirling dervishes are so characteristic of deserts and other dry country that Nevada's Gosiute Indians believed that they were born of the windblown dust, and that the whirlwinds embodied their ancestors' spirits.

Named for the dust that makes them visible and for their erratic, unpredictable courses, dust devils typically grow to 20 feet across and 100 feet tall and whirl only for a few minutes before running out of hot air. Their 20- to 30-mile-per-hour winds can easily loft TUMBLEWEEDS or even KANGAROO RATS, but are usually harmless. However, the sizzling summer temperatures of the Southwest's deserts and Great Basin's salt flats sometimes spawn giant dust devils that tower a half-mile high and pack destructive, 90-mile-per-hour winds, which can tear off roofs and collapse walls.

Dust devils are creatures of the sun. They form most often in spring and summer when the sun beats full strength on the soil, heating it up as much as 80°F hotter than the air temperature. The soil surface radiates heat, baking a thin layer of air near the ground. Eventually, a bubble of this hot air floats upward into the cooler layer. More hot surface air rushes in to take its place, developing a rising stream of hot air, or thermal.

To develop into a dust devil, a thermal needs something to give it a whirl. A thermal probably starts to spin when it hits an eddy, or area of turbulence, in the air. Once spinning, it sucks in more hot air and whirls faster. The thermal remains invisible until it vacuums up surface detritus— dry soil, tumbleweeds, trash, or other debris. Then a dust devil is born.

FOUR CORNERS Four Corners, where New Mexico, Colorado, Utah, and Arizona meet, is the only spot in the United States where a person can stand in four states at once. Bounded by the Paradox and San Juan basins to the north and east, the twisting Colorado River along the northwest edge, and the Monument Uplift and Black Mesa on the south and west, the Four Corners region is one of the most level portions of the COLORADO PLATEAU. Here, though, level does not mean monotonous. Water and wind have shaped the ivory-colored, 250-million-year-old Cedar Mesa sandstone and the rust-colored, 200-million-year-old Navajo sandstone into dramatic ARCHES and NATURAL BRIDGES, and colorful buttes, MESAS, and spires throughout the area, including MONUMENT VALLEY on the Arizona-Utah border in the Navajo Reservation and Natural Bridges National Monument west of Blanding, Utah. Winding canyons slice into the SLICKROCK, incised by the meandering San Juan River and its many tributaries. At Goosenecks State Park, west of Mexican Hat, Utah, the muddy river has carved its looping course more than a thousand feet deep into the rock layers, creating a Grand Canyon-like vista of multicolored, stair-stepping canyon walls.

With annual precipitation of less than 10 inches over most of the Four Corners region, plant growth is sparse; lichens or algae tint the rocks with a gray- or olive-green wash, without concealing their brilliant color. Shrubs such as blackbrush and SAGEBRUSH grow at lower elevations; thin lines of COTTONWOOD and willow trace the rare streams; PIÑON and JUNIPER woodlands dot the higher elevations. HAWKS soar high over the desolate landscape on hot summer days; JACKRABBITS, lizards, and RATTLENSAKES are common inhabitants.

Once home to the Southwest's dominant prehistoric culture, the Anasazi, the Four Corners encompasses thousands of Anasazi sites, including MESA VERDE and CHACO CANYON, the two most famous. The Massachusetts-sized Navajo Reservation now includes much of the southern Four Corners; Colorado's Ute Mountain Reservation takes in its eastern edge.

Today's Four Corners landscape is marked by incongruity. For example, the tall smokestacks of the giant Four Corners Power Plant, a coal-burning power plant responsible for the haze smudging the once-clear views, rise above the plateau not far from the dark landmark of SHIPROCK, a volcanic spire sacred to the Navajo people.

GILA WILDERNESS The Gila Wilderness Area, part of southwestern New Mexico's 3.3-million-acre Gila National Forest, was the nation's first wilderness area, established in 1924. The 75,000-acre wilderness encompasses the wild ridges and canyons of the Mogollon (MUG-ee-own) Mountains, once home to various groups of Apaches, including the great leaders Geronimo and Mangas Coloradas. Aldo Leopold, the naturalist and author of *A Sand County Almanac*, spent the early years of his forestry career in the Gila National Forest and was instrumental in establishing it as a wilderness.

Hundreds of miles of foot trails crisscross the dark forests and steep slopes of the Gila, part of a huge rectangle of mountains that rise thousands of feet above the surrounding deserts in central-western New Mexico. Created between 24 and 5 million years ago when a cluster of large volcanoes exploded, spewing out great quantities of ash and lava, these mountains include giant collapsed calderas as wide as 30 miles across. Precious metals—gold, silver, copper—found in large quantities around their edges have fueled brief booms, lasting until the ore bodies were mined out. COPPER is still mined from an enormous open pit south of the Gila, at Tyrone, New Mexico.

The wild country of the Gila shelters some of the Southwest's healthiest populations of mountain wildlife, such as Mexican spotted OWLS, COUGARS, and black BEARS. The Southwest's last grizzly bear was supposedly killed in the Gila in the 1930s.

GRAND CANYON The Grand Canyon of the Colorado River invites superlatives. After a trip into the mile-deep gorge, the largest in the United States, President Theodore Roosevelt declared it "the most impressive piece of scenery" he'd ever seen. He protected part of the 277-mile-long chasm as a national monument in 1908. Today a 1.2-million-acre national park, visited by several million people each year, encompasses most of the 4- to 13-mile-wide canyon.

The rocks that shape the Grand Canyon's stair-stepping walls provide a unique look into the earth's crust, telling of some 2 billion years of earth's evolution. The layers that form the COLORADO PLATEAU are exposed, from the youngest, the 250-million-year-old Kaibab limestone forming the striking white cliffs of the canyon's rim, to the oldest, the dark, contorted rocks of the 2-billion-year-old Vishnu schist, visible only in the narrow Inner Gorge.

The canyon itself, a geologic newborn just 5 million years old, is a story of piracy on the high plateau. The Colorado River once flowed south and eastward around a bulge in the Colorado Plateau, following the present course of the Little Colorado River but flowing in the opposite direction, and emptied into an interior basin in what is now northeastern Arizona. Then, some 5 million years ago, movement along California's San Andreas fault system opened the Gulf of California, creating a new, thousands-of-feet-lower outlet for Southwest streams, the pull of gravity multiplying their

Grand Canyon

down-cutting power. One such stream—which until then had its head-waters in the bulge, the area of the modern Grand Canyon—used its new power to cut through the bulge into the canyon of the Little Colorado, even-tually "capturing" the Colorado to flow westward down its channel. Over the next 1 to 2 million years, the mighty Colorado—now flowing westward as it does today—rapidly ground out the Grand Canyon.

Two undulating rims frame the canyon's east-west length. South of the gorge lies the more accessible South Rim, clothed in a rolling PIÑON-JUNIPER woodland. Across the wide canyon, the truncated edge of the Kaibab Plateau shapes the North Rim, some 1,500 feet higher than the South and supporting cool PONDEROSA PINE and FIR forests. Both rims give awesome views of the great gully, its slopes cut by fingering side canyons and ground away in debris-laden flash floods produced by summer thun-derstorms. The numerous spires, or "temples"—such as Isis Temple—that stand isolated from the canyon walls are products of just such erosion.

In a few short miles, the Grand Canyon embraces a span of ecosys-tems equal to a trip between Baja California and British Columbia. From subalpine spruce-fir forests at the highest parts of the North Rim, the canyon plummets to searing desert at 2,400 feet in the Inner Gorge. Each thousand-foot drop in elevation of the canyon walls is equivalent to a 300-mile move southward across flat country. In the canyon's Inner Gorge, summer daytime temperatures rise as high as 115°F, averaging 20 degrees higher than on the South Rim, with a scanty 8 inches of average annual precipitation. Desert animals and plants find homes here, including the endemic Grand Canyon RATTLESNAKE, a subspecies of the western rattle-snake that has evolved salmon-colored skin to blend in with the Inner Canyon's rocks.

Another Grand Canyon endemic, the black-bodied, white-tailed Kaibab squirrel, lives high above and a world away in the cool, shady conifer forests that clothe the North Rim and the Kaibab Plateau. Across the Grand Canyon on the lower and much drier South Rim lives the Kaibab squirrel's former sibling, the Abert's squirrel. The widening chasm separated the two squirrel populations.

People have lived in the Grand Canyon since around 2000 B.C. Today, some 250 Havasupai Indians still live in and around Havasu Canyon, an oases of springs, waterfalls, and azure-blue pools—and the only post office in the United States still to receive its mail on horseback.

See also COLORADO RIVER, DAMS, MAPLE, SQUAWFISH, TASSEL-EARED SQUIRREL.

HOODOO Hoodoos are dense congregations of grotesquely eroded rock pillars or spires. Often looking from a distance like eerily frozen crowds of giant human figures—sometimes tens of feet tall—hoodoos form when a layer of rock is cracked by a regular pattern of closely spaced vertical joints that intersect at right angles like a checkerboard. Wind and water erosion widens the joints, making free-standing pillars. Further erosion eats more quickly at softer areas of the rock, sculpting narrow "waists" below huge "heads" to form the bizarre hoodoo shapes.

Hoodoos formed in soft rock can be quite ephemeral, displaying geologic processes on "fast forward," while those in harder rocks may endure thousands of years. Rain literally sluices away the short-lived hoodoos formed in soft siltstones at Utah's BRYCE CANYON National Park. Photographs of "Queen Victoria," a hoodoo at Bryce, show dramatic changes in just thirty years. By contrast, the Needles in CANYONLANDS National Park, carved from Cedar Mesa sandstone, and the hoodoos in

Hoodoos

Arizona's CHIRICAHUA MOUNTAINS, shaped from layers of welded volcanic ash, are eroded by wind and sanded away slowly, grain by grain.

LIGHTNING Lightning is the Southwest's deadliest weather phenomenon. An average of 100 Americans are killed by lightning annually; more deaths by lightning occur in Colorado and New Mexico than in any other state. The SANGRE DE CRISTO MOUNTAINS around Cimarron, New Mexico, with a yearly average of 110 thunderstorms, are the nation's thunder and lightning capital. Lightning becomes art near Pie Town in western New Mexico, at the Lightning Field, a vast outdoor sculpture. Rods of varying lengths protrude from the ground, attracting the powerful, wild electricity in ever-changing patterns.

LLANO ESTACADO The Llano Estacado (pronounced YAH-no eh-stah-CAH-do, meaning "staked plains" in Spanish) of eastern New Mexico and the Texas Panhandle is part of the southern Great Plains. Its startlingly flat surface, shaped by level layers of underlying sediments, is capped by a layer of gravels that eroded 5 million years ago. Now cemented with CALICHE, this caprock is porous enough so that water sinks through its surface rather than forming streams to carve relief onto the flat surface. Only the Pecos River, at the Llano's western edge, has cut through the cemented gravels. The retreating edge nibbled by the Pecos forms a low line of bluffs, a prominent Great Plains landmark.

Several stories account for the name Llano Estacado. Some say that the stakes referred to were driven into the ground by local Comanches to guide the mythical "Great Chief" who was to come from the East and deliver the Indians from their enemies. Others maintain that yucca flower stalks rising above the shortgrass prairie looked like marker stakes. Since *estacada* also means "stockade" in Spanish, the stockadelike bluffs at the eroding Llano edge may have been the source of the name.

The Llano Estacado lies atop the southern end of the Ogallala Aquifer, the largest discrete underground reservoir of fresh water in the world. This huge body of water stretches underground from southern South Dakota to west Texas, and from Nebraska to eastern New Mexico. Once it contained some 3 billion acre-feet of water—enough to fill Lake Huron. Today, so much water is pumped from the aquifer for irrigation farming that withdrawals each year exceed recharge by 13 million acre-feet, an amount equal to the entire average annual flow of the COLORADO RIVER.

MALPAÍS Less than a thousand years ago, small volcanoes spewed forth basalt flows on the southern edge of the COLORADO PLATEAU in Arizona and at locations along the RIO GRANDE rift valley in New Mexico. Early Spanish explorers, finding the black landscapes of the lava flows hellishly hot in summer, and their tortuous and fractured surfaces painful to cross, named them *malpaís*, or "bad country." (In English, the term "badlands" refers to difficult-to-traverse landscapes of steep, bare slopes and narrow gullies formed from soft shale.)

> **Early Spanish explorers, finding the black landscapes of the lava flows hellishly hot in summer, named them *malpaís*, or "bad country."**

These basalt flows are so recent that they look fresh, as though frozen in mid-ooze. Their shiny surfaces are pocked with vesicles of popping gas bubbles and marked with ropy wrinkles formed when taffylike hot lava dragged along an already cooling surface skin. Pressure ridges and squeeze-ups show where molten lava pushed through breaks in the brittle crust. Tubes formed where liquid lava melted through already hardened areas. Cracks and fissures split the shrinking basalt as it cooled.

Although forbidding, these landscapes are not lifeless. Their black lava surfaces, in some places colonized by LICHENS, are too new to have weathered into soil. But pockets of wind-deposited sand and silt nurture drought-resistant shrubs, grasses, and flowers, and occasional twisted JUNIPERS, PONDEROSA PINES, and DOUGLAS FIRS.

One such malpaís fills a wide valley east of Grants, New Mexico, between the sandstone scarp of Ácoma Pueblo and the Zuñi mountains. The youngest flow in the malpaís, less than 1,000 years old, figures in Pueblo stories as the "fire rock" that buried the fields of their ancestors. Navajos call the malpaís "Monster's Blood," saying it was spilled when the hero twins, sons of Changing Woman, killed a giant, making the land safe for people. The oldest-known Rocky Mountain DOUGLAS FIR, 930 years old and only 30 feet tall, grows on this malpaís.

Valley of Fires, a large malpaís about 44 miles long and 4 or 5 miles wide, fills a valley west of Carrizozo, New Mexico. Small animals—such as rock squirrels, WOODRATS, mice, and lizards—living in this black landscape have evolved darker than normal coloring for camouflage. Just 70 miles south in White Sands' brilliant white dunes, the same species have evolved paler than normal coloring.

The Southwest's youngest malpaís may be a flow at Sunset Crater, near Flagstaff, Arizona. Tree-ring dating of charred pit house roof beams, constructed by the Sinagua (Spanish for "without water," referring to their dry-farming methods), dates this flow to the fall of 1064 or the winter of 1065, just 900 years ago. The accompanying rain of ash and cinders inundated 120 square miles of the surrounding landscape, enriching the soil and spurring a 150-year-long population boom as Anasazi and Hohokam people moved in to farm along with the Sinagua.

See also CASA GRANDE, CHACO CANYON, SAND DUNES, VOLCANOES.

MESA In the Southwest, a mesa (meaning "table" in Spanish) is a high, flat-topped hill or mountain with steeply sloping sides, capped by a resistant layer of rock, usually sandstone or dark basalt. Mesas are cut from elevated land masses by erosion nibbling away at soft underlying shales, siltstones, or other sediments undermining the hard caprock. Continuing

Mesa

erosion eats at the caprock, eventually shrinking mesas into buttes and then into narrow spires. Depending on the thickness of the rock formations that shape them, mesas rise from many tens of feet to a thousand or more above the surrounding landscape. Their horizontal extent varies, too. For example, MESA VERDE in southwestern Colorado is some 20 miles long by 30 miles wide, while the mesa atop which ÁCOMA PUEBLO perches measures less than a mile in each direction. With level, tablelike tops and steeply sloping or sheer sides, mesas are easily defensible and have long been choice sites for human settlements.

Mesas are defined in relation to other landforms. They are larger than buttes—isolated, flat-topped hills such as Mitten Butte in MONUMENT VALLEY—but smaller than plateaus—flat-topped tablelands like the COLO-RADO PLATEAU—which may cover hundreds of miles of landscape. "Mesa" is a common part of Southwest place names.

MESA VERDE Mesa Verde, known worldwide for its large and spectacular CLIFF DWELLINGS, encompasses nearly 4,000 archaeological sites, among them 200-plus-room Cliff Palace, the Southwest's largest cliff dwelling. So rich is its archaeology that Mesa Verde (Spanish for "green table") was named a World Heritage Site by the United Nations in 1978.

Mesa Verde is a great block of sedimentary rock—largely sandstone—some 20 miles long by 30 miles wide, which sits atop a 2,000-foot-thick layer of grayish, easily eroded shale. Streams cutting into the soft marine shale supporting the mesa have gradually sliced long, fingerlike canyons into the mesa. Carved into the canyon walls are soaring alcoves with vaulted ceilings, formed as water seeping through the 400-foot-thick upper layer of Cliffhouse sandstone eroded weaker layers below. Curving chunks fell away, leaving the alcoves into which the Anasazi and other ancient peoples built the walls and towers of their cliff dwellings.

The story of human occupation of this green mesa, rising several thousand feet above the FOUR CORNERS region in southwest Colorado at the edge of the COLORADO PLATEAU, echoes the stories of other Southwest places. Mesa Verde first attracted the Anasazi—"ancient ones" in Navajo—around A.D. 550 for its woodlands, DOUGLAS FIR forests, sheltered canyons, seeps and springs, and good soils. Around A.D. 750, the Anasazi began building pueblos of local rock atop the mesa. The ruins of these many-roomed, above-ground complexes—often ringed by external walls of finely laid rock—are still visible.

Sometime in the 1200s the Mesa Verde people moved out of their mesa-top pueblos and down into the vaulted alcoves in the cliffs lining the canyons. There they built the great multistoried cliff dwellings for which Mesa Verde is known—Cliff Palace, Spruce Tree House, Balcony House, Square Tower House, Long House, and others. All are constructed of nearby materials—sandstone blocks form the walls, tree trunks make the roof beams—which were carried up to the building sites via ladders and footholds chipped in the rock. Archaeological evidence shows that by then Mesa Verde's natural resources were wearing thin.

With no sign of struggle or disease, the Anasazi seem to have simply walked away from Mesa Verde, leaving possessions behind.

Roof beams were more often cut from inferior trees than from the straight trunks of Douglas fir. People's diets shifted from large animals such as deer and BIGHORN SHEEP to rabbits and squirrels. Perhaps the cliff dwellings were necessary to guard the fertile land around canyon springs and to take advantage of solar heating.

Less than a hundred years after building the cities in the cliffs, Mesa Verde's inhabitants left.

With no sign of struggle or disease, the Anasazi seem to have simply walked away from Mesa Verde, leaving behind mugs, pots full of corn, bows and arrows, jewelry, and in one case, crutches. As at CHACO CANYON and elsewhere, the shrunken rings of trees record a severe drought, which, combined with resource depletion, could have sent the ancient ones away in search of unspoiled territory.

Nearly 600 years later, in December 1888, Richard Wetherill, a Colorado rancher, found Mesa Verde's cliff dwellings. After hearing about the cliff cities from a Ute Indian, Wetherill and his brother-in-law spotted Cliff Palace while tracking cows in a snowstorm. Excited, the two men lashed together a ladder of logs, descended the sheer cliff, and explored the ruins. In 1906, Mesa Verde was declared America's sixth national park.

See also CHACO CANYON, CLIFF DWELLINGS.

MICROBIOTIC CRUSTS A curious community of microorganisms, called microbiotic crusts (also known as cryptogamic soil), compose up to 80 percent of the ground cover of some desert and arid-country soils. Forming a living web, these communities secure the particles in the top few inches of the soil against wind and water erosion, help soil absorb and retain water, and add nitrogen—essential to plant growth—to the soil. Microbiotic crusts give desert soils a characteristically spongy surface texture, a result of the gases produced by each living, breathing, digesting community member.

The pioneering members of microbiotic crusts are a kind of cyanobacteria, microscopic organisms that hatch from windblown spores and grow inside mucilaginous sheaths much thinner than a human hair. The sticky sheaths bind together the particles in the upper soil and persist for decades after their occupants die, resisting the eroding forces of wind and water.

Once the cyanobacteria have stabilized the soil surface, other organisms move in. FUNGUS bodies called mycorrhizae thread themselves between soil particles wherever plant roots grow, tapping into the roots to feed. The fungal threads in turn extend their host's root system, increasing the plant's absorbing surface as much as tenfold and delivering nutrients like phosphorus, zinc, and copper to the plant. Green algae grow in the soil pores, fixing nitrogen from the air while they grow, enriching the soil as they decay. Eventually, LICHENS, which also capture atmospheric nitrogen for the soil, and mosses colonize the surface layer, forming a living mulch.

Microbiotic crusts go dormant to survive the long months of drought. But after rains, when the spongy crusts swell with water, absorbing up to ten times their dry volume, the microorganisms spring to life again.

For all their ability to thrive in the harsh environment of desert soil surfaces, where temperatures may be as much as 50°F higher than the air temperature, microbiotic crusts are fragile. Repeated trampling by large animals, such as cows or people, and vehicle traffic can tear up and destroy this living web.

See also CANYONLANDS, FUNGUS, LICHEN.

MIRAGE Mirages are tricks of the desert, optical illusions caused when a layer of air next to the ground becomes superheated from heat stored in the soil or in dark pavement. The boundary between this hot (and therefore less dense) air and the cooler, denser air above it bends the light rays that strike it, acting like a giant mirror facing upward yet parallel to the ground.

Water mirages paint lakes across parched desert sands, deluding desert travelers. Mirages that look like puddles stretching across dry high-way pavement are produced when the boundary between superheated and normal air reflects the sky onto the ground, producing a very believable image of water on the ground. More complicated mirages result when viewers look at the distant horizon through the abrupt hot air–cold air boundary. It's like looking across the surface of a mirror: mesas seem to float free, separated from the land by a layer of blue sky. Mountain ranges clone themselves, growing upside-down mirror images attached at the peaks.

MOGOLLON RIM The Mogollon (MUG-ee-own) Rim, a rampart stretching for more than 200 miles across Arizona and western New Mexico and rising 2,000 feet in places, marks the southern edge of the COLORADO PLATEAU. Uplifted as part of that great raft of rock between 65 and 50 million years ago, the Mogollon Rim formed when southward-flowing streams eroded headward into the plateau's edge. Its cliffs are built of the same layers of limestone, sandstone, and shale exposed in the GRAND CANYON. "The Rim," as it is known locally, is not only a visual and geological boundary, it also divides the southern Southwest's deserts from the high plateau country of the north. Its cool, shady forests of tall PON-DEROSA PINE and DOUGLAS FIR provide a refuge from the searing heat of the basins below.

The name Mogollon commemorates Don Juan Ignacio Flores Mogollon, governor of the Spanish Province of New Mexico from 1712 to 1715.

See also MAPLE.

MONSOON Across most of the Southwest, the summer monsoon—the two-to-three-month rainy season—brings the majority of the annual pre-cipitation. In summer, the warm mass of the North American continent, especially the hot, dry Southwest, draws storm cells inland from the Gulf of Mexico. Moist, southerly winds blow across the Southwest beginning in late June in the southern Southwest and mid-July over the Rockies and COLORADO PLATEAU to the north, bringing the rain and raising the humid-ity to near-intolerable levels. Simmering heat and sticky, moist air combine to produce characteristic rains: intense, local, and often brief thunderstorms, occasionally dumping 4 inches in half an hour.

Accounting for as much as three-quarters of the annual precipitation, the monsoon is crucial to the lives of the Southwest's inhabitants. Plants respond to the ephemeral abundance of water with a frenzy of growth and reproduction. From QUAIL and peccaries to tiny FRESHWATER SHRIMP, many Southwest animals also time their breeding to bear young just before or during the monsoon. Traditional ceremonies such as Pueblo and Hopi rain dances, corn dances, and feasts, and Apache puberty rites, invite and celebrate the coming of the monsoon, bringing rain, and life, to the arid Southwest.

MONUMENT VALLEY

Monument Valley, on the Arizona–Utah border within the Navajo Reservation, is named for its spectacular formations, thousand-foot-high MESAS, buttes, cliffs, and spires. Rising from the sandy floor of the valley, the striking red-orange, sheer-walled monoliths have long drawn tourists, photographers, and filmmakers. Since trading post owner Harry Goulding persuaded director John Ford to shoot *Stagecoach* there in 1938, Monument Valley has been the location for numerous movies and, more recently, car commercials.

Monument Valley's starkly beautiful landscape is still evolving. Wind and water whittle the plateau edge into separate mesas, the mesas into

Monument Valley

smaller buttes, the buttes into fingerlike spires; the spires eventually disintegrate into sand dunes drifting across the valley floor. Wind's role brings the rock full circle: the monuments are carved in the thousand-plus-foot-thick de Chelly sandstone, deposited as great sweeping dunes by the Permian wind some 250 million years ago.

Monument Valley, made a Navajo tribal park in 1959, is part of the COLORADO PLATEAU.

NATURAL BRIDGES Natural bridges are rock ARCHES created when a stream has incised deep winding curves, called meanders, into a rock layer. At a point where a meander almost loops back on itself, a thin rock wall, called a fin, is formed. The stream continually erodes the rock, eventually breaching the fin, and creates a shorter, straighter course under a bridge of its own making. Streams slowly cutting down into the massive sandstone layers of the COLORADO PLATEAU have sculpted spectacular natural bridges.

Rainbow Bridge on the Utah–Arizona border is the world's largest natural bridge. Its 278-foot-wide span rises 309 feet—the height of a thirty-story building—above Bridge Creek. This graceful span is protected by the Southwest's smallest national monument: Rainbow Bridge National Monument, which encompasses only one-quarter square mile. Once accessible only via a spectacular 13-mile trail across the Navajo Reservation, the arch can now be reached by boaters floating Lake Powell.

Natural Bridges National Monument in southeastern Utah preserves three examples of the stages of natural bridge formation. Katchina Bridge is a "young" bridge, with a thick arch and relatively small opening. Sipapu Bridge is wide enough that the stream no longer eats away at its abutments—rain, wind, and frost are now its active sculptors. Owachomo Bridge is slender and more graceful, closer to the inevitable collapse that occurs when the sandstone span becomes too thin to support itself.

See also ARCHES, ZION CANYON.

PETRIFIED FOREST Petrified Forest near Holbrook in northern Arizona is not a forest at all. The "trees" studding this barren badland of eroded shale hills on the COLORADO PLATEAU are huge, rainbow-colored, fossil trunks washed here from long-vanished tropical forests.

The story of this forest in the desert begins more than 200 million years ago, when North America, part of the supercontinent Pangaea, was closer to the equator. Petrified Forest was then a marshy floodplain, with trees growing on small raised islands, much like the "hammocks" of Florida's Everglades. Nearby were mountains with tall forests—mostly of pinelike trees similar to Norfolk Island pine and monkey puzzle tree. The forests sheltered small, graceful DINOSAURS, crocodilelike phytosaurs, large, clumsy amphibians, and dragonflies as big as KESTRELS. Snails crawled among the tropical ferns on the forest floor.

VOLCANOES close to the mountains periodically erupted, spewing great quantities of ash and hot gas clouds that seared and knocked down the nearby forests. Post-eruption floods or mudflows carried logjams of downed trees down the floodplain, depositing Petrified Forest's logs. Quick burial by more layers of silt, sand, clay, and volcanic ash sealed the trees from oxygen and decay. Instead, silica-laden waters percolated through the sediments, gradually filling the pore spaces in the logs with silica and producing Petrified Forest's beautiful agatized "wood." Small amounts of iron tinted the glassy trunks red, orange, yellow, and brown; manganese yielded black and deep blue; other minerals gave other colors.

The "trees" studding this barren badland of eroded shale hills are huge, rainbow-colored, fossil trunks washed here from long-vanished tropical forests.

Much later, the whole area began to rise with the gradual uplift of the Colorado Plateau. Stresses and strains of uplift cracked the buried petrified trunks, "cutting" them like cordwood. Subsequent millennia of erosion sculpted the soft shales into badlands, exposing the beautiful Petrified Forest.

Petrified Forest is part of the Painted Desert, several hundred square miles of badlands in Arizona named for the delicate, mineral-derived colors that tint its banded shale layers blue, lavender, rusty red, white, ochre yellow, and moss green. Nearly barren of vegetation, the fine layers of mudstone, siltstone, claystone, and volcanic ash forming the badlands swell into a sticky coating when wet, then shrink and crack as they dry, crumbling easily into powdery dust.

Despite the desert's barren and formidable appearance, the Anasazi lived and farmed at its edge from about A.D. 500 to about A.D. 1400. Three hundred archaeological sites have been discovered here, among them the beautiful Agate House, a small pueblo built entirely of blocks of petrified wood. Newspaper Rock in Petrified Forest National Monument, named for its many PETROGLYPHS, contains some of the finest Anasazi rock art in the Southwest, including animals, god or spirit figures, solar calendars, and other symbols.

Beginning in the late 1880s, Petrified Forest's trees began to disappear by the railcar load to satisfy the fashion for agatized wood tables, pedestals, and other objects. In 1906, President Theodore Roosevelt preserved part of the area as a national monument, making collecting the wood illegal. Still, visitors to the current, larger Petrified Forest National Park who cannot resist "pocketing a small piece" steal some 12 tons of petrified wood each year.

Other petrified forests occur in similar-aged shales throughout the COLORADO PLATEAU, including at Bisti Badlands in northwestern New Mexico and Zion National Park in southwestern Utah. Zion's fossil logs are similar to those of Petrified Forest National Park, with one important difference: cavities in some of Zion's logs are tinted bright yellow with yellow-cake, radioactive URANIUM ore.

See also CHACO CANYON, DINOSAURS, ZION CANYON.

PETROGLYPHS AND PICTOGRAPHS As early as 3,000 years ago, people inhabiting the Southwest began chiseling and painting pictures on rocks and cliff walls. Preserved by the dry climate, much of this rock art, ranging from complicated geometric designs to huge, ghostly figures, remains to puzzle, astonish, and awe modern-day viewers. Southwest rock artists used two different media: petroglyphs (from the Greek *petros*, "rock," and *glyphe*, "carving") were created by pecking, chiseling, or scratching through the dark desert-varnish coating to expose the lighter rock underneath. Pigments painted on the rock produced pictographs (from the Latin *pictor*, "painter," and the Greek, *graphein*, "to write").

Petroglyph National Monument, established in 1990 just west of Albuquerque, New Mexico, is the first national monument devoted to prehistoric art. Fifteen thousand petroglyphs decorate the basalt boulders of a 17-mile-long serpentine mesa edge. Artists from two cultures—the Anasazi, from A.D. 700 to 1200, and their descendants, Tiwa-speaking Pueblo people—chiseled the sketchy images of animals, birds, masks, flute players, kachina figures, and ceremonial designs. The mesa, with a

Tsegi Canyon petroglyphs

splendid view across the wide Rio Grande Valley where Pueblo people still live and farm, and toward the 10,000-foot-high peaks of the Sandia Range, was likely a special site to the artists.

Dark basalt boulders capping a ridge at Three Rivers Petroglyph Site, south of Carrizozo, New Mexico, contain more than 500 vivid and lively petroglyphs. Images of human faces, BIGHORN SHEEP, grizzly BEAR footprints, fish, HORNED TOADS, BATS, and other animals, as well as complicated abstract designs decorate the rocks. The Jornada branch of the hunting and gathering Mogollon people chiseled this art between A.D. 900 and 1400.

Utah's Newspaper Rock, northwest of Monticello, in southeastern Utah, is named for the great density of petroglyphs—over 350 figures— pecked into one sandstone slab. Called *Tse' Hane'*, "rock that tells a story" in Navajo, Newspaper Rock records the sketches, scrawls, and stories of humans over an extraordinarily long span of time—3,000 years. The earliest petroglyphs are those of Archaic hunting and gathering peoples; the most recent, modern Ute and Navajo Indians and Hispanic and Anglo settlers.

Some of the finest pictographs in the Southwest decorate sandstone cliffs and overhangs in the SLICKROCK country of the COLORADO PLATEAU in southern Utah. CANYONLANDS National Park contains many pictograph panels, including galleries of larger-than-human-size figures called ghosts for their supernatural appearance. The painters, a hunting and gathering people who inhabited the area at least 1,500 years ago, used a variety of techniques to achieve the sophisticated effects. They spattered paint, stroked it on with their fingers, brushed with yucca brushes, blew pigment through reed tubes, and incised textural lines.

PLAYAS Playas (Spanish meaning "beaches")—dry, salty mud flats in undrained basins—are one of the flattest landforms in existence. Named by the early Spanish explorers for their resemblance to flat beaches, playas are actually the beds of shallow lakes that hold a skim of water only after heavy rains or snows. Hundreds of playas splotch the in-draining desert basins in the BASIN AND RANGE country of the Southwest—southern and central New Mexico and Arizona, and extreme western Utah.

> Named by the early Spanish explorers for their resemblance to flat beaches, playas are actually the beds of shallow lakes that hold water only after rains.

Most of the Southwest's playas formed during the Pleistocene, the glacial age that brought a cooler and wetter climate to the Southwest. Streams rushing from the many small mountain ranges dropped their boulders, cobbles, and gravel when they hit the level basins, forming evenly sloping BAJADAS at the edge of the mountains. Basins with no outlet filled with thousands of feet of finer silts and clays, atop which floated shallow lakes.

As the climate warmed and dried, the lakes evaporated, leaving their flat-floored beds to dry and harden to a cementlike consistency—a state we see altered after occasional heavy rains or snows when the ancient lakes, miles wide but only a few inches or feet deep, return briefly. For a few weeks, their salty waters teem with algae, FRESHWATER SHRIMP, brine flies, and other aquatic lives that survive the intervening months or years of drought.

When the water evaporates, it leaves acres of shiny, gooey mud flats, encrusted with a new coat of calcium, sodium, and other salts. As the pool-table-flat surfaces dry, the particles shrink together and crack into polygons. These curl upward as they dry, forming thin, hollow cylinders, thick curls, fanciful tubes, or shardlike plates. When the playa surface is again dry, winds scour the surface, creating dust storms thousands of feet high, and carrying the calcium and other salts uphill to bajadas and MESAS. The salty dust is washed into the soil, contributing to the formation of whitish, cementlike layers of CALICHE, which impede plants' roots.

See also SAND DUNES.

RIO GRANDE The 1,885-mile-long Rio Grande, North America's fifth-longest river, begins high in the cold, glacier-carved alpine ecosystems of southern Colorado's San Juan Mountains and ends by emptying into the Gulf of Mexico. Once it leaves the San Juans, the Rio Grande runs nearly straight south out of Colorado's San Luis Valley and through New Mexico. At El Paso, Texas, and Juárez, Mexico, the river turns abruptly southeast, forming the U.S.–Mexico boundary for 1,250 miles until it empties into the gulf.

The Rio Grande watershed encompasses half of the Southwest, much of northeastern New Mexico, and all of southwest Texas. But for all its length and enormous drainage area, the Rio is an inconstant desert river. A shallow, easily waded flow for much of the year (an easy crossing for the many illegal immigrants who frequently "commute" across the Rio between Texas and Mexico), the "Great River" lives up to its name when it suddenly swells to a raging brown torrent after summer thunderstorms. A flood in 1863 made the town of Mesilla, New Mexico, an island, with the river flowing on both sides. In another flood there in 1885, the whole river moved to the far side of Mesilla. During a flood in 1978, a hundred-plus-mile stretch upstream of Big Bend National Park, Texas, where the Rio often dries up completely, swelled to nearly a half-mile wide. No wonder, then, that in Mexico the Rio is known as the *Río Bravo del Norte*, the "Wild River of the North."

Dams built for irrigation and flood control now seem to tame the Rio Grande. One of the largest and oldest, Elephant Butte Dam holds back New Mexico's largest lake. The 45-mile-long reservoir and its 200 miles of shoreline form Elephant Butte State Park, New Mexico's most-visited state park, drawing thousands of sailors and powerboaters each year. Anglers fish for bass and perch stocked in the flat waters of the reservoir instead of the shovel-nosed STURGEON, humpbacked chub, and American EELS that plied the river before the dam was completed in 1916.

The Rio Grande traces an oddly straight north-south path through New Mexico, following a deep rift in the earth's crust that began forming some 30 million years ago when the North American plate began to ride up over the Pacific plate. A down-dropped wedge of crust between two parallel fault zones, the rift valley begins as a narrow slice in central Colorado and widens to about 30 miles near Albuquerque, New Mexico. In southern New Mexico, the rift valley stretches nearly 100 miles wide. Although the rift is 26,000 feet deep in places—nearly 5 miles!—the river has filled it with thousands of feet of sand, gravel, and other debris. In northern New Mexico and southern Colorado, the river has cut down through young basalt flows that top the debris layers, forming the spectacular, steep-walled Rio Grande gorge. Ranging from 200 to 800 feet deep, the narrow slot is a formidable barrier to travel. Only one bridge, rising 600 feet above the river near Taos, New Mexico, spans the gorge.

See also EEL, CRANE, STURGEON.

SALINIZATION Intensive irrigation of clayey, poorly drained Southwestern soils may result in salinization—soils toxically contaminated with salt. Salinization occurs when water dissolves out salts in the soil and wicks them up to the surface during evaporation, instead of leaching them downward out of the reach of plant roots. Eventually the soil surface becomes so salt-laden that it is toxic.

Salinization of irrigated land has cost billions of dollars in the Southwest. In the 1940s, the 75,000-acre, federally financed Wellton-Mohawk irrigation district in southern Arizona was abandoned just 20 years after it was installed. The cause: salinization. In the 1960s, federal dollars funded an expensive underground drainage system in the district, designed to flush the salts out of the soils, making farming possible again. However, the toxically salty runoff is now dumped into the COLORADO RIVER south of the Mexican border. In order to satisfy the terms of a water-quality treaty with Mexico, a $300-plus-million desalinization plant, built with federal money, will soon cleanse the agricultural runoff.

Salinization of arid-country soils is not a new problem in the Southwest. Between A.D. 300 and 1400, the Hohokam, the Arizona region's master farmers and irrigators, built hundreds of miles of irrigation canals by hand to water their farms in the Gila, Salt, Santa Cruz, and Verde valleys. But sometime around A.D. 1450, the Hohokam simply walked away, abandoning fields and villages alike. Archaeologists now think that increasingly saline soils led to crop failures. Unable to feed itself, the city-based society eventually disintegrated.

See also CALICHE, CASA GRANDE.

SAND DUNES For most people, the word "desert" conjures up images of endless vistas of undulating sand dunes, barren of all life. Yet only a fraction of the Southwest's thousands of square miles of desert are dune fields. Dunes form where there is a source of sand, winds blowing at least 15 miles per hour, and an area where the wind is forced to drop its cargo.

The dazzling dunes at White Sands, a 224-square-mile dune field near Alamogordo, New Mexico, are the largest of only three expanses of pure gypsum in the world. The blindingly white sands originate in thick layers of rock left when a landlocked arm of the ocean evaporated 250 million years ago. Runoff from snowmelt and thunderstorms erodes gypsum and other soluble minerals from the rock layers, now exposed by uplifting of the San Andres and Sacramento mountains, and deposits the minerals in a shallow, ephemeral PLAYA lake at the lowest spot in the basin, just downwind of the dune field. The dissolved gypsum recrystallizes on the surface of the playa, weathers into grains, and is carried up by the southwesterly spring winds to the dune field. Because the soft gypsum grains scratch easily, their furrowed surfaces scatter the light, resulting in their dazzling glare.

The roughly oval dune field at White Sands includes four kinds of dunes, distributed approximately at right angles to the winds. Nearest the playa, where the winds are strongest, massive, low, dome-shaped dunes dominate. Past these behemoths, where the wind loses some power, dunes with sharp ridge crests, called transverse dunes, form. When the constant wind breaks through these dunes, it pushes two curving horns of sand forward, reshaping the dunes into sinuous, crescent-shaped *barchans*, (from the Arabic word for "ram's horn"). At the margins of the dune field, where winds are not so strong, the now-slow-moving barchans reverse into massive parabolic dunes when their long trailing arms are caught and anchored by desert vegetation. Then the center of the dunes, not the horns, advances.

White Sands, established as a national monument by Congress in 1934, is surrounded by White Sands Army Missile Range, off limits to the public.

Great Sand Dunes, northeast of Alamosa in southern Colorado's San Luis Valley, is named for its 700-foot-tall dunes, among the tallest in the world. Southwesterly winds pick up sand-sized grains from the dry, flat-bottomed valley and drop them, forming the massive dunes, when the winds hit the wall formed by the SANGRE DE CRISTO MOUNTAINS.

A mix of sand grains, mostly quartz, with some dark grains from the volcanic rocks of the San Juan Mountains, gives the Great Sand Dunes their dark golden color. Because dark surfaces soak up more solar radiation than pale ones, the dune surfaces become searingly hot at midday in summer. Although individual dunes move, the whole field stands still, its forward momentum canceled each spring by the tremendous storm winds that swoop across the Sangre de Cristos from the northeast, the opposite direction from the winds that push the dunes the rest of the year.

SANGRE DE CRISTO MOUNTAINS

A finger of the Rocky Mountains that reaches into the Southwest, the Sangre de Cristo Mountains (meaning "blood of Christ" in Spanish) run south from Salida, Colorado, to Santa Fe, New Mexico. This imposing wall of peaks includes the Southwest's highest peak, 13,161-foot-high Mount Wheeler. The southern-most range of the Rockies and one of the youngest ranges in the United States, the Sangres began rising around 20 million years ago and are still being pushed upward. The fault that moves them is also dropping the east side of the RIO GRANDE rift, forming the San Luis Valley in Colorado and the Upper Rio Grande Valley in New Mexico.

Molybdenum, found in rocks intruded into a caldera that formed when a volcano collapsed some 25 million years ago, was extracted from the Sangre de Cristos until recently. The molybdenum mine near Questa, New Mexico, the Southwest's largest, is today closed because of falling mineral prices.

High in the Sangres above Taos Pueblo is Blue Lake, the site of annual religious ceremonies held by the people of Taos Pueblo. Made a part of the Carson National Forest when the forest was formed, Blue Lake was returned to Taos Pueblo in 1970 after sixty years of negotiation.

The Spaniards first called these mountains the *Sierra Madre*, or the "mother range." Beginning in the early 1800s, they acquired their modern name, probably from the Penitentes, a devout and secret sect of Catholicism that focuses on the torment and crucifixion of Jesus Christ.

SHIPROCK

Shiprock, a prominent landmark in the FOUR CORNERS region, rises 1,450 feet—twenty stories higher than the Empire State Building—above the surrounding arid landscape. Located in the northwestern New Mexico portion of the Navajo Reservation, Shiprock, a volcanic

Shiprock

monolith, got its English name from a fancied resemblance to a sailing ship with wind-filled sheets. But to the Navajo, this sacred rock tower is *Tsé Bit' a' í* (SAY-bid-a-ih), or "Rock with Wings," the remains of a giant bird that plummeted into the ground, bringing their ancestors to Navajo country.

Pictured in numerous geology texts, Shiprock is a classic example of a volcanic neck, the hard rock that cools, plugging the volcano's throat, and remains when the softer cone erodes away. Sheer-walled dikes, formed when molten rock flowed into narrow cracks, radiate from Shiprock's base. Smaller pinnacles near Shiprock are the necks of subsidiary volcanoes. Irregular vertical columns, produced when the rock shrank as it cooled, score the dark tower.

SKY ISLANDS Small, high mountain ranges rising above the Southwest's deserts and the SLICKROCK country of the COLORADO PLATEAU are called "sky islands." Because their summits catch extra moisture in both summer and winter, their slopes and canyons provide cool, moist environments for a host of species that cannot survive the surrounding hot, arid lowlands. Like islands in an ocean, these isolated landforms often contain endemic species found nowhere else. For instance, the Sierra Blanca lupine and Jemez Mountain SALAMANDER were once part of more widely distributed groups when cooler, wetter climates dominated the Southwest. Marooned on their islands when climates grew warmer and drier, they evolved into distinct species over millions of years, adapted only to their particular locations.

Mountain islands are also steppingstones, allowing more mobile species to traverse the Southwest's deserts and GRASSLANDS between larger mountain ranges. In the southern Southwest, the CHIRICAHUA MOUNTAINS and other small ranges provide highways for Mexican species such as COATIS and elegant trogons to move north from Mexico's Sierra Madre. Sky islands in the northern Southwest allow Rocky Mountain species to move south.

Mountain islands also form formidable walls dividing the populations of smaller animals—lizards or pocket mice, for instance—in adjacent desert basins. Such isolated populations may eventually evolve into separate species.

SLICKROCK A world of spectacularly sculptured sandstone, the slickrock country of the COLORADO PLATEAU in southern Utah and northern Arizona is not slick. Rather, the name refers to the naked smoothness of the largely unvegetated rock, and the shiny patina produced by blue-black DESERT VARNISH. Ancient dunes, deposited by the wind in a Sahara-like desert some 200 million years ago, later hardened into thick layers of rock, form typical slickrock landscapes.

The most spectacular scenery of the Colorado Plateau, the slickrock country includes not only well-known national parks, monuments, and recreation areas such as CANYONLANDS, ARCHES, and Glen Canyon, but also thousands of square miles of little-traveled plateaus, canyons, and sculptured rock landscapes.

See also NATURAL BRIDGES, WATERPOCKET FOLD, ZION.

SUNSETS The Southwest is known for its glorious, lingering sunsets, a result of the region's arid climate and relatively high elevations. Brilliant colors paint the western sky, tinting clouds, MESAS, and mountains in vivid shades as the sun slips below the horizon. An arid climate means fewer droplets of water in the air to bounce around and wash out the light's color; instead the colors remain clear and intense. Relatively high elevations mean a thinner atmosphere and longer views, so that after the sun disappears below the horizon, its rays remain visible for a long time.

The aerial debris from volcanic eruptions, even as far away as halfway around the world, periodically enhances Southwest sunsets. Most recently, in 1991, Mount Pinatubo in the Philippines spewed tens of tons of sulfur dioxide gas high into the atmosphere. The gas combines with water vapor to form a cloud of sulfuric acid droplets 16 miles above the earth's surface. After the sun sinks over the horizon, its rays strike the normally invisible cloud, producing a shimmering reddish glow that spreads high in the western sky and lasts up to half an hour. The cloud will take several years to disperse, delighting viewers with prolonged sunsets in the meantime.

TURQUOISE The Southwest's finest turquoise comes from New Mexico's Cerrillos Hills, between Albuquerque and Santa Fe. When the parallel faults of the RIO GRANDE rift sliced New Mexico from north to south, lava pushed up through the fault zone in many places, forcing hot, mineral-rich water through the surrounding rocks. At the Cerrillos Hills, the hot water dissolved alumina, phosphorus, and small amounts of copper, depositing the changed minerals as nodules of sky-blue turquoise.

Mined by Native Americans since A.D. 900 at least, Cerrillos Hills turquoise was so prized for jewelry and ceremonial uses that it was traded as far away as Teotihuacán, the Aztec capital. After the Spaniards conquered Teotihuacán—now Mexico City—Cerrillos turquoise was among the spoils taken by treasure galleon to Spain. The polished blue rocks ended up in the Spanish Royal Treasure, among the crown jewels. After the Spaniards reached the Southwest in the 1500s, they enslaved Native Americans to mine turquoise and lead in the Cerrillos Hills. The PIÑON-JUNIPER–studded hills still yield fine turquoise used in Navajo, Hopi, and Pueblo jewelry and fetishes; the highway winding through the Cerrillos is named the "Turquoise Trail."

Another mineral colored by copper and also found in the Southwest is also used in jewelry and can be confused with turquoise. Chrysocolla, a product of the oxidation of bodies of copper ore, is colored sky blue to greenish blue, like turquoise, but is much softer. Unlike turquoise, chrysocolla can be scratched with a knife; it lacks the porcelainlike luster of polished turquoise and is subject to cracking. Chrysocolla, always found in association with copper deposits, occurs widely in the Southwest. The Globe Mine at Globe, Arizona, has yielded especially fine specimens of chrysocolla.

URANIUM Uranium deposits are scattered throughout the Southwest, but the bulk of the Southwest's uranium is found in the eastern half of the

COLORADO PLATEAU, including the San Juan Basin, which contains one-sixth of the world's known reserves.

Uranium in the Southwest occurs in sedimentary rocks as part of the bright yellow mineral carnotite, or "yellowcake." Yellowcake is formed when water filtering through uranium-bearing volcanic rocks—for example, volcanic ash—picks up soluble uranium and redeposits it on organic matter in the rock. Most of the Southwest's uranium occurs in 150- to 200-million-year-old shales that also contain petrified wood and some of the world's greatest deposits of DINOSAUR bones.

Most of the Southwest's uranium occurs in the 150- to 200-million-year-old shales that also contain some of the world's greatest deposits of dinosaur bones.

The story of uranium mining in the Southwest is one of spectacular booms and equally impressive busts. In 1950, a Navajo sheepherder named Paddy Martínez found a strange-looking yellow rock near Grants, New Mexico. In the boom that followed, Grants labeled itself "The Uranium Capital of the World." Barely a decade later, the price of uranium dropped and most of the mines closed. After the mines opened again in the 1970s, the Grants area produced half of the uranium oxide in the United States. The 1980s brought a longer bust—most of the mines are still idle.

A destitute young geologist's strike on the day his drilling rig broke down in 1952 brought a similar boom to Moab, Utah, and the surrounding SLICKROCK country. Charlie Steen's "Mi Vida" strike touched off a rush that saw Moab quadruple in size. Prospectors swarmed over the slickrock country, building most of the area's Jeep roads, including the Burr Trail crossing WATERPOCKET FOLD. By 1956, however, the rush was over.

Unfortunately, each bust left more than idle mining and milling equipment and unemployed miners. In the heady days of the 1950s, despite the fact that cancer had been linked to radiation exposure, the Southwest's hundreds of mines lacked any measures to protect miners. Miners breathed radioactive dust, drank radioactive water, and handled radioactive ores daily. Three decades later, doctors began to report epidemic rates of fatal cancers among the largely Navajo and Pueblo miners. By then, the mines were closed and the companies gone.

The processing mills closed too, leaving behind millions of tons of dangerously radioactive, sandy tailings. Area residents, unaware of the danger, used the sand to build playgrounds, mixed it in cement for homes and other buildings; the ever-present winds dispersed it widely. Then came disaster: in 1979, a tailings pond dam at the United Nuclear Corporation mill near Church Rock, New Mexico, broke, pouring a flash flood containing 95 million gallons of radioactive water and 1,100 tons of radioactive mud down the Puerco River. Among the victims of this radioactive flood was a woman sheepherder who waded the receding flood to rescue her sheep. After the skin sloughed from her feet and lower legs, she died.

Unreclaimed uranium mines and tailings piles still dot the FOUR CORNERS region.

See also PETRIFIED FOREST, ZION CANYON.

VOLCANOES Within the past several million years—just a few minutes in geologic time—the earth under the Southwest has belched forth fire and molten rock, splotching the landscape with dark lava flows or MALPAÍS, blanketing the region with thick layers of ash, and raining cinders over wide areas. Most Southwest volcanism either occurs in a north-south line from southern Colorado to El Paso, Texas, along the parallel fault zones that scribe the RIO GRANDE rift, or in a wavy-margined ring around the COLORADO PLATEAU. Among the hundreds of landforms created by recent Southwest volcanism are three especially spectacular volcanoes: the San Francisco Peaks, Mount Taylor, and the Jemez Caldera.

San Francisco Peaks, a trio of peaks rising out of the southern margin of the Colorado Plateau near Flagstaff, Arizona, are all that remain of a tall, symmetrical, Fujiyama-like volcano. Several million years ago, the graceful cone exploded, blowing out its northeast side, and collapsed on itself. The three peaks, remnants of the volcano's slopes, include 12,670-foot-tall Humphreys Peak, the highest point in Arizona. Navajo and Hopi people regard these prominent and often snow-covered landmarks as sacred places. The Hopi believe that San Francisco Peaks are the home of their kachinas, holy beings.

Mount Taylor, north of Grants, New Mexico, also began to form about 4 million years ago as a result of Colorado Plateau uplift. Like the San Francisco Peaks, Mount Taylor built itself up out of successive lava and ash flows over about 2 million years before destroying itself in a spectacular sideways explosion. At 11,301 feet, Mount Taylor, *Tsoodzil* (SOOD-zih) in Navajo, towers over the surrounding mesas. Mount Taylor is one of the four sacred peaks that mark the four corners of *Diné Bikéyah* (Dih-NEH

Bih-KEH-yah), "the Land of the People," Navajo country.

A much more recent and violent eruption about 1 million years ago created a huge caldera in the Jemez Mountains, west of Los Alamos in northern New Mexico. Jemez Caldera or Valle Grande ("Big Valley" in Spanish) is a roughly circular, flat-floored valley 14 miles across. The Jemez volcano exploded twice, releasing more than 50 cubic miles of ash, pumice, and broken rock—100 times that spewed out by Mount St. Helens—and then collapsed, forming the Jemez Caldera.

WATERPOCKET FOLD Waterpocket Fold is a hundred-mile-long single fold, or monocline, in the normally horizontal rock layers of the COLORADO PLATEAU that splits south-central Utah like a huge standing wave of rock. Less than 3 miles wide through most of its length, the great fold, locally called a reef, still presents a formidable barrier. Only four canyons, all subject to flash floods, penetrate it. Only one paved road crosses it. Unpaved Burr Trail winds over the fold near its south end.

Formed when uplift of the Colorado Plateau raised one block and dropped an adjacent one, Waterpocket Fold was like a giant stairstep in the rocks. Rather than breaking, the great rock layers, mostly sandstones with some shales, simply drooped over the displacement. Subsequent millennia of erosion have forged a parallel array of ridges (erosion-resistant rocks) and valleys (softer rocks) in the fold. Along its west side, Waterpocket Fold is marked by a high, angular cliff of red-tinted sandstone that rises above the slopes of soft green and purple shale.

Waterpocket Fold is named for rainwater-collecting potholes—"water pockets"—that pock its sandstones. Slight depressions in the surface are enlarged by the prying action of frost, eventually deepening enough that they provide habitat for the pothole ecosystem, a community of aquatic organisms that thrive despite months when the pothole is bone dry. Adult red and SPADEFOOT TOADS survive the drought burrowed deep in the dried mud. Gnat larvae simply dehydrate, losing up to 92 percent of their body weight, and swarm to life when water fills the pothole. FRESHWATER SHRIMP eggs stay viable for decades in the dried pothole dust, hatching after the first substantial rain. The aquatic community enlarges its watery home by secreting acidic metabolic wastes, which dissolve the limy cement of the sandstone.

Since 1971, most of Waterpocket Fold has been protected by Capitol

Reef National Park, 378-square-mile park named for the domes of cream- and gold-colored Navajo sandstone topping the highest ridge in the fold. This sandstone erodes grain by grain, leaving smooth, cone-shaped remnants. One that resembles the United States Capitol gives the park its name.

ZION CANYON

Zion Canyon, carved in the southern end of the Markagunt Plateau in extreme southwestern Utah, boasts some of the highest sheer cliffs in America, soaring 2,000 feet from the valley floor to the plateau top. So steep are the massive sandstone walls that trails traversing them climb at an invigorating 500 feet per mile, and the only road tunnels through the cliffs in order to gain the plateau. The West Rim Trail, climbing 3,070 feet in just over 6 miles, includes a section of tight switchbacks named "Walter's Wiggles" for a former park superintendent. When hewed from the cliffs in 1919, Walter's Wiggles required twenty-one switchbacks to climb one 600-foot stretch.

A drop of up to 80 feet per mile in places—ten times as great as that of the COLORADO RIVER in the GRAND CANYON—gives the Virgin River the power to carve Zion Canyon. Originating at around 9,000 feet elevation on the Markagunt Plateau, the Virgin tumbles to just over 4,000 feet in the canyon bottom. When summer thunderstorms or spring snowmelt swell its normally clear, low flow, the Virgin picks up powerful grinding tools: sand, gravel, and even boulders.

Great Arch of Zion

The river's power is especially evident in the Narrows, the river's aptly named upper canyon. The canyon walls close in places to just 20 feet apart, yet rise 2,000 feet to the narrow slot of sky. The Paiute call this canyon *Ioogoon*, or "arrow quiver," for its narrowness. Here, as in the rest of Zion Canyon, summer downpours can cause awesome flash floods. In one such storm in 1954, the Virgin swelled fiftyfold in just 15 minutes.

Zion Canyon's walls and enormous buttes, such as Great White Throne, are sculpted in the 2,000-plus-foot-thick layer of Navajo sandstone. This massive rock layer was laid down by winds sweeping a broad plain some 200 million years ago, depositing Sahara-like sand dunes from what is now northern Arizona to southern Wyoming. The shape of the dunes is still traced by cross-bedding lines, slanting parallel lines sweeping across the sheer rock faces. Where the sandstone walls fracture along the curving cross-bedding lines, ARCHES form, such as the Great Arch of Zion. (Although called arches, most are actually enormous wall alcoves, not true freestanding spans.)

Underlying this massive layer of hardened dunes is its weak spot: a thick layer of easily eroded silt and mudstone. Where the river has worn through to this rust-colored layer, the canyon widens abruptly, since the mudstone dissolves, undermining the sandstone above it.

The silt and mudstones are responsible for another of Zion's distinctive features. Groundwater from rains and snowmelt percolates slowly through the thick Navajo sandstones, but is stopped by the impervious mudstones. Moving laterally along the contact between the two formations, the water emerges as a "spring line" bisecting canyon walls. Alcoves and side canyons shelter hanging gardens of lush, water-loving plants like ferns and COLUMBINES, which grow along the spring line.

Anasazi sites, including a large pueblo from A.D. 750, show that the ancient ones farmed the southern part of the canyon until about 1200. Fremont hunter-gatherers ranged over the northern part and the plateau tops at the same time, leaving many PETROGLYPHS, including some of BIGHORN SHEEP. When Mormon settlers arrived and began to farm the fertile soils of the lower canyon after the 1860s, Paiutes lived in the area, but not in the tight confines of the upper canyon, the home of *Wai-no-pits*, the "Evil One," and other sacred beings. A Mormon settler gave Zion its English name after the temples in the Biblical city of David.

See also PETRIFIED FOREST.

FURTHER READING

GENERAL GUIDES

Chilton, Lance, et al. *New Mexico: A New Guide to the Colorful State*. Albuquerque: University of New Mexico Press, 1984. *The* book on New Mexico. This revised and expanded version of the WPA Guide issued in the 1930s has introductory chapters on New Mexico's varied cultures and natural history, followed by road tours packed with information.

MacMahon, James A. *The Audubon Society Nature Guides: Deserts*. New York: Alfred A. Knopf, 1985. A field guide with photographs and descriptions of the most common animals and plants of the Southwest deserts. A good basic introduction to deserts, especially to the four North American deserts.

Pavitt, Irene, ed. *The Sierra Club Guides to the National Parks: Desert Southwest*. New York: Stewart, Tabori and Chang, 1984. Describes the national parks of the Southwest and western Texas—from Arches to Zion—including geology, plants and animals, human history, and facilities. Beautiful photographs.

ANIMALS AND PLANTS

Dodge, Natt N. *Flowers of the Southwest Deserts*. Tucson: Southwest Parks and Monuments Association, 1985. Describes the most common desert plants, with anecdotes about historic usage. (Other books in the series include *Shrubs and Trees of the Southwest Uplands* and *Flowers of the Southwest Mountains*.)

Olin, George. *Mammals of the Southwest Deserts*. Tucson: Southwest Parks and Monuments Association, 1982. Lovely illustrations and anecdotal descriptions of the more common mammals.

Phillips III, Arthur M., and John Richardson. *Grand Canyon Wildflowers*. Tucson: Southwest Parks and Monuments Association, 1990. Gorgeous photographs make this worth the price. Applies to much of the Colorado Plateau.

GEOLOGY

Chronic, Halka. *Roadside Geology of . . . Series*. Missoula: Mountain Press. One volume each for Arizona, Colorado, New Mexico and Utah. Concise descriptions of geology as seen along the Southwest's highways. An easy way to learn what shapes the landscape.

CULTURAL HISTORY

Durham, Michael S. *The Smithsonian Guide to Historic America: The Desert States*. New York: Stewart, Tabori and Chang, 1990. Well-written, place-by-place histories—with only occasional factual errors—accompanied by splendid photographs. Oddly, "Notes on Architecture" does not include the region's unique Indian architecture. The guide does not cover Colorado.

Noble, David Grant. *Ancient Ruins of the Southwest: An Archaeological Guide*. Flagstaff: Northland Press, 1981. Valuable introduction to early Southwest Indian cultures. Descriptions of over fifty sites, from well-known Mesa Verde to those off the well-traveled routes.

GOOD READING

Gelbach, Frederick R. *Mountain Islands and Desert Seas*. College Station: Texas A&M University Press, 1981. A naturalist travels along and describes the United States–Mexican border, with comments on the changes wrought by growing human populations.

Krutch, Joseph Wood. *The Desert Year*. Tucson: University of Arizona Press, 1985. This story of a year in Arizona's Sonoran Desert, first published in 1951, is a classic.

Nabhan, Gary Paul. *Gathering the Desert*. Tucson: University of Arizona Press, 1987. "Biographies" of twelve important Sonoran Desert plants, weaving science and human history with lively story-telling.

Reisner, Marc. *Cadillac Desert*. New York: Viking Penguin Books, 1986. The story of water, and its use and abuse, in the arid West.

Silko, Leslie Marmon. *Ceremony*. New York: Viking Penguin Books, 1977. A powerful story of a Laguna Pueblo man's struggle to return to harmony with his life and culture after being a prisoner of the Japanese in World War II.

Williams, Terry Tempest. *Coyote's Canyon*. Salt Lake City: Peregrine Smith Books, 1989. Magical stories and exquisite photographs bring the reader into the heart, and soul, of the canyon country of the Colorado Plateau.

Zwinger, Ann Haymond. *The Mysterious Lands*. New York: Truman Talley/Plume, 1989. Beautifully written and illustrated book on the four North American deserts. An excellent way to get to know the desert.

INDEX

ABOUT THE AUTHOR

Susan J. Tweit is a writer, naturalist, and radio commentator. Her book, *Pieces of Light: A Year on Colorado's Front Range* (1990), is an intimate account of the wild, hidden side of Boulder, Colorado. Her nature essays have appeared in several publications, including *Harrowsmith, Sierra,* and *New Mexico* magazines. "Wild Lives," her natural history radio commentaries, are broadcast each week on New Mexico public radio.

Susan lives in Las Cruces, New Mexco, with her husband, Richard, and stepdaughter, Molly. She is now working on a book about New Mexico's Chihuahuan Desert.